I0828106

CHIARA TERZUOLO
ILLUSTRATED BY JUSTINE WONG

HIDDEN JAPAN

Smith Street Books

Contents

Tokyo

& Beyond

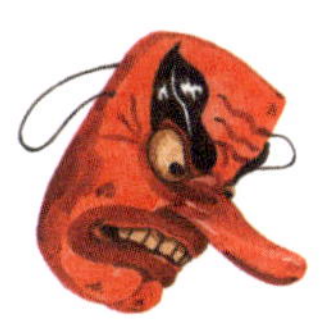

A Little Bit About This Book

When you're travelling, do you find yourself distracted by intriguing signs down a side street, wandering into random galleries or ducking into curious little shops, completely forgetting about the main attraction you were on your way to see? If this sounds like you, then you're going to love Japan. Sure, it's got some spectacular major attractions, but it's those curious 'only-in-Japan' experiences you find off the beaten path that are really going to make their mark on your memory.

There is a *lot* of information about Tokyo. That's because it's the first port of call for most visitors to Japan and, to be honest, you could spend months exploring the capital's diverse cityscapes, foodie spots and hidden gems alone. This is not a comprehensive guide to Japan. Instead, think of it as a carefully curated selection of magical highlights and fascinating discoveries that a local wants to share with you.

For almost every region, I have included walks that take you away from the big-ticket sights and towards a more local and authentic side of the city. Japan is one of the best places in the world to walk, from wandering through city side streets jammed with quirky businesses and kooky spots, to hiking the trails and former ancient roads that crisscross the country and its rural charms.

Of course, as with any travel guide, information can be subject to change. Businesses close, prices fluctuate, and new branches pop up, so do a quick check online before you set out to avoid disappointment – or potentially find a new and unexpected treasure.

So, are you ready? Pull on your walking shoes, download a map app, bring your appetite, and let's go!

TOKYO

WELCOME TO TOKYO

One of the best ways to explain Tokyo is through the concept of *machi*, meaning 'city' or 'town'. Tokyo itself isn't administered as a single city. It's one of Japan's 47 prefectures and it consists of 23 central 'special wards' and more than two dozen cities and towns further out, which all have their own local governments.

There is no single Tokyo but, rather, a collection of distinct, modern villages, each with its own specific history and quirks. Tokyo has been my home for over a decade now and I've tried a bunch of the city's eclectic neighbourhoods on for size, getting to know each of them and their charms. That's why I've divided the Tokyo section of this book into categories: retro; foodie; nature; art and fashion; quirky; and late night ... Whatever you may be, there is a Tokyo for you.

Don't know where to start? That's okay; just follow me.

レトロ東京

Retro Tokyo

DESPITE ITS SPRAWLING size now, Tokyo wasn't always Japan's capital. It was once a small fishing village called Edo, but its excellent river connections did not go unnoticed by the 'great unifier', Tokugawa Ieyasu. He was the legendary leader who became the country's first shogun and began the Tokugawa shogunate, which ruled the country from 1603 until its fall from power during the Meiji Restoration in 1868.

Tokyo originally centred around Edo Castle, which extended far further than the small remaining section that currently houses the Imperial Palace grounds and gardens. The city grew quickly, expanding all the way to the ocean and mountains and into the impressive sprawl it is today.

Due to traditional architecture being made of wood, a lot of Tokyo's older buildings didn't survive the effects of fires, bombings and earthquakes. Add to that the massive drive to build new structures during Japan's economic Bubble Era and it can be difficult to imagine the Tokyo/Edo of yore, which is more easily done in places like Kyoto and Nara. However, if you know where to look, there is still plenty of history to discover and places where you can get a feel for Edo (1603–1868), Meiji (1868–1912), Taisho (1912–1926) and Showa (1926–1989) eras in Tokyo.

BEST HISTORY-FILLED NEIGHBOURHOODS IN TOKYO

So where should you go to experience a bit of old Edo? Why, the shitamachi and yamanote of course!

Technically, shitamachi refers to the lower city (rather than the 'old city' as it is sometimes erroneously translated) and is the opposite of the yamanote, or higher city, where you'll find the Imperial Palace and East Gardens. Basically, during the Edo period, lower-class folks tended to live in low-lying areas that were more prone to flooding, while the samurai and lords lived in the safer spots on higher ground.

However, the shitamachi now has a more cultural connotation and in Japanese is used to refer to areas of the city that have charming alleyways, twisty streets, low wooden houses, craft workshops and a definite air of having been forgotten by time. Let's take a rundown of some of the famous places in these areas.

ASAKUSA

No guide to Tokyo would be complete without this famous neighbourhood, centred around iconic Sensoji Temple and its huge 'thunder gate'. During the Edo period, this was *the* place to go for entertainment. There were geisha-frequented tea houses, kabuki theatres and comedic rakugo storytellers, as well as the Yoshiwara red light district that abuts it (which, in a much more limited capacity, is still in existence today). There are shops and restaurants here that have operated for centuries, and tempura in particular is closely associated with the area.

You can find a full rundown of things to see and do in Asakusa on page 18.

IMPERIAL PALACE & EAST GARDENS

The gardens and home of Japan's imperial family are on a small part of what was once Edo Castle. The East Gardens are open to the public and have seasonal sights such as plum trees that bloom in February, and cherry blossoms in the spring. The majestic gates and towering walls of carefully stacked stones hint at the power and protection around these innermost circles of the castle: the honmaru, where the rulers lived, and ninomaru, where they met with visiting lords. If you want to go deeper, register in advance for a free guided tour to a part of the grounds that is closer to where the emperor and his family currently live.

The grounds are just a fraction of what they once were, as this was once the largest castle in the world. The inner compound alone had an 8 km (5 mile) circumference, with the outer ring extending for 16 km (10 miles). You can still see parts of the outermost moat in modern-day Akihabara, Ochanomizu and Kanda.

SHIBAMATA

Despite being just 20 minutes by train from the soaring Tokyo SkyTree, the stone pavements and wooden buildings of Shibamata are a total blast from the past. Although best known in Japan as the location of a longstanding film series, *It's Tough Being a Man* (you will see bronze statues of the characters outside the station), you don't have to be an expert on the series to enjoy this cute township.

The shopping street approaching Shibamata Taishakuten Temple is lined with shops selling snacks, toys and candy, along with restaurants serving freshly grilled eel, a local specialty. On your way to the temple, stop at Shibamata Haikara Yokocho (look for the robot vending machine) to experience a *dagashiya* (old-school candy shop) and play some of the original vintage games. After visiting the temple, take a look at Yamamoto-tei, a former merchant's residence with a lovely garden, and then head to the river to experience Yagiri no Watashi, Tokyo's last traditional boat crossing.

YANAKA

Yanaka, near Nippori Station, was mostly untouched by the air raids during WWII, so it has retained a tranquillity and charm usually reserved for country towns. The area is a treasure trove of old wooden buildings, temples and surprises. One of the highlights is Yanaka Ginza, an old-fashioned shopping street of mom-and-pop shops and some of the best street food in Tokyo.

The Yanaka Cemetery is filled with the graves of intriguing historical figures, including the writer Ichiyo Higuchi, who is featured on the ¥5000 note, and Michio Miyagi, a famous koto musician. Many members of the Tokugawa family, which ruled Japan for over two centuries, are also buried here. Of particular interest is the grave of Oden Takahashi, an infamous 19th-century murderess. It's said that she was buried near the public toilet as a form of posthumous punishment following her beheading!

You can find a guided walk around the greater YaNeSen (Yanaka, Nezu and Sendagi) area in the Arts & Fashion Tokyo chapter on page 96.

Yanaka Ginza shopfront ◆

OPEN

Asakusa Backstreet Walk

For most first-time visitors to Tokyo, Sensoji Temple is a major spot to tick off the 'must-see' list, but make sure you explore the little side streets around the area, too.

On your approach to Tokyo's oldest and most iconic temple, you'll pass through the massive Kaminarimon (Thunder Gate) with its 700 kg (1534 lb) lantern and navigate the busy Nakamise shopping street, full of colourful souvenirs. It can be a bit of a sensory overload, and a lot of the souvenirs here are quite commercial, so keep an eye out for more interesting and authentic gifts elsewhere.

Two spots where you can get a literal taste of history are right by Kaminarimon. For more than 200 years, Tokiwado, a shop just to the left of the bright-red gate, has made kaminari okoshi, a crunchy sweet made from puffed rice and sugar. Make sure to order the freshly made ones! In the shopping arcade to the right of the gate is Sansada, Japan's oldest tempura restaurant (opened in 1837, when samurai still walked the streets of Edo). Opt for the special tendon, a bowl of rice topped with their most prized tempura varieties, for the full experience.

Sensoji Temple legendarily dates back to 645 AD, when it was built to house a golden statue of Kannon, the goddess of mercy, that two brothers found in their nets while fishing in the Sumida River. The former temple building was destroyed during WWII but was rebuilt thanks to donations from people across the country, becoming a symbol of rebirth for the capital. Before going in to pay your respects to the goddess, stop by the massive incense burner and absorb the aroma, as the smoke is believed to have healing powers.

Off the Nakamise shopping street is Denboin Dori, a wider street lined with stores and workshops, many of which have been honing their craft for centuries. If you are visiting between mid-March and early May, make a detour to one of the lesser-known parts of the temple, hidden in plain sight: the Denboin Gardens. Most visitors skip this, due to the limited opening times and ¥300 entrance fee, but the cherry trees and peaceful pond frame Sensoji's five-storey pagoda beautifully.

A nearby hidden treasure is the tiny Sensoji Chingodo Shrine, at the intersection of Denboin, Rokoku and Hoppy streets. This shrine is dedicated to the legendary tanuki, mischievous raccoon dogs with magical powers (and large testicles). People come to this quiet spot to pray for help to find lost objects or for protection from fire.

Heading from the gate and straight down to Rokuku Street, you should see Mokuhankan coming up on your left. Owned by passionate printmaker David Bull, this is not only a place to sell his and other artists' woodblock prints, but also his effort to keep this traditional art alive and relevant.

For a little taste of more recent history, head to the front of the Ekimise building near the Tobu Railway Asakusa Station. Look for a sign with a mole on it and follow the stairs down to the distinctly retro Asakusa Underground Shopping Centre. Built in 1955, the feel and prices don't seem to have changed much since and, while it is most active in the evening (including a curious ninja bar), the vintage vibe makes it worth a quick detour.

Once you have exhausted the main sights and shopping streets of Asakusa, you'll probably need some coffee. Head to Asakusa Station and walk down Asakusa Dori avenue towards the nearby station of Tawaramachi, then take a left down Kotobuki Kodomoen Dori street. Continue until you find the elegant From Afar, a cafe housed in a former print shop from the 1960s. The gleaming dark wood, whimsical antique decor and bookcases filled with art and design books give it a timeless, old academia feel, with coffee served in fancy Arita, Imari and William Morris porcelain cups. The same company operates several other small businesses in the area, all with the same aesthetic and concept of bringing new life to older buildings. Check out nearby Nobori, where you can find beautiful crockery and glassware.

From here, make your way back to the main road and take a left. You should soon see why this is often called Butsudan Dori, as the road is lined with stores selling elaborate (*butsudan*) Buddhist altars and other funerary accessories. Keep going until you see a large chef's head appear on the horizon, which is the sign that you have reached Kappabashi, the cookware district.

The stores lining this long street and its many crossroads have everything you could possibly imagine (and more) dedicated to the art of good food. Many folks come looking for high-quality Japanese knives. Kamata is a good choice for beginners, as there is a good range and you can watch the masters sharpening the knives of Tokyo's best chefs. Bakers will love Majimaya, which specialises in everything pastry and confectionery related, and whose walls are covered with over 1000 different types of cookie cutters. There are a few shops offering beautiful mugs and enough plates, bowls and adorable chopstick holders to last a lifetime.

Retro Eats in Asakusa

TENGOKU

↘ 1 Chome-41-9 Asakusa, Taito City, Tokyo

A 10-minute walk down Hoppy Street and through some smaller shopping arcades is Tengoku, a little *kissaten* (old-school coffee house), whose name literally means 'heaven'. There are several retro hotdog options on the menu (and cute astrological fortune-telling gadgets on the tables), but the thing to order is the owner's famous hotcakes, stamped with the kanji for 'heaven'. Be sure to get a cup of coffee, as when you get to the bottom you will find out your fortune.

FUKUCHAN

↘ 1 Chome-1-12 Asakusa, Taito City, Tokyo

For a retro Asakusa flavour that is easy on the wallet, head to Fukuchan in the Asakusa Underground Shopping Centre, where a plate of stir-fried yakisoba noodles is just ¥350 (but I recommend splurging an extra ¥100 to get a sunnyside egg on top).

LEMON PIE

↘ 2 Chome-4-6 Kotobuki, Taito City, Tokyo

Just a few steps away from From Afar (see page 19), the cheerful yellow frontage of Lemon Pie reflects their most famous confection, which is, unsurprisingly, a beautifully fluffy and tart lemon meringue pie. They have been serving this and other nostalgic cakes since 1981 and are a local favourite, so you are likely to see a number of birthday cakes in the cool cases, just waiting for their owners to pick them up.

COOLEST SHRINES & TEMPLES IN TOKYO

There are over 4000 shrines and temples in Tokyo, ranging from world-famous spots like Sensoji Temple to tiny neighbourhood shrines mainly frequented by pensioners looking for a quiet place to read their newspapers. The sheer number of sights can be overwhelming, so here are a few personal favourites worth a detour.

MEIJI JINGU SHRINE

The location of this famous shrine couldn't be any better, right by Harajuku Station and a short walk from Shibuya and other popular sightseeing spots. It's the main imperial shrine, surrounded by 70 hectares (173 acres) of sacred forest that was planted in dedication to Emperor Meiji and Empress Shoken in 1920. The massive torii gates, impressive collection of barrels of sake donated by breweries across the country, pretty gardens and regular wedding processions give the area a sacred feeling, despite being in the middle of a busy city. The less visited section by the North Pond is also well worth a wander.

GOTOKUJI TEMPLE

This is known as the *manekineko* (lucky cat) temple, and the area to the left of the main hall is covered with hundreds of the famous beckoning cats, from tiny palm-sized statuettes to life-sized versions. Check out the cute carvings on the Sanju no To pagoda, featuring more cats, mice and critters from the Japanese zodiac.

According to legend, the feline connection goes back hundreds of years. This temple was a humble place tended by an elderly monk and his beloved kitty. One day, the cat beckoned to a samurai caught in a storm, who was impressed with the kindness and spirit of the monk, who invited him to shelter in the temple. The samurai turned out to be a great lord, who made Gotokuji his family temple, changing its fortunes.

After the lucky cat died, the monk blessed its grave and manekineko statues soon became symbols of good luck and prosperity.

A visit to this temple is best combined with a visit to Shimokitazawa, a couple of stops and a short walk away on the Odakyu Line. The shopping street that leads to Gotokuji is also quite charming, with several excellent sweet shops.

TOYOKAWA INARI BETSUIN TEMPLE

This 1828 hideaway is another fun temple, dedicated to the adorable kitsune foxes. As you follow the bright-red flags into the inner sanctuary, hundreds of different statues of the pointy-eared critters of all ages and sizes appear. It's a magical experience in this relatively office building–filled area of Tokyo.

The closest station is Akasaka Mitsuke, making this an easy detour if you decide to book a tour of the National Diet Building or Akasaka Palace State Guest House, both intriguing, offbeat spots where you can learn a bit about Japan's political system and ambitions.

HIE SHRINE

This very vertical shrine is just a 15-minute walk from the Toyokawa Inari Betsuin Temple. You'll also find more interesting animal imagery here, with the shrine guarded by monkeys in dashing red capes. This shrine was once a favourite of the Tokugawa shogunate, which had it moved first to within the castle keep and then, later, to its current location so all citizens could pay their respects to Oyamakui-no-kami, the guardian god of Edo. Perched on a hilltop and overlooked by vertiginous skyscrapers, it has a distinct old-meets-new feel.

TSUKIJI HONGANJI TEMPLE

This incongruous, soaring Indian-inspired structure has a very different feel from your average temple. It's a relatively recent creation, completed in 1934, with Western-inspired touches like stained-glass windows, a pipe organ and a massive, gold leaf–covered main altar.

The architect was known for having a love of yokai, the creatures of Japanese legends, and you can find them in the carvings, along with grotesques, phoenixes, winged lions and other animals.

Early birds may be interested in popping by for breakfast at Tsumugi, the temple's cafe. They open at 8 am and availability is limited.

HISTORY & RETRO MUSEUMS

Like any self-respecting capital, Tokyo is full of museums for history fiends to get lost in.

EDO-TOKYO MUSEUM

This is the perfect place to learn about how modern Tokyo evolved from the Edo period into the captivating capital it is today. The incongruous exterior, with its Space Invaders feel, gives way to immersive exhibits, including a reconstruction of the original Nihonbashi bridge, a full-scale kabuki theatre and a reproduction of Edo/Tokyo homes throughout the ages. (Please note that the museum is under renovation until 2025/early 2026.)

TOKYO NATIONAL MUSEUM

This massive museum, spread across six buildings in Ueno Park, has the country's largest collection of art and historical artifacts – over 100,000 items. The *honkan* (main building) is dedicated to Japanese arts and cultural items, while the Horyuji Homotsukan houses a treasure trove of religious figures donated by Horyuji Temple in Nara. The most beautiful is the Hyokeikan, which was built in 1909 and is a wonderful example of Western-influenced Meiji period architecture.

SHITAMACHI MUSEUM

Right on the bank of Shinobazu Pond in Ueno Park, this immersive little museum gives you a taste of what life was like for regular folks during the early 1900s in Tokyo. Enter the houses of a merchant, a shoemaker, a coppersmith and a regular family.

NATIONAL SHOWA MEMORIAL MUSEUM

If you're interested in more recent Japanese history, this dramatic structure is dedicated to the Showa period, with a particular emphasis on the daily life and hardships of Japanese citizens during WWII. The two floors of exhibits give a touching look into a Japan that is now difficult to imagine.

EDO-TOKYO OPEN AIR ARCHITECTURAL MUSEUM

It's a bit of a ride on the Chuo Line to Koganei Park, but the collection of Meiji period and more recent buildings make it worth the trip, as they were moved here to preserve important examples of architectural history under threat of fires, earthquakes or redevelopment. The traditional farmhouses, photo studio and former residence of Hachirouemon Mitsui are particularly impressive, as is the recreated shopping street.

NEZU MUSEUM

The experience here starts with the building itself, an airy, minimalist marvel by Kengo Kuma, and continues in the gorgeous sunken garden, complete with several tea houses. The collection of pre-modern Japanese and East Asian arts, with its particular emphasis on ceramics and tea ceremony utensils, calligraphy and sculptures, was once owned by railway tycoon, Kaichiro Nezu. The museum's location, near the fashionable Omotesando shopping street, offers a quiet retreat from the city.

TRADITIONAL TOKYO EXPERIENCES

Tea ceremonies, kimono rentals and ninja trick houses have become common around Japan, so it is easy to find and book an experience. But how about something a little more unique and interactive, where you can get a feel for how the people of Edo used to let loose?

SEE SOME KABUKI

Kabuki is one of Japan's flashiest traditional performing arts. It's completely over the top with its costumes and staging, movement and vocalisations. Kabuki was originally performed by females during the early Edo period, but the shogunate, worried about public morals, decided to switch it to the all-male art we see today. Actors specialise in either masculine or female roles, with many of the latter (known as 'onna-gata') attracting legions of dedicated fans.

Stories and styles vary widely, from traditional plays focusing on themes of filial piety and doomed love, to modern super kabuki, in which popular manga, animation and movies are given a glitzy makeover for the stage. Performances are often between 3 and 5 hours long, but at the lovely Kabukiza Theatre in Ginza, you can get inexpensive tickets for a single act.

Kabukiza Theatre is accessible directly from Higashi Ginza Station, and you'll see the day's shows listed near the ticket window. One-act tickets cost around ¥1000–¥1500 and evening tickets around ¥2000, depending on who's performing. Get to the theatre 20 minutes before the show starts, take the elevator to the fourth floor, and grab an unreserved seat. A word of warning: if you go on the official website (kabukiweb.net) to see what's on and book a ticket, be careful, as this site is the booking point for kabuki theatres all around the country.

WATCH A SUMO TOURNAMENT

The sumo we see today was formed during the Edo period, when matches became popularised as a way to raise money for temples and shrines.

The Tokyo tournaments take place over two weeks in both January and May, with ticket sales starting about one month in advance. Matches run from 10 am to 6 pm, with the higher-ranked wrestlers starting their bouts around 2 pm. The festive atmosphere, energy from the ring and awesome snacks definitely give the Kokugikan building a timeless atmosphere, and you don't need to know the rules of sumo to enjoy a day out at the tournament.

It's easy to book regular free seats up on the second floor via the official website, but my favourite way to watch sumo is from the *masu* (box) seats closer to the ring. Prices start at around ¥40,000 per box, which can hold four people (tightly – two or three is comfier), but with some help from a concierge or Japanese-speaking friend, you can get special tickets from one of the 20 *ochaya* (tea houses). These include tons of only-in-Ryogoku foods and free-flowing drink service from the *dekata* (staff dressed in traditional clothing). Don't forget to tip them at least ¥2000 – an unusual experience itself in tip-free Japan!

YAKATABUNE DINNER CRUISE

You're likely to see these long, low and lantern-festooned boats by the riverside in Asakusa. Yakatabune have been around since the Heian period (794–1185) as the pleasure boats of wealthy lords but became more available (and the scene of raucous parties) during the Edo period. A night out on a yakatabune is a lot of fun, and particularly popular during the summer firework festivals. Inside, they usually have tatami floors, free-flowing drinks and low tables heaving with a feast of tempura and tasty tidbits. If you're lucky, you might get to buy ice cream or *tsukudani* (soy-simmered foods) from vendors who sell boat-to-boat like in the olden days!

There are a lot of yakatabune companies to choose from; however, Harumiya is a good bet for international visitors, as all its boats have horikotatsu, where the floor is sunken underneath the low tables, so you don't have to sit cross-legged for the entire journey.

Jindaiji Temple Escape Walk

Jindaiji Temple, hidden away in the western outskirts of Tokyo, is just 40 minutes from Shinjuku (via the Keio Line train to Chofu Station or the Chuo or Inokashira Line to Kichijoji Station), but it feels like another city. A trip to this temple goes well with a romp around fashionable Kichijoji and a visit to the Ghibli Museum, followed by a bus ride towards Jindaiji.

Most buses will drop you off near the entrance to the Jindai Botanical Garden, so buy a ticket and head through the wickets. This is Tokyo's main botanical garden, and home to the biggest rose garden in the city, with about 400 varieties that bloom in late May and mid-October. The late-winter plum trees and spring cherry blossoms, and the colourful azalea-covered hills that bloom from mid-April to June, are all lovely. With no tall buildings in sight, you will feel miles away from the metropolis.

Continue your exploration by exiting via the Jindaiji gate, from which a short trail through trees, smaller sub-temples and little tea houses will take you to Tokyo's second-oldest temple, dating back to 733 AD (although it has been rebuilt several times since). If you stop by at 11 am or 2 pm on weekdays (or 11 am, 1 pm or 2 pm on weekends) you can catch the Goma Fire Ritual in the Ganzan Daishi hall, where wooden sticks that represent human desires and other symbolic offerings are set aflame. On 3–4 March, the Jindaiji Daruma Doll Festival is held here, with hundreds of vendors selling the round, red good-luck dolls.

One of the loveliest parts of Jindaiji is the flagstone walkway in front of the temple. It's lined with soba restaurants, ponds, waterwheels and shops with old-fashioned treats. You must have soba noodles here, as buckwheat has been a major part of the area's appeal since the Edo period. Tenant farmers would pay their dues to the temple with bags of buckwheat for the temple cooks to turn into soba noodles. Try Aokiya for its fast service and outdoor tables with pond views. Suzume no Yado is a little more upmarket and offers lovely, fresh tempura, *tamagoyaki* (rolled omelette), coffee and kuzumochi jelly.

If you're just looking for a quick bite, head to Ameya, near the pond, for unique street food. Their most popular item is the soba pan bread, stuffed with takana veggie stir-fry, red bean paste, curry or simmered daikon radish ... or with soft-serve ice cream for those with a sweet tooth. If you are lucky, they might have packs of karameyaki, a truly retro treat made of puffed, crunchy caramel.

When walking towards Jindaiji Dori avenue, anime and manga fans may recognise the characters from the series *Gegege no Kitaro* peeking out from the corners and rooftop of the Kitaro Chaya tea house. For those less familiar: this popular series features yokai, the spirits and supernatural entities of Japanese folklore, which vary from the terrifying to the merely perplexing (like living rolls of cotton cloth or anthropomorphic paper lanterns).

From the Jindaiji Information Centre, you have a couple of options. Go left, and you can stroll around the Jindai Botanical Aquatic Garden, where irises bloom from late May to mid-June. Follow the street to the right, passing waterwheels and attractive houses, and you will end up at Daruma no Ouchi, a shop that specialises in daruma dolls, considered symbols of perseverance and luck. If you book in advance, you can even learn how to make your own.

A particularly fun side trip is to Yumori no Sato, a beloved local hot spring. Take a left at the Jindaiji Information Centre, then a left at the first stoplight. Follow the hilly little road for about 5 minutes, go left when you hit a larger road, and look for the green sign.

This is not a *sento* (a public bath with regular heated water) but an actual onsen hot spring, with the mineral-rich dark-brown water typical of the Kanto area. Submerging yourself for the first time in the dark water feels a bit odd – almost like bathing in soy sauce! – but the outdoor pools with Ghibli-esque touches and the higgledy-piggledy nature of the retro wooden building are all charm. Say hello to the resident rabbit and get some ice cream topped with a candied grasshopper at the little concession stand.

FOODIE WONDERS OF JINDAIJI

Foodies looking for a real hidden gem should head to sleek and airy Maruta, about a 5-minute walk from the Jindai Botanical Garden main entrance. The lunch and dinner courses are not cheap (around ¥18,000), but the quality of the food is extraordinary. Ingredients are grown in their own garden, sourced from Chofu farms or, in the case of their ultra-fresh fish, flown in from the Izu Islands. The modern interior makes a stunning contrast to the dishes, which are all cooked over a wood fire. Book in advance, and understand that the hyper-seasonal, locavore menu means that they don't make substitutions for allergies or special diets.

◆ *Jindaiji Temple*

WHY IS THERE SO LITTLE OF OLD TOKYO LEFT?

You might be surprised by all the prefab homes and drab apartment blocks that surround the splendour of the historical monuments, temples and shrines of Tokyo. While there are remnants of the beautiful wooden architecture of 'old Japan' in smaller towns and some pockets of the city, there are a few reasons why so much of it didn't survive.

—

NATURAL DISASTERS – Japan is frequently hit by earthquakes, tsunamis and (in earlier times) fires, which have given a very different cultural understanding of ownership and permanence. While older buildings can stand for centuries in places like Europe, a more permanent structure was not usually a possibility for people in Japan, so traditions and locations become more important than the structure itself. This is why you will often visit temples and shrines that have been in the same place for hundreds (or even thousands) of years, but the buildings will be much more recent.

WWII – The atomic bombing of Hiroshima and Nagasaki feature heavily in history books, but the fire bombings of Tokyo and other major cities during WWII were (terrifyingly) even more devastating. In just one night, over 40 hectares (99 acres) of Tokyo were burned to the ground and around 100,000 people perished. There was similar devastation in other major cities and ports such as Osaka, Nagoya and Kobe. As most structures were built from wood, the fires burned sections of the cities to the ground.

NEW = BETTER – After the devastation of the war, there was an immediate need for a lot of housing. Tons of cheap houses were created, without much thought to how long they would last. This set off a cycle of erecting buildings that were not meant to be used long term but, instead, razed and rebuilt within a generation or two, using the latest technology, particularly regarding earthquake-damage prevention.

DEPRECIATION – Buying a pre-owned house is less common in Japan than in other countries. While there is a growing trend towards buying and restoring traditional Japanese houses, more modern homes are often built of relatively flimsy materials and it's only the land they are built on that retains its value. As such, many people don't see the point in renovating or keeping their house current and compliant with earthquake regulations.

SPIRITS – Albeit a minor part of the puzzle, the long tradition of animism means that some people in Japan believe that objects and places that have been important to others can become imbued with the soul or feelings of those who used them, which can make people wary of moving into a second-hand house. This is the same reason you may see people bringing chopsticks, dolls, needles and other beloved items to temples to be ritually burned ... just in case!

美食の東京

Foodie Tokyo

JAPAN HAS A DEEP OBSESSION WITH FOOD. The thought and craft that go into the cuisine make it truly magical and, as Tokyo has the most Michelin-approved restaurants in the world, the proof is really in the pudding.

Tokyo is hard to beat when it comes to price and quality. You can get a soulful bowl of noodles for under ¥400 and even modest budgets will buy you memorable meals.

The flipside is trying to decide where to eat in a city so packed with restaurants that they are often stacked one on top of the other over multiple floors. The sheer choice and number can be overwhelming and, if you want to eat out at less touristy places, the lack of English signage can make ordering with confidence a bit of a challenge. So let me break down the best areas for you. Don't worry: you'll never get a bad meal in Tokyo.

TOKYO'S BEST STREET FOOD AREAS

While Tokyo doesn't have the nightly street markets of neighbours like Taipei and Bangkok or the hawker centres of Singapore, there are certainly parts of the city where you can enjoy strolling around and sampling all kinds of Japanese morsels.

I've covered some street eats in the guided walks in Togoshi Ginza (page 42), Harajuku (page 44), Sugamo (page 52) and Yanaka (page 97), but here are some other foodie spots to try.

NAKAMISE DORI

This famous street that leads to the iconic Sensoji Temple should be renamed 'Temptation Alley'. You'll find stalls selling everything from 200-year-old traditional sweets to the latest foodie craze, with even more interesting options along the side streets.

You really can't go wrong, but I love the ridiculously over-the-top mochi skewers from Soratsuki. These sweet rice dumplings are doused with different toppings, shiny sprinkles and sweet strawberries. Look for the stall's strawberry decor, about halfway between the Kaminarimon Gate and the temple itself. Or turn right at the end of Nakamise Dori and look for the green shades of Sawawa, dedicated to all things matcha (the filled pancakes – dorayaki – and ice cream are fantastic). For something savoury, Toyofuku's curry bread is the perfect winter treat. Take a left a little after Soratsuki to find this tiny stall on nearby Denpoin Street.

AMEYOKO

After WWII, this was where the black-market trade in American goods and other hard-to-get foods was centred. Shopping options have certainly expanded since then but, running along and below the train tracks of Ueno Station, it still has a bit of that wild, unregulated feel, which attracts lots of visitors in search of interesting eats.

At Hyakken, you can get sticks of ultra-sweet seasonal fruit (the melon, mango and strawberries are particularly good). At standing bar Uokusa (look for the red shark) they offer fresh seafood with a glass of sake for around ¥500–¥1000 a pop. Niku no Oyama's ¥400 wagyu beef croquette is considered one of the must-eats by Japanese visitors, although I think the meat-free ameyokoyaki – which tastes like okonomiyaki and is redolent of post-war cheap eats – is more unique. Keep an eye out for the cart that shows up whenever the owner feels like it! You'll also find plenty of popular imports like bubble tea, Chinese dumplings and Korean cheese-covered, deep-fried hotdogs here as well.

YANAKA GINZA

This charming little shopping street, just a short walk from Nippori Station, packs a lot into a small area – especially for cat lovers. There are statues and shops celebrating the local cats, and you can even get treats like taiyaki pancakes in the shape of lucky manekineko cats at Manekiya and donuts shaped like cat tails at Shippoya.

In a side street to the left just after the Yuyake Dandan staircase is Himitsudo, a kakigori (shaved ice) spot open all year round, with seasonal specials. It's tiny and gets incredibly busy on the weekends, so aim to stop by on a weekday. There are several shops with savoury snacks like meat croquettes and battered and grilled squid but, overall, Yanaka is definitely a sweet tooth's dream.

SUNAMACHI GINZA

This truly old-school shopping street is still very much under the radar, as it's not conveniently located near a station. It's not far from the hip and historic Fukagawa area and, with a map app and a bus ride, the excellent and budget-friendly food scene here is definitely accessible.

This area is known for clam-based cuisine, so try the *asari gohan* (clam rice) from Asariya. Okada, recognisable by the dozens of bright signs with prices, is famous for its *yakitori* (grilled chicken skewers). Look for the steaming vats at Masuei Shoten, where you can try oden, a steaming broth bobbing with daikon, eggs and a huge variety of surimi-based bites.

EATING LIKE A LOCAL

While sushi, tempura and the glorious excess of kaiseki course meals are wonderful, these aren't considered everyday meals in Japan. Many staples are localised versions of dishes inspired by international cuisines. Others are so deceptively simple, they never make it onto restaurant menus outside of Japan.

Get a taste of what people in Japan actually cook and eat at home with these favourites.

CURRY

Pronounced 'car-eh' in Japanese, this is definitely one of the top three local comfort foods and a perennial favourite with children. Japanese-style curry does include some Indian spices, but it's not too hot, just a little sweet and has a thicker texture than traditional curries. The most common ingredients are potatoes, carrots, onions and meat, but this varies in each household.

Cheap and cheerful *kare raisu* (curry and rice) is available at a number of chains, with nationwide CoCo Ichibanya being particularly good for vegan and allergen-free options. For something a little more special, head to the book district of Jimbocho and line up at Kitchen Nankai for their black curry, a beloved recipe that goes back over 60 years. If you're struggling with Japanese translations, make it easy on yourself and just ask for the chicken katsu curry.

MABO TOFU

The Japanese version of the popular Sichuan dish is absolutely everywhere, from restaurant menus to supermarket shelves. It's a warming, spicy delight, with tofu and ground meat in a thick sauce made from doubanjiang chilli paste, garlic, ginger, spring onions (scallions) and Sichuan pepper.

If you want a version that's lighter on the spice (and vegan!), head to Izakaya Masaka, in the basement of the Parco department store in Shibuya. For a more fiery experience, the Ryu no Ko restaurant not far from Togo Shrine in Harajuku is particularly popular with Tokyo foodies.

NAPOLITAN

This pillar of *yoshoku* (Western-style cuisine) is a real love-it-or-hate-it dish: spaghetti flavoured with a thick, ketchup-laced sauce with ham, green bell peppers (capsicums) and onions. This post-WWII American-influenced dish was created at the elegant Hotel New Grand in Yokohama, and originally had a complex tomato paste–based sauce. That was a bit too expensive for less elite restaurants to copy, so they subbed in ketchup instead, which was readily available from military stocks.

You can get a good napolitan at the retro Coffee House Rose, tucked behind the Takashimaya department store a short walk from Tokyo Station. For an even more historical spot, try Denkiya Hall, a great kissaten established in 1903. It's just a 5-minute walk from Sensoji Temple in Asakusa, so go for the retro arcade table games, a bowl of napolitan and other Showa period favourites.

NIKUJAGA

Most people have never heard of this staple of Japanese home cooking, which directly translates to 'meat and potatoes'. This stew consists of (no surprise) meat, potatoes and onion cooked in sweetened soy sauce and mirin. It's thought to be a Japanese version of British beef stew, brought back by a navy commander in the late 1800s. Many Japanese people associate nikujaga with their childhoods and cook this comfort food at home.

Try this dish at Sake no Ana, a hidden gem in Ginza and just a short walk from the fancy Matsuya department store. They do a roaring trade at both lunch and dinner and have a truly impressive sake selection. Their okonomi lunch set includes three dishes from the monthly line-up (which usually includes a generous serve of nikujaga) for just ¥1200.

HIYASHI CHUKA

No two ways about it, summer in Tokyo is hot and humid. Enter hiyashi chuka, a great chilled ramen dish with curly noodles, sliced vegetables, egg and ham, all doused in either a black vinegar or a creamy sesame sauce. The dish is said to have been created in the late 1930s by the chef of a Chinese restaurant in Sendai as a way for folks to enjoy his cuisine even during the summer heat.

You can pick up a pre-made pack of hiyashi chuka at convenience stores and supermarkets throughout the summer, but it's best enjoyed fresh at one of the capital's many ramen joints. One particularly good spot is Nihonbashi Sapporoya, a basement ramen restaurant a short walk from the Yaesu Exit of Tokyo Station. While most famous for their Hokkaido-style miso ramen, during the summer months it is the huge plates of gomadare hiyashi ramen (their version of sesame hiyashi chuka) that keep me coming back. Look for the red sign and arrow leading to the basement of this unfussy, salarymen-beloved spot.

AN ODE TO KONBINI

When you find yourself jet-lagged and starving at odd hours of the night or early morning, Japan's incredible convenience stores (locally known as *konbini*) come to the rescue. A definite step above their non-Asian counterparts, these 24-hour businesses are like shining beacons, attracting hungry folks and caffeine seekers like moths to a flame.

The most common are 7-Eleven and FamilyMart, the former best known for its large range of cold prepared foods, and the latter most closely associated with fried chicken and other hot foods. Lawson's dessert selection is the most impressive, while MiniStop has a range of seasonal ice cream floats. My personal favourite is the rarer Natural Lawson, which is better in terms of health-conscious and vegan options and is generally found in the more hip areas of Tokyo.

To truly go local, buy a cup of spicy noodles and a precooked egg, along with your drink of choice. Konbini have a wide range of regular and alcoholic beverages, but a canned, fruit-flavoured *chu-hai* (shochu highball) is a traditional choice. Fill your ramen cup with hot water at the counter, drop in the egg and then wander over to the nearest park for the quintessential Japanese snack. This is particularly nice during the cherry blossom season after dark, when you can enjoy your ramen under a canopy of ghostly blossoms fluttering in the dark.

Old-to-new Foodie Adventure

For dedicated foodies who want to experience *all the things*, here's an itinerary that will take you from the traditional to the contemporary, ending with a well-deserved, self-guided sake tasting.

Fuel up on coffee and a light breakfast then aim for Togoshi Ginza shopping street, which is near Togoshi Station on the Toei Asakusa Line, or Togoshi-Ginza Station on the Tokyu Ikegami Line. Alternatively, it's about a 15-minute walk from Osaki Station via Mitsugi Street.

This old-school shopping street is the longest in Tokyo, stretching over 1.3 km (0.8 miles), and retains its character thanks to the enlightened decision to bury the power lines that so often crisscross above your head. This is one of the capital's lesser-known street-food havens, offering snacks of all varieties. No need to hurry here, as most shops open between 10 and 11 am, so you can fit in some morning sightseeing if you're feeling ambitious.

Perhaps the most iconic food to try is the *korokke* (potato croquettes) at Nakamura Tadashi Shoten, where the perfectly fried crunchy exterior gives way to a generous portion of fluffy mashed potato. At Henteco, you can buy intricate animal-shaped cookies and bear-shaped pancakes. Unlike a lot of cute dessert spots, here they put a huge emphasis on natural ingredients and avoid using preservatives and food colouring, so the treats are as good as they look. For those with gluten allergies (or those who are just curious), stop at Beicon for their rice flour–based curry bread, cookies and melonpan. Harimaya offers an 'ultra-spicy' curry bread as well, if you want to test your taste buds.

Some other fun things to try are the okonomi-taiyaki at Omedetaiyaki, which blend the heft of savoury pancakes with the famous fish-shaped taiyaki cakes. The very affordable coffee at Compass Coffee pairs nicely with the soft navona cookie sandwiches filled with cream, jam or fruit from longstanding sweets-maker Kameya Mannendo. This is just a small sample of the dozens of treats available, so go wandering before you make your decisions! While you're at it, keep an eye out for the statues of the shopping street's mascot, a cartoon tiger(-ish) creature called Gin-chan.

Work up your next appetite by visiting nearby Togoshi Hachiman Shrine and its cute bunny statue, said to make your dreams come true. A little further away is Togoshi Park, an Edo-style strolling garden with ponds, a waterfall and plum, cherry and ginkgo trees.

Ready for more? Follow Togoshi Ginza (past Togoshi-Ginza Station) until you hit the large Nakahara Kaido Road. Cross, then go left until you see a side street to your right and the entrance to the Palm shopping arcade. (Look for the two weirdly anthropomorphic, squirrel-like characters.) At around 800 metres (½ mile) long, it's the longest covered arcade in Tokyo, and gives you a good feel for how Japanese shopping streets evolved over the years, as many of these popped up in the 1950s, influenced by Western architecture.

This area is a great rainy-day alternative to Togoshi Ginza. Try the yakitori at Toriyu, which has been in business since 1926, or get a matcha or hojicha latte and something from the quirky toast menu at Saryo Bakery, a little outpost of the famous tea house in snazzy Kagurazaka.

If it's a hot day, stop at the unusual Dessert Inn, an intriguing little hole-in-the-wall that sells school uniforms and, for some reason, extremely good gelato. The yoghurt and citrus flavours are especially refreshing. Keep an eye out for the shop selling Buddhist altars, as they often have candles shaped like beer, sake or cups of green tea, which make for interesting souvenirs.

After this in-depth taste of the old, it's time to check out the new! Hop on the train towards Meguro at Musashi Koyama Station, then switch to the Yamanote Line and get off at either Shibuya or Harajuku Station. In either case, your first destination should be Miyashita Park, which is about a 10-minute walk from either station.

This modernist three-storey shopping complex, with its stores, cafes and rooftop gardens, is a magnet for Tokyo's young and fashion-obsessed. Wander around the bright shops and up to the second floor of the south building for an organic tea break at The Matcha Tokyo. The cold matcha served over ice has a pleasant natural sweetness and it's fun to watch the staff do an abbreviated version of the tea ceremony for certain drinks. The rich green tea ice cream is also excellent.

From Miyashita Park, it's just a short walk to the Omotesando/ Harajuku area. Go via fashion-forward Cat Street (look for the giant golden egg at the entrance – it's the symbol of Pink Dragon, a rockabilly clothing store popular with famous retro dancers who strut their stuff in nearby Yoyogi Park). Take a peek at the 'dragon museum' for a bit of odd whimsy.

The broad streets of Omotesando (sometimes nicknamed the 'Champs-Élysées of Tokyo') are lined with shop after glittering shop of famous designer brands, while just a couple of side streets away is Harajuku, with teenagers looking for bright, cheap fashion. This entire area is where the latest 'it' desserts and treats tend to pop up, and you can usually figure out the latest craze by the lengths of the lines. Food trends in Tokyo change very quickly, so staying on top of the latest must-try is best done via social media, but there are plenty of long-standing favourites too. Will it be a giant rainbow of cotton candy or a massive everything-and-the-kitchen-sink crepe in Harajuku? The vegan donuts at the Good Town bakery or vegan cookies at Ovgo? A total chocolate attack at Jean Paul-Hevin or the insanely artistic mille-feuille rounds at Gariguette? This is the sweetest agony of choice.

For a kitschy treat, check out Madosh! Cafe, just a few steps from the Design Festa art gallery. This cheerful joint is run by an owner completely obsessed with avocados, and every dish features the delicious green fruit, including the creamy avocado cappuccino. This can be a good option for an early dinner, to line your stomach for the final stop of the day.

Before making your way to Meiji-jingumae Station, detour to Togo Shrine, a little oasis of traditional Japan surrounded by the bright chaos of subculture fashion and boba stands. Despite its distance from the sea, it's dedicated to a legendary navy admiral, Heihachiro Togo, and there are some monuments dedicated to mariners and submariners on the grounds. The walkways over the koi-filled pond are popular spots for wedding photos, and you may well see posing couples decked out in kimono.

Take the Fukutoshin Line from Meiji-jingumae Station (there are entrances dotted along Omotesando) to Shinjuku-sanchome Station for the last delicious stop of the day: an all-you-can-drink sake tasting!

First, pick up some snacks to go with your sake. Head for exits B3 or B5, which will lead you straight to the Isetan department store and its legendary basement food hall. The sheer range of this foodie wonderland can be overwhelming; to simplify things, sake tends to pair well with foods with deep, umami flavours, so look for interesting pickles, robust fish or meat dishes, smoked nuts, Chinese food or funky cheese. Chocolate, fruity desserts and Japanese wagashi sweets also work well.

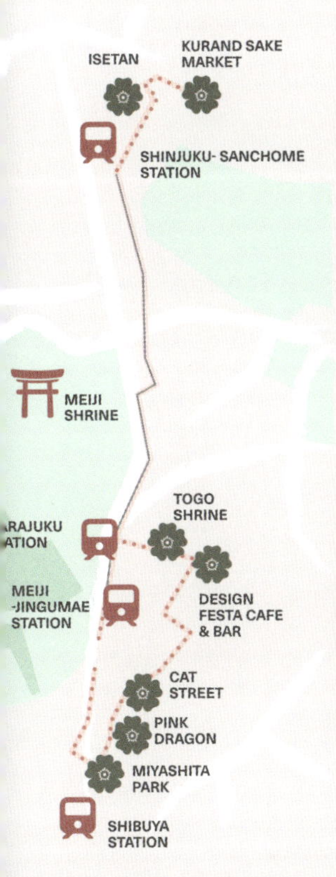

All stocked up? Just a couple of minutes from the department store is the Kurand Sake Market, tucked away on the sixth floor of a building right in front of the C8 Exit of Shinjuku-sanchome Station. From 6 pm to 11 pm, you can pay ¥3600 for unlimited self-service access to over 100 different types of craft sakes, as well as umeshu plum wine, fruit-based liqueurs and shochu. It's a bring-your-own-food system, so set up your nibbles then hit the bottle-filled fridges. If you're new to sake and want some guidance, the staff are incredibly helpful and can curate a little tasting flight to get you started. (If several hours of sake sounds a bit intense, they also have cheaper 30-minute and 90-minute sessions available.) Book in advance, especially for Fridays and weekends.

Where to Savour Retro Tokyo

If you're hungry for a bit of gastronomic time travel, Tokyo does not disappoint. There are restaurants here that have been in operation for well over 100 years. These interesting spots are often a bit hidden, and so well established that they don't need to advertise, so let me show you where to find a taste of Tokyo past.

SAVOURY

OIWAKE

↘ 3-28-11 Nishi-Asakusa, Taito-ku, Tokyo
5.30 pm–midnight, performances usually start around 7 pm, closed Mondays

Located in Iriya, not far from the major sightseeing hub of Asakusa, this legendary *minyo sakaba* (folksong pub) is definitely off the beaten track. With live performances by the talented staff (some of whom have gone on to become famous recording artists) and a casual, tatami-floored dining area, it feels like you've slipped back to the 1950s. The tone and singing styles of minyo vary from high-pitched to gravelly, depending on where they originated from, and are usually accompanied by a *shamisen* (a shovel-shaped string instrument).

— Unless you speak Japanese, you'll need help booking a table, as they only accept reservations by phone. Ask your hotel concierge or guide to call for you.

FUCHA BON

↘ 1-2-11 Ryusen, Taito-ku, Tokyo
Lunch and dinner daily, closed Wednesdays

Also near Iriya, this elegant restaurant serves fucha cuisine, a Chinese version of Japanese shojin ryori Buddhist meals. The restaurant has been around since 1972 and each meal is a procession of delicate, intricate vegan dishes. After being shown to your private room, the experience begins with tea and a pressed-sugar sweet, and then takes off into a folly of seasonal tastes. A few staples of fucha are present in every meal, such as unpen, a ginger-laced, thickened soup made with veggies, and the restaurant's famous fried eggplant in a hearty miso sauce. It's a lot of food, so light eaters and those on a budget should opt for weekday lunch courses.

OTAKO

↘ Otako Bldg, 2-2-3 Nihonbashi, Chuo-ku, Tokyo
5 pm–10 pm, closed Sundays

Just a short walk from the Yaesu Exit of sprawling Tokyo Station, Otako is an unpretentious oden restaurant that has been around since 1936. They specialise in Tokyo-style oden, laden with *hanpen* (a pillowy surimi fish cake), eggs, daikon and shirataki noodles that are stewed for hours in a savoury broth. You can also get your selection of oden to go, packed in the most adorable, vintage-style red canister: a meal and souvenir all in one.

RENGATEI

↘ 3 Chome-5-16 Ginza, Chuo-ku, Tokyo
Lunch 11.15 am–2.30 pm, dinner 4.40 pm–8.30 pm, closed Sundays

This Ginza staple has been in business since 1895 and the signage and exterior don't look like they've changed much since then. It's considered one of the major birthplaces of *yoshoku* (Western-style cuisine) in Japan. Their other claim to fame is inventing tonkatsu, the incredibly popular crumbed and fried pork cutlet that was a lighter twist on the French *côtelette de veau* (veal cutlet). They are also thought to be the originators of the omurice, an omelette filled with tomato ketchup–flavoured rice, which is still a favourite for kids (and adults) in Japan. The shrimp gratin is also very good, and just the thing after a winter walk around Ginza.

初音

SWEET

MONT BLANC

↘ 1-29-3 Jiyugaoka, Meguro-ku, Tokyo
10 am–6 pm, closed Tuesdays

The unassuming entrance to this legendary tearoom is close to the central gate of Jiyugaoka Station. The shop opened in 1933, and the murals, original paintings and Art Deco chrome detailing are a real trip back to the 1930s.

This is where Japan's beloved chestnut-filled Mont Blanc cake originated and their version is particularly tall and complex, with multiple layers of castella cake, buttercream and golden chestnut paste. Their old-fashioned cookies are also lovely, like something you'd find at a European Christmas market.

Note that Mont Blanc is undergoing a four-year renovation from the start of 2023, but you can still get your cake fix from a small shop inside the nearby Iwatate Textile Museum building (1-25-13 Jiyugaoka, Meguro-ku, Tokyo).

HATSUNE

↘ 1-15-6 Nihonbashiningyocho, Chuo-ku, Tokyo
11.30 am–5.30 pm

Hatsune, on the main road in the Ningyocho area, dates all the way back to 1837. This *kanmidokoro* (literally translating to 'sweet place') specialises in traditional Japanese desserts heavy on red beans, rice flour dumplings, agar jelly cubes and black sugar syrup. The cream anmitsu has all of these, along with a generous dollop of vanilla ice cream. My personal favourites are their summer-only *anzu kakigori* (shaved ice with homemade apricot syrup), and the matcha shiratama, a dish of sweet red beans, glutinous rice dumplings and matcha ice cream. For a small bite, go for the simple yet tasty *isobemaki* (grilled rectangles of mochi wrapped in dried seaweed that you dip in soy sauce).

◆ *Hatusne*

COOKING EXPERIENCES IN TOKYO

Has *washoku* (Japanese cuisine) stolen your heart? Take one of these classes so you can recreate your favourite dishes at home.

RAMEN

It's pretty hard to beat a piping-hot bowl of fragrant broth and noodles. However, making ramen is not the work of one afternoon, and the broth itself takes hours, and sometimes days, to create. Get a chef's-eye view of the ramen-making experience by booking a special 'behind the counter' tour. You'll learn what goes into making the all-important broth, the proper way to cook and drain the noodles, and how to rapidly assemble the perfect bowl. Book this and other ramen-focused tours online at Tokyo Ramen Tours.

HOME COOKING

Buddha Bellies Cooking School has been around for over 10 years, run by Ayuko and her pro sushi chef husband. The homely, welcoming atmosphere is a huge part of the charm of her classes, and the fact that she can also accommodate vegetarian, vegan and halal needs is another.

While you may be tempted by the fancy sushi classes, go for the standard washoku course, in which you'll learn how to make a homestyle Japanese main dish and three side dishes that can be easily recreated at home. Go to their website for more information on classes and how to book.

MOCHI DESSERTS

For a light and vegan-friendly sweet treat, why not learn how to make soft mochi rice-paste dumplings filled with seasonal fruit? At Chagohan, conveniently located in the major sightseeing haven of Asakusa, you can learn how to make the base for these iconic Japanese sweets, which you then get to snarf down after the class, along with a bowl of freshly prepared matcha tea.

REAL HOME COOKING

If you are more interested in learning about typical life in Japan and what kinds of foods people usually eat at home, sign up for Nagomi Visit. Run by an NPO, this organisation seeks to create international bonds and friendship through food, so you will be paired with one of the hosts and enjoy a couple of hours cooking, chatting and experiencing regular life in Japan at their home.

A Taste for Tradition – A Foodie's Garden Walk in the Old City

Sure, Japan has an impressive line in Instagrammable foods like those over-the-top crepes of Harajuku, but traditional Japanese aesthetics, which extend to food, go for a more subtle approach. While the very Edo period ethos of being *iki* – effortlessly stylish and elegant – now often gets overshadowed by the more bombastic parts of Japan's culture and subcultures, it's certainly not gone. Take this walk in the old city, with plenty of treats to tempt you along the way, and you'll see. This pleasant stroll through a quieter part of town encapsulates a slower pace and time.

Take the Yamanote Line to Komagome Station, take the South Exit and follow the signs to Rikugien Gardens, a few minutes by foot from the station.

Rikugien literally means 'garden of six poems'. Created in the 1700s for the shogun of the time, this is a traditional strolling garden, meant to show different landscapes from various angles. Autumn is considered one of the best times to visit, when they also host evening illumination events, but I'm partial to early summer, when the azalea bushes are in bloom. Stop for green tea and rakugan, a pretty seasonal sweet treat made from fine sugar and rice flour, at Fukiage Chaya tea house overlooking the pond.

After getting your fill of pretty gardens and flowers, head to Sugamo. Sure, it's only one stop away on the Yamanote Line, but it's more fun to take the 20-minute walk through the side streets. Cat lovers should stop on the way at Komagome Myogi Shrine, a beloved cherry blossom spot in the spring, to hunt around for the cat statues and pick up a cat-themed *omamori* (lucky charm) or a *goshuin* (shrine/temple stamp).

Rikugien Gardens ♦

After arriving near Sugamo Station, your first stop must be Sennari Monaka, just a few steps away from exit A3. While their namesake *monaka* (red bean paste or other sweet filling in a crispy wafer shell) is certainly good, get a dorayaki, in which the red bean paste is sandwiched between two pancakes. When they're served warm and straight off the grill, they're magical in their simplicity.

Next up, take a left and make your way to the Jizo Dori shopping street, which is affectionately known as 'granny's Harajuku'. While supposedly catering to the elderly, the charming retro feel attracts all ages.

Togenuki Temple has been the heart of the neighbourhood since 1891 and is known for the Arai Kannon statue. According to legend, this statue can help you recover from injury. Just pray as you wash the part of the statue that corresponds with the site of your pain, and you'll recover. Buy a small white hand towel for ¥100 and then wait your turn to rinse the statue and then wipe it down.

A couple of minutes' walk from the temple is Maruji, a shop that exclusively sells bright-red garments and goods, most famously underwear. In Japan, red is an auspicious colour, thought to bring

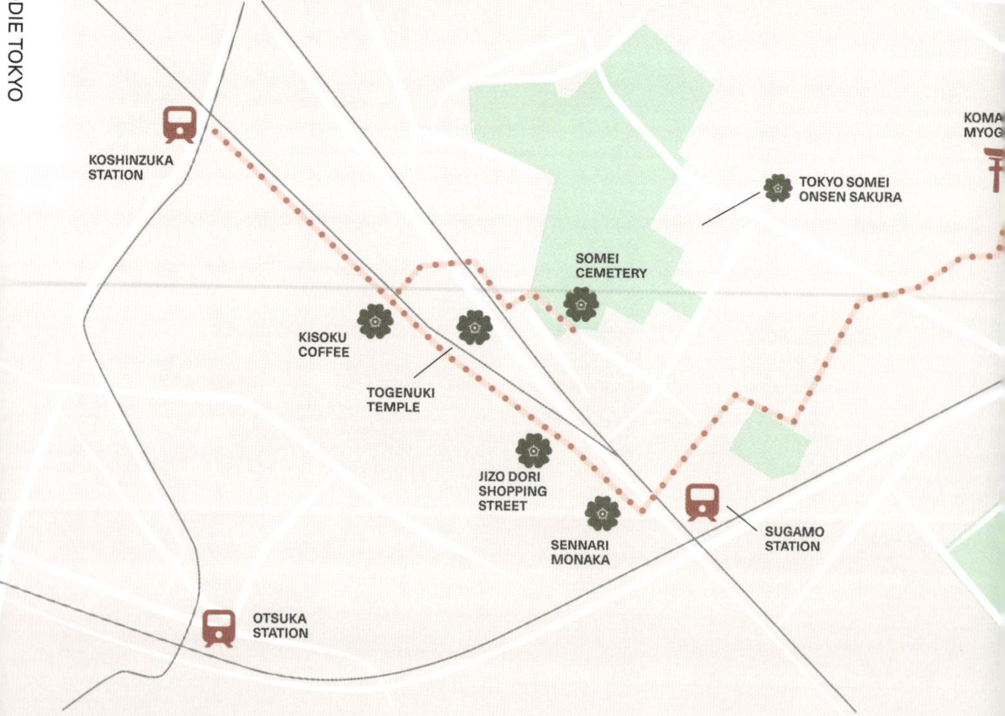

good luck and longevity. When people turn 60 in Japan, they are celebrated with a kanreki party, for which they wear a special red hat and vest as a prayer for longevity. Older people wear this bright-red underwear in the hope of a long life! You can even get underwear with the 12 signs of the Chinese zodiac if you want a pair for your birth year.

By now, it's probably time for coffee. Head to the charmingly old-school Kisoku Coffee, where iced coffee is served in giant silver goblets. If you want something more substantial, stop at Konaya for curry udon, a Japanese comfort dish rarely found outside the country. Konaya is tucked down a side street just before the entrance to Togenuki Temple and they've been serving their creamy, rich bowls of curry broth and noodles topped with seasonal tempura for almost 40 years.

There are a lot of quirky little things to see (and taste) in Sugamo, so take your time walking around Jizo Dori. For a final retro flourish, ride on the Arakawa Line tram, one of only two tram lines left in Tokyo. If you are visiting during the cherry blossom season, take the short tram ride to the Somei Cemetery or large Asakusayama Park, which are both local favourites for seeing Japan's famous cherry trees in bloom. During the cooler seasons, walk to Somei Onsen Sakura, where you can bathe in hot springs and get the feel of a ryokan inn stay without the price tag.

HIGH-END DINING DILEMMAS

When you're planning your culinary trip to Japan, you might find that a lot of the more high-end restaurants don't offer online bookings or email reservations. Often a phone call (or fax!) is the only option, and the lack of English-speaking staff can make it very difficult to get a spot at the dining destination of your dreams.

—

FOODIE TOKYO

Why the seemingly cold shoulder? Chefs may state they wish to protect the quality and tradition of the dining experience for their longstanding patrons. This is not entirely unfounded. The rise in popularity of Japan as a travel destination has definitely brought an influx of tourists who are happy to splash the cash on an upscale meal without understanding the etiquette of Japanese fine dining.

This rule isn't just aimed at international visitors, but at first-time Japanese guests as well. Not unlike the rules of the geisha-frequented tea houses of Kyoto – *ichigensan okotowari* (no entry without introduction) – this policy requires potential guests to first be invited by an already-known patron of the establishment. While most definitely elitist, it does protect restaurants (and tea houses) from potentially troublesome guests and ensures that there is someone to vouch for them.

If you're absolutely desperate to book a table at a prized restaurant, some of the fancier establishments will still accept bookings from concierges at high-end hotels, but the very top batters have actually stopped taking bookings of that type as well. If you know someone who managed to get a spot, ask them to book a table for you at the end of their meal (although admittedly this is a pretty rare occurrence). If you have business connections in Japan, they may be able to help, or you can use online booking services like My Concierge or Pocket Concierge to get a spot.

But if this process leaves a bad taste in your mouth, don't worry. There are many fantastic restaurants, including Michelin-starred ones, in Tokyo that do accept reservations, so forget the hype and try traditional spots like Tempura Kondo, the innovative kaiseki at Narisawa or Edo-style sushi at Hanabusa instead.

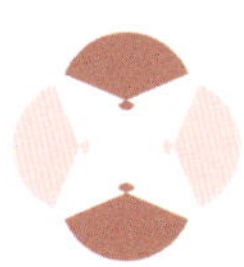

東京の自然

Nature Tokyo

BELIEVE IT OR NOT, about 40 per cent of the Tokyo area is covered in forest. Admittedly, most of this greenery is concentrated in the westernmost part of the region, in the mountainous slopes of the Tama area, but you don't have to be an avid hiker to enjoy little natural hubs in central Tokyo.

The deep obsession with seasonality, as well as the many parks, gardens and tree-lined riversides dotted around the city, means you can experience Japan's fluffy pink cherry blossoms, Photoshop-bright autumn colours and rainy-season hydrangeas alongside the sights and sounds of the city.

In this chapter, I'll show you the best spots for a blast of plant life in Tokyo, from wild parks and perfectly manicured traditional gardens to photogenic flower-filled cafes and a dip into the culture of bonsai.

PARKS & GARDENS AROUND TOKYO

Tokyo is densely populated, and it can feel like every tiny pocket of the urban expanse is packed to the max with tall buildings and office towers. But there is actually a surprising amount of space dedicated to greenery in the capital, with about 80 sq km (31 sq miles) of parks and gardens open to the public.

Many of the most famous ones once belonged to powerful lords or even the imperial family and have since been reclaimed, so you don't need a title to enjoy a bit of nature in the city.

Here's a carefully curated selection of Tokyo parks with stunning views. You'll also find more park recommendations throughout this guide, including Rikugien (page 52) and Inokashira Park (page 75).

SHINJUKU GYOEN NATIONAL GARDEN

This famous spot is Tokyo's equivalent to New York's Central Park: a lush, green expanse bang in the middle of the city, flanked by a backdrop of shimmering skyscrapers. It used to be the house and grounds of a feudal lord during the Edo period, before it became a public park in 1949. The grounds include Japanese, English and French gardens (with a touch of Taipei) and are considered among the top places to see *sakura* (cherry blossoms), as the large variety of cherry trees means that you can catch the blossoms from mid-March to mid-April.

The garden is a short walk from Shinjuku Station, and the entry fee is ¥500 for adults.

UENO PARK

This huge park is on the former grounds of Kaneiji Temple, which was once one of the biggest (and wealthiest) temples in the city. After the Meiji Restoration, the grounds were transformed into one of Japan's first Western-style parks and opened to the public in 1873. It's dotted with shrines, temples, museums and intriguing memorial monuments dedicated to fugu, chickens and knives. If you visit in July and August, you can see lotus flowers in bloom on the Shinobazu pond. Thousands

flock to Ueno Park for *hanami* (cherry blossom viewing) when over 1000 trees are in bloom.

The park is right next to Ueno Station and is free (although some of the museums have entry fees).

KOISHIKAWA KORAKUEN

Along with Rikugien and Hama Rikyu, this is one of the oldest gardens in Tokyo, dating back to the Edo period, when it was part of the residence of a member of the ruling Tokugawa family. Like many traditional strolling gardens, Koishikawa Korakuen is dotted with recreations of landscapes from Japanese and Chinese poetry, and walking paths that meander among them. The 'full moon' bridge that reflects on the stream below is particularly pretty in autumn.

The garden is a 10-minute walk from Iidabashi Station, which connects you to nearby sightseeing spots like Tokyo Station and Akihabara. The entry fee is ¥300.

SHOWA MEMORIAL PARK

This is the largest park in Tokyo, and relatively new, opening in 1983 to celebrate the 50th anniversary of the reign of the Showa emperor. The grounds are massive, to the point that there are bicycle rentals available to help you get around. Besides the many walking trails, there are Japanese and European-style gardens, traditional farmhouses, a bonsai museum, a boating pond and flower fields with yellow canola flowers, carpets of tulips, bright poppies and azaleas taking turns to bloom in the warmer months. There are also plenty of cherry trees and autumn colours in season.

The park is quite out of the way in western Tokyo, about a 15-minute walk from Tachikawa Station on the Chuo Line, which also connects with Kichijoji and Musashi Koganei, home to the Edo-Tokyo Open Air Architectural Museum. The entrance fee is ¥450.

KOISHIKAWA BOTANICAL GARDEN

Owned by the University of Tokyo, this park often gets overlooked due to it being a bit off the regular tourist route, but it's one of the most underrated cherry blossom, autumn leaves and iris spots in the city. It was once a medicinal herb garden established by the Tokugawa shogunate, and now has a living collection of around 1400 different plants from across East Asia. The garden is also home to offspring of both the apple tree said to have inspired Isaac Newton, and the grapevines Gregor Mendel used in his research. Although it's been closed since 2021, it's still worth stopping by the Koishikawa Annex, the university's museum of architecture, which looks stunning framed by the nearby pond.

The garden is a 15-minute walk from Myogadani Station on the Marunouchi Line and the entry fee is ¥500. During the spring, take the route that passes via Harimazaka Sakura Namiki, a street lined with cherry trees.

OTAGURO PARK

Once the home of Motoo Otaguro, a music critic who introduced composers like Debussy to Japan, this tasteful little spot is at its best during the autumn foliage season. The stone-paved approach to the garden is lined with glowing yellow ginkgo trees, and the grounds are dotted with maple trees that frame the koi-filled pond and little streams. During the spring, there are a handful of cherry trees in bloom as well, but for the rest of the year it is pretty quiet and tranquil.

The park is an 8-minute walk from Ogikubo Station on the Chuo or Marunouchi Line, close to sightseeing spots like Nakano and Kichijoji. Entry is free, except for the evening illuminations in the autumn, which cost ¥300.

FOREST BATHING AROUND TOKYO

Shinrinyoku, or forest bathing, has attracted a lot of attention, but comes from a simple premise: those of us who live and work in major cities do not spend enough time in nature, and need some quiet time among the trees to reduce stress and improve mental health. It first popped up in the 1980s, with a particularly strong base in mountainous Nagano Prefecture, but has now become a common term in Japan and, increasingly, around the world.

Despite the name, this is not about bathing in a stream deep in the forest. Interestingly, even hiking doesn't necessarily count. Shinrinyoku is more of a nature-based mindfulness practice, in which you experience the forest with all five senses, slowing down to soak up the natural world and (supposedly) phytoncides, substances that plants release to protect themselves.

From a commonsense perspective, spending some time in nature, far away from screens and stress, sounds like a no-brainer, and there are studies showing that forest bathing can help strengthen your immune system and alleviate anxiety, depression and anger.

So where can you find some place quiet enough to be at one with the trees when you're in a city as frenetic as Tokyo?

INSTITUTE FOR NATURE STUDY

A real departure from the perfectly manicured grounds of traditional Japanese gardens, this unusually wild spot will transport you miles from the city. The 20 hectare (49 acre) forest and marshland belongs to the National Museum of Nature and Science, whose staff study and preserve the flora and fauna here. These grounds once belonged to a lord, and you can still see the ruins of his villa as you wander through, passing by the Hyotan Pond and the Mizudori Marsh. There are large, old cherry trees, dramatic 300-year-old pines, and plenty of benches where you can sit and relax to the sound of the birds singing and the leaves rustling.

The preserve is a 10-minute walk from Meguro Station, and the entry fee is ¥310. They only allow 300 people in at a time, so you'll have plenty of personal space.

SHAKUJI PARK

Despite being one of Tokyo's largest parks, this oasis seems to fly under the tourist radar. It's a significant sanctuary for many native birds and feels tranquil and quite remote. Paths circle the Sanpoji and Shakuji ponds, the latter lined with weeping cherry trees and gorgeous houses of various styles, from traditional Japanese to modern and even Victorian-inspired mansions. Go forest bathing in the trees around the Sanpoji Pond and marshland area, or combine some forest bathing with *hanami* (flower viewing) when the park's 300 cherry trees are in bloom.

The easiest way to get to the park is to walk from Shakuji-koen Station on the Seibu line, which also connects to the town of Kawagoe, a popular day-trip destination.

TODOROKI VALLEY

If you just need a quick top-up of nature's healing power while sightseeing in central Tokyo, then this riverside walk should do the trick. This miniature valley follows the Yazawa River for 1.2 km (¾ mile) and feels so serene, as it's sunken below street level and covered by a thick canopy of trees. Breathe in the greenery, listen to the soothing river sounds, then wander around to see a waterfall, shrine and temple. While not directly related to forest bathing, the cheerful welcome and tasty fruit sandwiches at nearby cafe Haluuu have their own healing powers.

Get to Todoroki Valley by taking an Oimachi Line train to Todoroki Station – just hop on a Toyoko Line train in Shibuya and switch at Jiyugaoka, a haven for sweet lovers.

Todoroki Valley ➧

One-day Hiking & Nature Adventure in Tokyo

After days of subway rides, museums, temples, shrines and more good food than you can shake a stick at, you might start craving a slightly less urban adventure. No problem: a large section of westernmost Tokyo is part of Chichibu-Tama-Kai National Park. Head to the Okutama area for a bit of rural Tokyo sightseeing and a gentle hike of Mount Mitake. (There are more challenging peaks if you're up to it.) Make sure to wear suitable footwear, especially if you plan to take on the more advanced hikes.

It takes just under 2 hours from Shinjuku Station on the Chuo and Ome lines, then a short bus ride, to get to the Mount Mitake cable car. While you can technically hike up from here, it isn't particularly noteworthy and takes quite a while, so spring for the 10-minute cable car ride that will drop you off in a little village above the clouds.

The houses and lodgings here are all associated with Mitake Musashi Shrine, built on the top of 929 metre (3047 foot) Mount Mitake and from where, on a clear day, you can see Mount Fuji. For something a bit special, book an overnight stay in shukubo lodgings run by Shinto priests. Komadori Sanso is particularly popular, as the priest also offers *takigyo* (waterfall meditation) experiences!

A little road winds up towards the shrine through the various houses and eateries, where you can get bowls of soba and other traditional fare. Pick up a few things to eat if you intend to do one of the longer hikes, as well as a map at the visitor information centre, just in case.

A number of hiking trails start at the foot of the shrine's long stone staircase. For a pleasant, not overly taxing hike that will leave you plenty of time to explore other spots in the Okutama/Ome area, I recommend doing the Rock Garden loop, which takes about 2 hours in total. The well-marked trail takes you down into a tapering, forested valley where

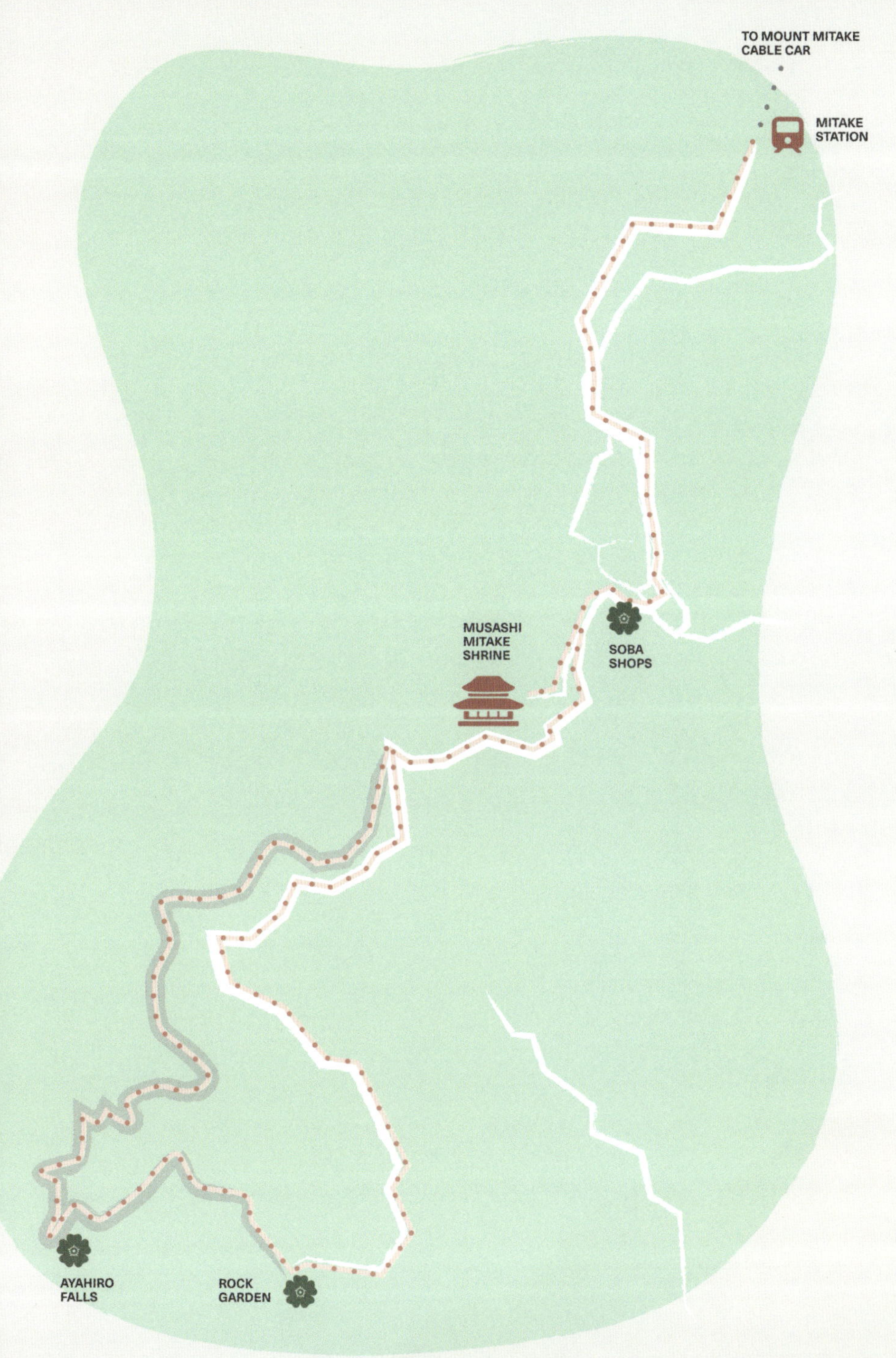
TO MOUNT MITAKE
CABLE CAR
MITAKE
STATION
MUSASHI
MITAKE
SHRINE
SOBA
SHOPS
AYAHIRO
FALLS
ROCK
GARDEN

you follow a pretty stream to multiple spots with stones and boulders lushly covered in moss, until you reach a sacred waterfall.

Before heading down the mountain, climb up to the shrine to pay your respects. You may notice a number of dog statues (and people visiting with their pooches). This is because the deity enshrined here is Oinu-sama, the wolf who accompanied Yamato Takeru, a hero from ancient Japanese legends.

Take the cable car and bus back down the mountain, then look for a little street leading down towards the river (it's between the bus stop and the bridge). This 1.5 km (0.9 mile) riverside trail is well paved and offers great views of the river and sneak peeks into well-tended private gardens and wooden homes along the banks. Keep going until you reach the Sawanoi sake brewery and the suspension bridge right by it.

Sawanoi is the oldest brewery in the Tokyo area, dating back to 1702. They offer four daily brewery tours that end with free tastings and, while the tours are held in Japanese, they do offer English brochures. Book in advance via their website.

If you don't have time for a tour, the brewery's garden and covered terraces overlooking the river are open to the public, along with a counter where you can try their clean, smooth brews for around ¥200–¥500. Get a few varieties, then order a few dishes from the stall next door. Their fresh homemade tofu and fluffy manju dumplings go especially well with the sake and the views. They also have an equally idyllic coffee shop called Shizuku. The restaurants and brewery are closed on Mondays, so plan accordingly.

There are several spots nearby where, with a little scrambling, you can get down to the river. During summer, you'll see people swimming in the cool, clean water, and I can definitely recommend taking a dip. There is a public bathroom on the Sawanoi grounds where you can change. Alternatively, take a stroll over the suspension bridge and stop by nearby Kanzanji Temple.

To make your way back to Tokyo, climb up the hill away from the river and follow the signs for Sawai Station, which usually has a train service every hour. You can either switch directly to the Chuo Line at Ome Station or take a look around this former weaving and indigo-dyeing town.

The main highlight is a handful of period buildings and museums near the station, instantly recognisable by the large, hand-painted movie billboards. The Showa Retro Good Museum and Showa Gento-kan Museum are both worth a visit for a bit of vintage goodness, particularly the latter, which features dioramas populated with cat people!

Craft beer fans should stop at nearby Ome Bakushu. This woodsy, vinyl-spinning joint offers an ever-changing array of Japanese craft brews, including varieties from the Vertere brewery in nearby Okutama and Bright Blue Brewing at the foot of Mount Fuji. They have a beer-friendly menu of burgers and pizza too.

Flower & Plant Cafes

Ranging from Instagram-famous locales to little shops tucked away in the backstreets, get your chloro-fill (get it?) of tea and greenery at these verdant cafes. Visit early on weekdays or the weekend queues will really knock the bloom off your rose.

AOYAMA FLOWER MARKET TEA HOUSE

↘ 5-1-2 Minami Aoyama Minato-ku, Tokyo

Run by a flower company of the same name (so make sure you have the right address for the cafe, not the florist), Aoyama Flower Market Tea House is like a colourful greenhouse, with glass tables, vaulting bouquets of fresh seasonal flowers and vines trailing down from above. The menu is small, but always features interesting blended teas and desserts inspired by the flowers of the season.

The main branch is in Aoyama, a short walk from exit A5 of Omotesando Station. It's the largest branch, but also the best known, so you'll be competing for a seat. The Akasaka branch is also pretty and airy and is a good option if you are visiting the nearby Hie Shrine or taking a tour of the surprisingly attractive National Diet Building. There's also a smaller branch in Kichijoji but, while the flowers are still lovely, its location in the basement of the Atre department store makes it feel a bit less dreamy than the other two.

CAFE NOMU

↘ 5-7-2 Minami-Aoyama, Minato-ku, Tokyo

This Scandi-style cafe, just a short walk from the Aoyama Flower Market Tea House, is covered in avant-garde floral arrangements designed by Nicolai Bergemann. The highlight is the incredible seasonal arrangement that covers the entire back wall. Soak up the floral wonders while deciding between the open-faced Danish sandwiches, salads, smoothies and fruit tarts.

NEZU CAFE

↘ 6 Chome-5-1 Minamiaoyama, Minato City, Tokyo

While not a 'plant cafe' per se, this glass-walled spot is in the heart of the Nezu Museum's garden, also in the Aoyama area. You'll need to buy a ticket to enter the museum, which is well worth the price for its collection of ceramics and gardens alone. The menu, mainly featuring dishes like meat pies and beef stew, doesn't quite gel with the surroundings, but the matcha and yuzu-flavoured drinks and desserts (especially the cheesecake) are more in keeping with the serene interior and view. This is one cafe where going solo is actually a plus, as you'll get a seat at the long counter with a picture window directly facing the lush greenery outside.

TOKYO GARDEN

↘ 6-1-27, Meguro-ku, Tokyo

If you need a bit of a breather after a trip to the infamous Meguro Parasitological Museum (see page 108) , Tokyo Garden is just a short walk away. This florist/furniture shop/cafe is a quiet retreat, certainly less crowded than more central cafes, with lots of leafy green plants taking over every corner and minimalist but chic flower arrangements gracing the sleek wooden tables. The menu has the usual Japanese cafe standards, although the seasonal doria rice gratin is particularly satisfying. Leave room for dessert, as the cakes from neighbouring patisserie Antoine Carême are spectacular.

ROUTE BOOKS

↘ 4 Chome-14-3 Higashiueno, Taito City, Tokyo

Blend a bookstore with a cafe, add a cool industrial design and a ton of plants and you've got Route Books. Books are the main focus here (largely in Japanese), but you are welcome to bring your own and relax in the vintage chairs scattered across the two floors. The limited menu includes good coffee and baked treats from the associated Route Bakery. The cafe is a 7-minute walk from the Iriya Exit of Ueno Station. The area does feel a bit run down, which makes Route Books seem even more like a diamond in the rough.

TOKYO IN BLOOM

Planning on chasing the cherry blossoms or seeking the sunset colours of hydrangeas? Find out some of the best lesser-known spots to see Tokyo's colours in all seasons.

WINTER

Thanks to relatively mild winters, when temperatures during the day rarely go below freezing, a winter visit to Tokyo does not preclude you from catching some early blooms.

The earliest trees to come into colour are the bright-yellow wintersweet, with an unmistakable sweet scent that carries on the chilly wind from mid-January to mid-February. Most of the famous spots to see this hardy number are a bit of a trek, such as Mount Hodo in neighbouring Saitama Prefecture, Matsuda Yadoriki Park not too far from Odawara, and Hakone in Kanagawa Prefecture. However, you can also catch some in the far more central Hama Rikyu gardens.

In February, the plum trees add a burst of colour to gardens all around Tokyo and, while often mistaken for cherry trees, the *ume* have a much greater range of colours, with some very dramatic reds, magentas and even mixed colours on some trees. One easy spot to see them is within the East Gardens of the Imperial Palace, where the Bairin-zaka (plum hill) has 50 trees that bloom near the massive protective walls of Edo Castle. Hanegi Park, just a couple of stations away from fashionable Shimokitazawa, has over 600 trees of 65 varieties that flower around mid-February.

Another often overlooked winter flower is the camellia, which blooms from early February to mid-March. The large, dramatic blossoms usually fall to the ground whole, carpeting the ground with stunning effect. Check out the gardens of the elegant Hotel Chinzanso in an area once called *Tsubakiyama* (Camellia Mountain). It's free to enter the garden, and its hill, with 2300 camellias of about 100 varieties, is worth the 10-minute walk from Edogawabashi Station (which is a few stops away from Ikebukuro Station or not too far from the Koishikawa Korakuen garden).

SPRING

It is impossible to read about Japan and not hear about the joys, beauty (and crowds) of the country in spring and its cherry blossom season. You'll see the popular cherry trees no matter where you go, but there are some spots off the tourist radar where you can quietly immerse yourself in these joyful, soothing blooms.

Cherry blossom season varies a bit due to the weather but, generally, it's at its best between late March and early April. Any major park will have a section dedicated to these iconic blossoms, but Shinjuku Gyoen National Garden has one of the longest blooming periods, due to the diversity of the cherry trees. Right next to Kudanshita Station, the trifecta of Chidorigafuchi (the moat of former Edo Castle), Kitanomaru Park and controversial Yasukuni Shrine is very pretty, particularly early in the morning.

For a spot well off the beaten path, check out the long park that flanks the Zenpukuji River, which is lined with over 500 cherry trees, creating a fluffy pink tunnel. It's a 15-minute walk from either Minami-asagaya Station on the Marunouchi Line or Hamadayama Station on the Inokashira Line. You can extend your walk to Omiya Hachimangu Shrine, with its dramatic approach and huge torii gate.

But cherry blossoms are not the only harbingers of spring. The bright-yellow carpets of canola flowers bring an early burst of cheer to the season. Usually at their best in late February and throughout March, you can see 300,000 of them in bloom at the famous Hama Rikyu gardens near Shiodome Station. You will also find them a bit later in the season, around mid- to late April, at Showa Memorial Park.

If you missed the sakura season, don't worry: azalea season kicks off straight afterwards, usually starting in mid-April and blooming to early May. Nezu Shrine is one of the best spots to see them, with 3000 plants of 100 varieties creating a technicolour mosaic. If you're planning a day trip to the hiking trails of the Ome or Okutama areas, make a small detour to Shiofune Kannonji Temple (a short bus ride from Kabe Station on the Chuo Line), as it's entirely surrounded by a multicoloured slope covered in 20,000 azalea bushes, creating a landscape that looks straight out of Dr Seuss.

SUMMER

Early summer in Tokyo can be pretty wet and grey, as the monsoon season makes itself felt. Once that passes, it's hot and sunny until the end of September, resulting in tons of flowers to see throughout the season.

One of the major consolations of the rainy season is that cooler, wet weather allows hydrangeas to bloom prolifically. The Bunkyo Hydrangea Festival, held from early to mid-June at Hakusan Shrine, celebrates the 3000 bushes that beguile with their sunset colours. In Asakusa, Sumida Park has a 2 km (1.2 mile) promenade where over 7000 hydrangeas bloom, overlooked by the towering Tokyo SkyTree. If you're as obsessed with these flowers as I am, take a day trip to Kamakura, where there are four temples known for their purple-blue blooms: Hasedera, Tokeiji, Jochiji and Meigetsuin.

Summer is also iris season, and the inner garden of Meiji Jingu Shrine is one of the easiest places to catch them, with 1500 plants and a cute thatched cottage that make you completely forget you're in the middle of a city. The lesser-known Horikiri Shobuen garden has been around since the Edo period and features some 6000 irises that bloom in many shades of purple and lavender. It's a short train ride (and a bit of a walk) from Asakusa Station.

While July and August are sunflower season, most of the prettiest fields tend to be a bit of a hike from central Tokyo. One potential option in July is the large field of 15,000 sunflowers (complete with windmill) at Sakura Furusato Square in the city of Sakura, just a few stops away from Narita Airport by train on the Keisei Line.

AUTUMN

While cherry blossoms tend to steal the spotlight, I personally think autumn in Japan is the prettiest time to visit. Beautiful weather, autumn flowers, trees dappled in the richest shades of red, gold, orange and rust ... you'll come home with a 1000 photos.

A lot of people are surprised by how late autumn begins in Tokyo, as the autumn foliage season usually doesn't get started until late November, running to mid-December. Get peak views at Inokashira Park, where the red and gold maple trees line the walkway around the large pond at the centre. If you are visiting Ginza or the Imperial Palace, take a quick detour to Hibiya Park for a fabulous photo op of the maples (and skyscraper) reflecting in Kumogata Pond, and the massive sun-yellow ginkgo by the Matsumotoro restaurant. The stunning 300 metre (980 foot) long avenue of ginkgo trees at Meiji Jingu Gaien in Aoyama attracts a massive tourist crowd, but you can find a less crowded version at Showa Memorial Park.

If you're visiting in mid- to late September, you'll have to go further north, to the Tohoku region, to catch any autumn colours, but you can get your fill of bright reds with the kooky and aptly named spider lilies. Enjoy a carpet of these unusual blooms at Kinchakuda Park in neighbouring Saitama Prefecture, a short walk from Koma Station. With 5 million of the red (and occasionally white) spider lilies in bloom and plenty of pleasant hiking trails nearby, this is a great day out for nature lovers. If you can't make the trek, you will find patches of the flowers in Koishikawa Korakuen as well.

DAY TRIPS FOR ONLY-IN-JAPAN NATURE EXPERIENCES

When your time in a city is limited, a day trip has to be worth the pay off. These spots combine natural beauty with experiences you can only have in Japan.

MOUNT TAKAO

Just an hour by train from Shinjuku Station, Takao is the closest mountain to Tokyo with the easiest access and, in late November, it's also one of the top autumn foliage spots.

One of the great things about Takao is that you can customise your route. Want to avoid the initial climb up? There is a cable car and a chair lift. Prefer to take a longer, scenic route to the top? Opt for the 3.5 km (2.2 mile) Biwa Waterfall Trail/Trail 6 to go up (and the Inariyama Trail going down).

Make sure to visit Yakuo-in Temple (most directly accessed via trails 1 and 3), which was founded in 744 AD and has captivating, colourful carvings. You will also spot many statues of tengu, mythical beings who live on sacred mountains, acting as messengers for the gods and punishing evildoers while protecting the good. After your hike, grab lunch at one of the many soba restaurants in the area. Tororo soba – noodles topped with grated mountain potato – is the most famous local specialty.

Mount Takao's proximity to the city means it gets very crowded on weekends, especially during the autumn foliage season. Visiting on weekdays and slightly overcast days is the best bet for avoiding crowds.

OMIYA BONSAI VILLAGE

This 'village' with six different nurseries is centred around the Omiya Bonsai Art Museum, which has a gallery and garden featuring around 60–70 bonsai on display which are rotated seasonally. They also offer classes, but you have to book at least two months in advance.

The nurseries are all within walking distance of each other and have different specialties. Seiko-en is one of the most attractive, as the bonsai are displayed against the backdrop of traditional buildings. Fuyo-en has some of the most impressive bonsai, with quite large, dramatic shapes. Make sure you stick to the rules regarding photography, as most nurseries don't allow people to take photos of their prized potted wonders.

This plant-filled area is about an hour from central Tokyo, with the closest station being Omiya-koen Station on the Tobu Noda Line. The museum and nurseries are closed on Thursdays. For a cute detour, book a ticket to the nearby Railway Museum, which has a huge collection of retired trains that you can enter and explore.

HAKONE

Hakone has been Tokyoites' favourite hot spring retreat for centuries, and there's a lot to do here, so start early to make the most of your day.

If you want to see both nature and art in Hakone, hop on the Hakone Tozan Railway (particularly gorgeous in hydrangea season) after arriving at the main hub of Hakone Yumoto and start the day with a visit to the Hakone Open Air Museum. Enormous modern sculptures pepper the 70 hectare (173 acre) gardens overlooking the mountains, so you can have the ultimate al fresco artistic experience.

Next, head up to Gora Station, switch to the cable car and then take the ropeway up to Owakudani for a truly volcanic vibe. Take in the views, sulfurous fumes and bubbling hot springs on a 30-minute route around this crater. Book in advance, as numbers are limited for safety reasons, due to the active volcanic nature of the area.

Use the ropeway to get down to Togendai and take a gorgeous scenic cruise to Hakone Machi area. If you're lucky, you may be able to ride on one of the 'pirate ships' and get a view of Mount Fuji.

Once in Hakone Machi, follow the footsteps of the travellers of yore by hiking along the old Tokaido Highway. Near the former Hakone Checkpoint, you'll find the Cedar Avenue. Follow it until Moto Hakone, where the best-preserved section with original stone pavement will lead you on a 90-minute hike to Hatajuku. On the way, stop for snacks at the thatched Amasake Chaya tea house. From Hatajuku, there are a couple of buses per hour back to Hakone Yumoto.

The fastest, easiest way to get to Hakone is by taking the Romancecar (Odakyu Line) from Shinjuku Station to Hakone Yumoto. It takes about 75 minutes. You can buy special passes at Shinjuku Station that give you a full day of public transport for a flat fee.

Hakone ◆

Nature Craft Experiences

In the crowded capital, having an outdoor garden of your own is rare, so folks have found ways of bringing nature indoors and miniaturising it instead!

IKEBANA

Perfect in its asymmetry and minimalism, Japanese flower arranging is always striking and, with a few basic tips and rules, you can recreate credible versions at home, too. There are several ikebana schools that offer classes in English. The most famous is the Sogetsu school, which has a gorgeous building in Akasaka. On Monday mornings, they offer an 'international class', and you can book a trial lesson for just ¥3300 from their English website.

For something even more special, you can book a private lesson with Mika Otani, a famous ikebana artist. She offers a special class held in a beautiful ryokan for ¥15,000 per person. The personal attention and tranquil atmosphere make it well worth the splurge. Book via her website.

BONSAI

The Shunkaen Bonsai Museum was created by multi-award-winning bonsai artist Kunio Kobayashi. The garden and tatami rooms display around 1000 bonsai, each a perfect tiny landscape. Maple, plum and cherry trees showcase themselves in the colours of the seasons, all in miniature.

They offer basic, 1-hour bonsai-tending classes in both English and Chinese, so visitors can experience first-hand the delicate touch required for this ancient art. This temple to bonsai is a bit out of the way, requiring a short bus ride from either Koiwa or Ichinoe Station. Book your experience via email from their website.

A BIT ABOUT BONSAI

Like many of Japan's oldest arts, bonsai was brought from China in around the 13th century. It is linked to the Taoist belief in the power of miniaturised things, most iconically miniature gardens populated with small plants, and mountains made from carefully selected rocks. These tiny gardens were used for contemplation and as a way to travel without moving. Bonsai became very fashionable in Edo (now Tokyo) as, even as early as 1700, the population was densely packed and the miniature trees allowed people to have a garden (and contact with nature) in very limited space.

Bonsai are not dwarf trees but, rather, regular ones that have been kept small via specific pruning, watering and fertilising techniques. However, the greatest artistry is in how the practitioners shape the trees. The aim is not to keep the trees small, but to style them so that they give a feeling of being shaped by wind and time in the wild. Some lean dramatically, some have the majesty and solidity of trees many times their size, and some seem to rise like dragons.

Bonsai masters carefully cut off branches and bend the remaining ones using copper wire to slowly coax the trees into shape. The trimmed roots and limited soil also mean that bonsai must be watered multiple times a day, so you could almost see them as pets rather than plants! This is an art that requires dedication, as it can take decades to transform a tree into a work of art.

TIPS FOR TACKLING MOUNT FUJI

The most iconic view in Japan, Mount Fuji's perfectly conical shape draped in snow has inspired artists for centuries. There are great train and bus connections and a plethora of organised tours that can take you for a day trip to the country's most famous peak. So, does a visit live up to the hype? Well, that depends on whether you want to see the mountain, or climb the mountain.

–

CLIMBING MOUNT FUJI – Many visitors dream of climbing Fuji-san to see the sunrise from the very top of Japan and, while the views are indeed magical, the hike itself is definitely for experienced climbers only. At 3776 metres (12,388 feet), Mount Fuji is the country's tallest peak, and the climb is long and strenuous. The air gets noticeably thinner as you go up, and the temperatures plummet (especially at night). There are a few huts along the way (which require reservations), but the mountainside is completely exposed, which means really good rain gear and waterproof hiking boots are a must. You don't want to be one of those unprepared sorts who have to be evacuated down the mountain at great expense.

As the summit gets covered in snow, the climbing season is limited, which also means that it can get quite crowded, especially around weekends and holidays. The Yoshida Trail is usually open from 1 July to 10 September, while the Subashiri, Gotemba and Fujinomiya trails are open from 10 July to 10 September.

If you do have the endurance for it, I actually recommend climbing from the very bottom, on the trail that starts by gorgeous Sengen Shrine. From there until the fifth station, you will slowly make your way up through thick forest that will remind you why Mount Fuji is considered sacred.

At the fifth station, you will join the major Yoshida Trail, from which point the mountainside is completely bare and covered with switchbacks, so having that initial scenic trek through the woods is definitely mentally soothing. Overnight at one of the huts, the higher the better, then attack the summit at least 2 or 3 hours before dawn. This is about 12–13 hours of hiking on a constantly upward slope, so know your fitness levels before you attempt it.

SEEING MOUNT FUJI – If you want great views of the mountain, it is actually best to stay in the foothills rather than go to the fifth station (as many organised tours do). The Fuji Five Lakes area is particularly good if you're chasing that perfect shot, as there are a number of cute, recreated villages, a shrine and the lakes themselves. The Fujikyuko bus company has regular buses that can take you around the sights of the five lakes, but keep in mind that the distances mean you should plan carefully. The largest of the lakes, Kawaguchiko, has the highest concentration of attractions and museums (the Ichiku Kubota Museum is especially memorable), while Lake Saiko next door gives access to the more natural sights, like the beautiful (but also somewhat infamous) Aokigahara Forest and the wind and ice caves.

A more active way of seeing the highlights and getting shots off the traditional tourist path is by biking around the area. You can do it on your own (there are bike rental shops near major stations), but to make the most of your time and avoid getting lost, it may be worth opting for a guided tour, such as those offered by the friendly folks at Fuji Bike Tour.

Keep in mind that Mount Fuji is notoriously 'shy'. The mountain makes its own weather, and so is often covered by clouds. You'll have a higher chance of seeing it during the colder months rather than in spring or summer, as the clouds tend to disperse in the morning and evening.

アートな東京

Art & Fashion Tokyo

TRYING TO SUM UP what makes Japanese art and fashion so special is a daunting task. The sheer number of arts and crafts, which command the same level of respect in Japan, can be overwhelming.

Many of the more traditional arts are deeply influenced by the philosophy of wabi sabi, which means finding perfection in imperfections and accepting transience. This concept can be understood in the beauty of the unfinished edges of a tea bowl or the natural asymmetries of an ikebana arrangement. But this contrasts with the elaborate designs of hand-embroidered kimono or the bright colours of regional crafts. Hanging scrolls embellished with just a few artful black ink characters find their opposite in the detailed ukiyoe prints. And this is even before you get to modern Japanese art and architecture, in which ideas from other countries are revamped with a sensibility that is purely Japanese.

As for fashion, transforming yourself into a walking work of art is certainly not a new concept in Japan. Think of the maiko and geisha, talented artists draped with elaborate (and seasonally changing) kimono, who bring an air of refinement and tradition to any event. These days, the more dramatic subculture fashions do very much the same thing, with Lolita, visual kei and even more extreme street fashions making people walking expressions of their inner worlds and aesthetics.

In this chapter, you'll find tips on where to get your fill of Japanese art and fashion, both old and new, and walks that will inspire your own creative process.

BEST JAPANESE ART MUSEUMS

If you love art, you are going to love Tokyo. Japan's capital has over 1800 established museums and galleries dedicated to every possible art you can think of, with hundreds of smaller pop-up events happening all over the city every day.

Aside from the most famous spots, such as the Mori Art Museum, Tokyo Metropolitan Art Museum and National Art Centre, which mainly host temporary exhibitions, take the opportunity to focus on more local art and see the world through the eyes of Japanese artists. Besides this list, which combines a good mix of both old and new, check out the walks later in this chapter for other lesser-known museums and galleries you won't want to miss.

NATIONAL MUSEUM OF MODERN ART, TOKYO

This gallery has one of the largest collections of Japanese art in the country, with over 13,000 works in a variety of media, dating from the end of the 19th century to the present day. The permanent exhibits are great value, with entry at just ¥500, although special exhibitions can be much pricier. The museum is close to the Imperial Palace and gardens, an easy detour to see the evolution of Japanese art over the past century.

OTA MEMORIAL MUSEUM OF ART

In a side street just off Omotesando (and not too far from the famous Meiji Jingu Shrine), this little gem shows creative exhibits of its 14,000 ukiyoe block prints. The exhibitions change monthly, with themes that range from works of the great masters to scary Japanese legends, animals and connections with other countries. The ¥800–¥1200 entrance fee is worth it to get a feel for the breadth of expression possible in ukiyoe.

YAYOI KUSAMA MUSEUM

While the renowned artist's main works are housed in a museum in her hometown of Matsumoto in Nagano Prefecture, this little outpost located halfway between Waseda and Kagurazaka has some larger-scale works, including the immersive experiences she is known for. Book a ticket in advance – it might feel a bit pricey, but worth the effort if you are a fan.

KAIKAI KIKI GALLERY

Those interested in emerging artists, both Japanese and international, should seek out Kaikai Kiki Gallery. The entrance can be hard to spot, tucked away down a flight of stairs in a nondescript office building behind Arisugawa-no-Miya Memorial Park in hipster Hiroo. Established by global phenomenon Takashi Murakami in 2008, this relaxed gallery is free and offers visitors the chance to see the works of up-and-coming artists. It's only open when there's an exhibition on, so check the website first.

JAPAN FOLK CRAFTS MUSEUM

With its kooky location near Komaba-todaimae Station, this traditional stucco and tile-roofed building from 1936 is often missed by visitors, but it houses a lovingly chosen collection of Japanese folk art. Nearby, you'll find an eye-catching, dark, 19th-century gatehouse and the entrance to Komaba Park, once the estate of the powerful Marquis Maeda. It's free to visit his elegant Western-style mansion and Japanese-style residence.

SUMIDA HOKUSAI MUSEUM

This new museum dedicated to Japan's most famous ukiyoe artist has a real wow factor, with its asymmetrical, reflective walls almost blending into the sky. The permanent collection and special exhibitions showcase an impressive selection of the artist's work, along with a cool recreation of his house/workshop. It's a 5-minute walk from Ryogoku Station, not far from the Kokugikan sumo stadium.

Nakameguro Art Walk

Nakameguro is one of the most sought after places to live in Tokyo, with artists, TV personalities and fashion identities living in homes or apartments overlooking the tree-lined riverside. Just one train stop away from Ebisu and a couple of stops from Shibuya, the atmosphere around here is decidedly tranquil and sophisticated.

During spring and winter, it can get busy with people strolling under the blossoming riverside trees but, if you avoid peak times, it can be a beautiful, peaceful path to wander. Thanks to the thick tree cover, it also feels somehow cooler than the rest of Tokyo during the hot summers.

Down a side street along the river, just a couple of minutes from Nakameguro Station, is one of the city's most charming, hidden art spots, the Sato Sakura Museum. Look for its stunning black ironwork frontage. This little museum houses a permanent exhibition of four large-scale paintings of cherry blossoms. There are revolving exhibitions that change every couple of months but always feature nihonga, post-1900 works that align with Japanese artistic conventions, techniques and materials, mostly dating back to the Showa period (1926–1989). The entrance fee is just ¥500, and the curation is superb.

Return to the riverside and take a right. Just beyond the fourth bridge is Haute Couture Cafe, on the second floor of the chic Sakura Garden building. It is known for being one of Tokyo's most photogenic spots, and the over-the-top decor changes to match the seasons. In the spring you can enjoy their elaborate afternoon teas surrounded by boughs of (faux) cherry blossoms or curtains of purple lilacs, while in the autumn they create a tunnel of maple leaves, for a magical feel that also makes for incredible photos. Unlike a lot of themed cafes, where the food is mediocre at best, the adorable sweets and savoury bites actually taste as good as they look. They don't accept walk-ins, so book in advance, especially for weekends.

If you prefer something a little more streamlined and contemporary, take a right onto the side street before Haute Couture, then take the next left. Look for a pleasingly asymmetrical wooden door, the entrance to 311ONZ. This collaboration between a famous sushi chef and a modern art gallery is a free art gallery in the afternoon, featuring Japanese and international artists, and a spectacular restaurant at night. Michelin-starred chef Saito's team offers world-class sushi omakase for just eight people a night – and around ¥33,000 per course!

If you continue meandering along the riverside long enough, you'll eventually reach the Ikejiri Ohashi area, home to one of the city's most unusual gardens. The massive, circular walls of Ohashi Junction, which connects two major expressways, are already dramatic enough in their own right, but take the elevator next to the bank up to the top floor and you'll discover the Meguro Sky Garden on the roof of the actual junction. This intriguing urban design solution protects residents from traffic noise while also providing them with a 7000 sq metre (1¾ acre) garden boasting 1000 trees (including cherries and wonderfully twisty pines), a fruit and veggie garden with a tiny rice paddy, and views of Mount Fuji on clear days.

For the second half of your adventure, find your way back to Nakameguro Station. With your back to the South Exit, take the way out to your left and then an immediate right. Walk until you reach a street with lots of restaurants and bars. Turn left and take the first alley – you should soon find Onibus Coffee, which occupies a renovated traditional home. The Tokyo-based roastery has a few shops dotted around the city and is passionate about its craft. The brews are always smooth and the daily specials interesting and well sourced.

Once you're suitably caffeinated, retrace your steps out of the alley and take a right. The second street on your right is Meguro Ginza, the main shopping and eating hub of Nakameguro. It's a bustling wonderland of wine bars, restaurants, vintage clothing stores, tea shops and other old-school businesses. There are so many options (and so much competition!) that finding a good spot for lunch is as easy as following your nose.

For a lunch with a distinctly only-in-Japan twist, stretch your explorations to nearby Yutenji. Once you get to the end of Meguro Ginza, take a right (passing under the train tracks) and then an immediate left into an alley. At the next crossroad, take a left, going back under the tracks once more, and take the first right. Keep on going straight as much as possible, as there are a few little kinks in the road, and you should soon see the unmistakable front of Curry Station Niagara. The retro Japanese curries served match the decor, which includes an impressive collection of vintage train memorabilia. Some of the simpler curries are even delivered to you by a model train. Ask for help from the staff to buy the correct ticket if you want to experience this. All in all, it is a charming tribute to the late owner's love of the railways!

This corner of Tokyo is home to some really niche museums. Those fascinated with fashion can take a left from Curry Station Niagara, doing a quick loop under the tracks then continuing straight on the main road for 5 minutes to the Accessory Museum. This homely private collection features jewellery and other accessories from the Victorian to the avant-garde, and often holds incredibly specific exhibitions, like a recent one dedicated to 'regrettable fashion' (featuring pieces that, for social, ecological or other reasons, are no longer acceptable). The entrance fee is ¥1000.

Taking a right from Curry Station Niagara, about 15–20 minutes away, are two more museums that offer a lot of bang for their buck. The Museum of Contemporary Sculpture is free and has an indoor and outdoor collection of 200 pieces by 56 different Japanese artists, with some of the wooden works being particularly remarkable. For something on the stranger end of the scale, the (in)famous Meguro Parasitological Museum is not too far away. This bizarrely popular date spot features more examples of unusual parasites than you can shake a can of bug spray at.

Retrace your steps back to Nakameguro Station, perhaps making a side quest to Traveler's Factory, hidden in a residential backstreet just a couple of minutes from the station. This beloved stationery and travel-goods shop has beautiful notebooks, stamps and other paraphernalia, all perfect for helping you document your adventures. Right across from them you will also find Hill Valley, where you can pick up gourmet popcorn in seasonal flavours such as purple potato, strawberry shortcake or cookies and dark chocolate.

Alternatively, during cherry blossom season, make the long-ish riverside walk back to Nakameguro Station, or go directly to closer Meguro Statio, from where you can catch the Yamanote Line to your next destination.

ART EXPERIENCES IN TOKYO

These are some of the coolest, most under-the-radar artistic experiences in the capital that go beyond the surface and give you deeper connections to traditional arts.

SUMI-E INK PAINTING

When travelling around Japan, you are certain to see at least one sumi-e, or Japanese ink painting, in which just a few, seemingly careless strokes of black ink and carefully curated white space create a powerful piece of art. The small, relaxed classes run by Yuta Honda, the son of famous sumi-e artist Toyokuni Honda, cover the basics of the ink and brush techniques, but he also gives insight into the philosophy behind it, and he's absolutely great with kids. Being such a minimalist style, sumi-e gives lots of scope for self-expression, and Yuta's own adorable sumi-e paintings are just one example. Book via his website.

INDIGO DYEING

The deep, rich blue of kimono, traditional textiles and renowned Japanese denim all come from the same source: indigo. Samurai once prized *aizome* (as it is known in Japanese) because, besides the beauty of the colour, the dye also has antimicrobial properties. While there used to be hundreds of indigo dyers around Tokyo, numbers have dwindled, but you can still try this form of natural, colour-fast dyeing in Asakusa at Wanariya. The experiences usually run for about an hour, and they offer both the shibori style (similar to tie dyeing) and wax dyeing on a variety of tenugui towels, handkerchiefs and t-shirts. The canvas bag is a handy option, or you could splurge on a dress shirt to make a totally personalised indigo creation you can wear for years. The website is a bit eccentric, but they do have an online booking system.

KINTSUGI GOLD JOINERY

The art of repairing broken pottery with lacquer dusted or mixed with powdered gold, kintsugi is a perfect expression of the wabi sabi aesthetic that treats damage and repair as an important part of the history of the object, rather than something to hide. The technique popped up in the late 15th century, and it is said that some collectors became so smitten with the gorgeous results that they deliberately smashed their expensive ceramics just to have them repaired using kintsugi.

There are a few studios that offer classes in this elegant art, but one of the friendliest is Kuge Crafts, a 15-minute walk from Shin-Koenji Station. Hidden away in a residential area, the husband and wife team are super sweet, speak basic English and have come up with a way to allow you to take your repaired cup home on the same day (rather than having to wait for it to dry). You can also bring your own ceramics to repair, giving beloved objects a second life. Email them to book a class.

Shopping for Arts & Crafts in Tokyo

If you are more of a collector than a hands-on artist, you are likely to need a second suitcase to hold all your finds for your trip back home, particularly if you have an interest in more traditional Japanese arts. As older generations pass away, their collections of kimono, porcelain and wooden crafts find their way onto the market and they are often quite reasonably priced, as younger generations don't seem to have the inclination (or space) to hold on to them.

TRADITIONAL

YAMADA SHOTEN

↘ 1-8 Jinbocho, Kanda, Chiyoda-ku, Tokyo

Woodblock prints are a great souvenir option for art-loving visitors, as they are light, pack flat and are easy to frame when you get home. My top source for finding a wide variety of prints is Yamada Shoten, located in the Jimbocho book district. This multi-storey shop has English assistance and is well organised, arranging their prints in drawers by period and artist. Besides the more common Edo and Meiji period prints, they also have a fantastic selection of shin hanga (prints with Japanese themes influenced by Impressionism) and moody sosaku hanga, for which the artists draw, carve and print everything themselves. Be sure to check out the modern prints, to see how the latest generation of artists is reimagining this old-school technique. While there are some expensive treasures, expect to pay ¥10,000–¥30,000 per original print and around ¥4000 for copies of famous masterpieces. If you just can't get enough, nearby Gallery Soumei-do is also chock full of printed treasures.

YAMAMOTO SHOTEN

↘ 5-6-3 Kitazawa, Setagaya-ku, Tokyo

If you are more interested in interior design and decor, this massive vintage and antique furniture store is a 10–15-minute walk from hip Shimokitazawa. Stretching over three floors, part of the fun is hunting for treasures among the many gleaming wood tansu chests that take up most of the floor space. This is a good place to look for carved wooden statuettes, porcelain, inlaid boxes and other decor that used to be commonly found in Japanese homes.

TOMIOKA HACHIMANGU ANTIQUE MARKET

↘ 1-20-3 Tomioka, Koto-ku, Tokyo

Browsing for treasures is particularly fun at this outdoor market, which is regularly held on the first, second, fourth and fifth Sundays of the month on the grounds of Tomioka Hachimangu Shrine, right by Monzennakacho Station. The vendors here have a little bit of everything, from kimono and obi sashes to scrolls, old coins, ceramics and masks. A personal favourite is the gentleman who sells vintage postcards, which are inexpensive and look fabulous when framed in pairs. Be sure to check out nearby Fukagawa Fudodo Temple, included in the Quirky Tokyo chapter on page 111.

CONTEMPORARY

DESIGN FESTA GALLERY

↘ 3-20-18 Jingumae, Shibuya-ku, Tokyo

Delve into the side streets of Harajuku to find this colourful spot, part of the small Harajuku Art Village complex. This free gallery opened in 1998 and has dozens of rooms with a continually changing roster of artists and styles, from manga-inspired pop art to photography, mixed media and handmade jewellery. If you want a one-of-a-kind piece that doesn't break the budget, you'll probably find it here!

WALLS TOKYO

↘ 6-2-41 Yanaka, Taito-ku, Tokyo

Serious art collectors with serious budgets should make a stop at this curated gallery, tucked away in the Yanaka area featured in the YaNeSen walk on page 97. While they do have a selection of works in the ¥10,000–¥100,000 range, this gallery tends to feature artists who already have earned both national and international recognition and higher price tags. However, the vibe remains friendly, and the exhibits change regularly. Check out their line-up online to see if anything catches your fancy.

GALLERY HANA SHIMOKITAZAWA

↘ 3-26-2 Kitazawa, Setagaya City, Tokyo

This tiny neighbourhood gallery is a must-see if you are in the area. Usually focusing on single-artist exhibitions, it seems to attract creators with a lighter, more whimsical touch. Whether the works on show are available for sale or not depends on the artist; however, it is always worth asking the friendly owner, who may be able to negotiate on your behalf.

YaNeSen Arts & Crafts Walk

Many of the city's best museums and art spots tend to be in busy areas, housed in stunning creations of glass, steel and concrete. But don't worry: there are still some pockets where you can feel a bit of old Tokyo and still get your fill of artsy goodness. One of the best spots to get this vibe is in the triangle created by the neighbourhoods of Yanaka, Nezu and Sendagi (hence the nickname YaNeSen). Very walkable and fun in either direction, this is a go-to when I have art-loving visitors who have gotten a bit overwhelmed by the multi-storey nature of most of the capital.

For simplicity's sake, this walk starts in Nezu Station, which is quite close to the major museums of Ueno Park. From Exit 1, go straight then take a left at the third traffic light for the 5-minute walk to Nezu Shrine, one of the city's oldest. People come here to wander through the line of orange torii gates that snakes through the garden, which is particularly spectacular in April, when 3000 azalea bushes of 100 varieties bloom, creating an adorably rounded painting of pink, red and white blossoms.

Retrace your steps to the torii gate at the entrance, then go left. Take the pedestrian crossing and continue straight until the next small intersection; here, you'll take another left, which will lead you into the cute side streets of Nezu. However, you may want to make a stop at Imojin (on your right), where they serve ice cream sandwiched in crispy monaka wafer shells or showayaki, with a fluffy pancake-like shell filled with a dollop of sweet red bean paste.

After taking the left, keep going straight, passing unique little businesses like the one selling Japanese-style paintbrushes of every size and type imaginable. After a bit, the road will end, so go right, then right again, and you should soon see Gallery KINGYO, a small art space with free exhibitions of modern art. If you peek into the narrow side street right across from the gallery, you'll spot Bonjour Mojo2, a bakery making adorable Japanese breads shaped like crabs, koalas and bunnies. It's right next door to elegant Maruhi, a gallery housed in a building from 1917.

After KINGYO, take a left onto Hebimichi, or 'Snake Street', named for its tight curves. Follow this road, which is dotted with more galleries, shops and retro homes, until you reach a main road. Turn right, and you should soon see the large courtesan on the sign above Isetatsu. This lovely paper shop has been in business since 1864, and sells traditional chiyogami paper still made by hand, just like it was during the Edo period. The bright, colourful prints may come as a bit of a surprise to those who think Japanese paper arts are subtle and subdued, but they are a true snippet of the brash and over-the-top aesthetic of the period.

As you get into the Yanaka area, there are even more enchanting little shops. Just in front and to the side of Isetatsu, you'll find Hakoyoshi, which exclusively sells boxes made of paulownia wood, and Biscuit, a miniature shop packed with vintage curios. Retrace your steps until you are in front of cosy Petticoat Lane, a homely cafe with a friendly owner. Cross the street and take Yomise Street, peeking into the various shops and cafes, until you see Yanaka Ginza on the right.

This old-fashioned shopping street hasn't changed much since the 1950s, and has a delightful mishmash of shops, from vegetable stands to more recent additions. You'll quickly spot Waguriya, thanks to the chestnut roaster outside the shop. This popular dessert shop celebrates sweet Japanese chestnuts in varied forms, from elegant Mont Blanc–inspired parfaits to cakes and even drinks.

Towards the entrance to the street from the staircase side is Shinimonogurui, a shop that creates interesting *hanko* (the personal seals often used in Japan instead of signatures) with your choice of cute critters added in. They can do English seals too, and you can admire the pricey (but detailed) sweatshirts that transform you into a bunny or a penguin. Just across the street is Midoriya, a more traditional shop that dates back to 1908. Here, you'll find bamboo crafts created by celebrated artist Suikou Buseki. His larger bamboo art may be out of budget, but the smaller, more affordable creations, such as cute bamboo animal statuettes, chopsticks or coasters, are made with equal care and devotion.

Once you have gotten your fill of the tasty foods and intriguing shops hidden down all the side alleys, climb the stairs (keeping an eye out for the cat-themed shop Neko Action and nearby Matsunoya, which sells

gorgeous handmade baskets and homewares). Take a right before the temple gate and wander down until you see the dramatic black walls of the Asakura Museum of Sculpture. Often thought of as the 'Rodin of Japan', Fumio Asakura designed this house and studio, which is now an ode to his work and filled with his sculptures, including some rather wonderful ones of (once again) cats.

Right across the street is Yakuzen Curry Jinenjo, where the outgoing owner-chef creates delicious Japanese-style curries that include medicinal herbs and spices, an ideal lunch on a chilly autumn or winter day.

You can continue following the street, vaguely reminiscent of Kyoto with its small temples along the way, or take one of the side streets to the left, which lead to the large Yanaka Cemetery, the final resting place of many illustrious historical figures. This peaceful and leafy cemetery is particularly pretty in spring, when the cherry trees blossom among the gravestones.

For one last blast of art before heading to your next destination, go to the very furthest edge of the cemetery (heading towards Ueno Park) for a quick, free visit to SCAI The Bathhouse. This old-school sento bathhouse has been transformed into a contemporary art gallery with regularly changing exhibitions.

◆ Isetatsu paper shop

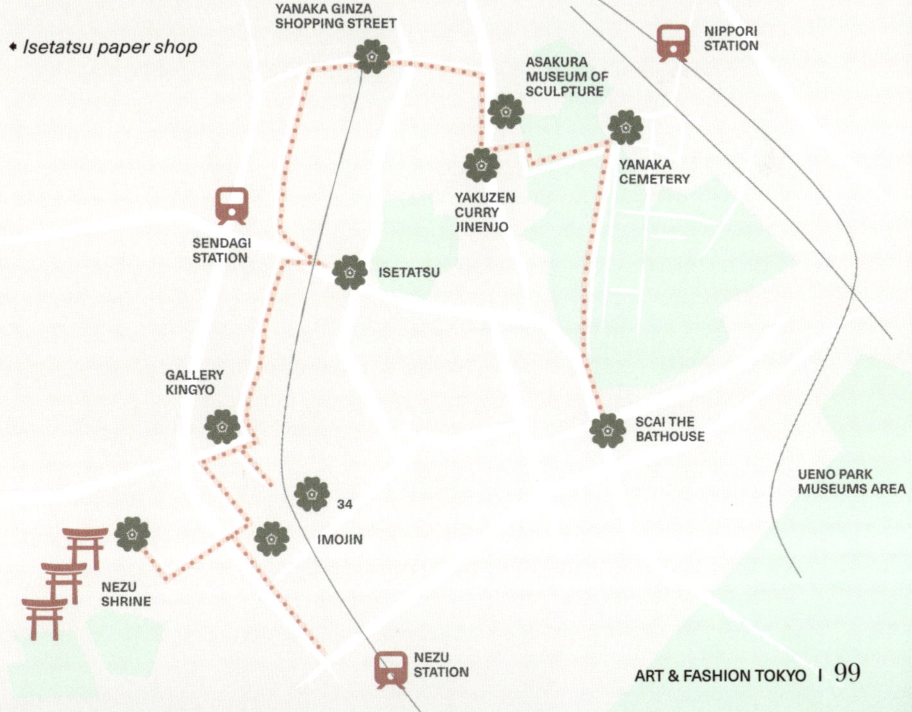

FASHION EXPERIENCES BY NEIGHBOURHOOD

Considering the size of Tokyo, there's no end to the opportunities to simply wander and stumble into interesting enclaves with their own points of view. Here are some captivating fashion-centric areas well worth exploring.

OMOTESANDO & HARAJUKU: FASHION CENTRAL

Often called the Champs Élysées of Tokyo, fashionable Omotesando glitters with luxury fashion stores and fancy restaurants, with a constant parade of fashionistas strolling down the wide, tree-lined avenue. Even if you can't afford the price tags, it's worth exploring the area for the amazing architecture, as brands compete with each other to have the most dramatic storefronts. To get a feel for more only-in-Japan fashion, take a whirl through the Laforet Harajuku department store, where Lolita fashions, all-black tech wear and kimono reinventions reign.

Despite running parallel to this temple to high fashion, Takeshita Dori street has a very different vibe. Although chain stores have encroached on this hub of youth and subculture fashion in the past few years, the vibrant colours, high energy and tantalising crepe shops still remain.

Want to experience the whole range of Japanese street fashion, with the occasional subculture outfit thrown in for good measure? Then head to Cat Street, which spans from the Miyashita Koen complex in Shibuya all the way to the residential side of Harajuku. The Shibuya side tends to have more classic or outdoorsy international brands and select shops, with Converse's White Atelier – where you can get your shoes customised with prints and charms – being particularly popular. If you need a break from shopping, grab a matcha latte and a seat at Chop Coffee, just off Cat Street as you approach Omotesando.

Once you cross the broad Omotesando road and head into the Harajuku section, the looks tend to get wilder. Check out the creative takes on Japan's traditional clothing at Kimono by Nadeshiko, and keep in mind that competition here is fierce, so stores may move or go out of business quickly. Keep an eye out for Stephen Powers' graphic *Now Is Forever* graffiti art, which you should be able to see if you look down one of the larger side streets in Harajuku. It's bold and colourful and a popular photo spot.

KURAMAE: ARTISANAL EVERYTHING

In the Edo period Kuramae was lined with the rice granaries of wealthy merchants and the craftspeople who catered to them. While there are still some traditional workshops, the neighbourhood has become a popular spot for a younger generation of artisans and businesses, giving it the somewhat overblown title of 'Tokyo's Brooklyn'. Nonetheless, it is an interesting little corner of the city with a lot of creative energy and it's just a 15-minute walk from Asakusa.

Indulge in bean-to-bar chocolate at Dandelion, or artisanal teas from the people at Tea Nakamura, who revamped a more than 100-year-old shop and now sell great organic green tea in canisters printed with the exact coordinates of where the leaves were grown. For something stronger, the Tokyo Riverside Distillery specialises in top-notch 'ethical spirits', making inventive craft gin and other drinks from food that would otherwise be wasted. (Their restaurant-bar, Stage, opens at 6 pm and is a romantic spot for a date night.)

Take a wander down Kokusai Street to Kakimori, which, besides having the most beautifully curated selection of pens, notebooks, stationery and ink in the city, also offers a made-to-order notebook service. You choose the paper, cover, bindings and other details, and they will create a one-of-a-kind notebook for you. (Be aware that the wait can get long on weekends.) You can also have them mix a personalised ink colour for you. Just across the street is Maito, where the craftspeople use natural materials and local dyes (such as cherry blossoms, indigo, ume plum and tea) to create their handmade clothes.

To finish your visit, take a walk along the Sumida River towards Umayabashi Bridge (and Kuramae Station) to see an artsy public restroom that looks like four faces in profile.

SHIMOKITAZAWA: SECOND-HAND PARADISE

If digging for vintage gold is your idea of heaven, then hightail it to Shimokita (as the locals call it). This pedestrian-friendly neighbourhood was once home to a thriving black market after WWII and, while the shops have since gone legit, the warren of poky streets and tiny shops still has a bit of that joyfully chaotic feel, although there have been some fancy additions in the past few years.

On weekends, the area in front of the station hosts an outdoor craft and flea market, while the areas near the entrance have been revamped with indoor food stalls, fancy coffee shops and an underground bazaar of second-hand clothes shops and a maze of handmade jewellery stalls.

For cheap and cheerful second-hand fashion, go to the station's Central or East exit and look for the shopping street with a blue-green arch at the entrance. This street is lined with stores selling affordable street fashion. Just off the six-way intersection at the end of the street you can find a bunch of quirky spots like Good Heavens!, a British pub that regularly hosts quiz and comedy nights, Tollywood, a pint-sized indie movie theatre, and RBL, a reading cafe with a small selection of English books. Serious coffee fiends should walk a bit further, to Coffea Exlibris, for some boundary-pushing single-origin coffees.

The stores get a little more upmarket towards the northern side of the station. For well-curated, high-quality vintage menswear, Monk Vintage Archive has a great selection; just keep your eyes peeled for the yellow sign, as it's hidden away below floor level. Further down the street is Little Trip to Heaven, which has vintage fashions, with a particularly good selection of purses and knits. Across the road is Florida, a local icon that you can spot thanks to the giant flamingos, which tends to have a little bit of everything. Just keep in mind that, as with anywhere, the grass is always greener away from home, so many of the second-hand clothing stores mainly stock pieces imported from the US or Europe.

Shimokitazawa shopping street ➧

30

Shopping for Unique Clothes in Tokyo

Like most major cities, the shopping streets of Tokyo are crowded with fast fashion, ubiquitous international brands and boutiques that (while adorable) don't really sell anything that screams 'Japan'. While you could just pick up a t-shirt with kanji characters or cherry blossoms, there are better options for wearing your travels.

JAPANESE DENIM

Combine a long history of indigo dyeing with the Japanese focus on quality and attention to detail, and it is no surprise Japanese denim is internationally revered. With proper care, these hardy jeans can last over a decade, which perhaps makes the price tag (around ¥20,000–¥60,000) a bit easier to justify.

MOMOTARO

↘ Ao 2F, 3-11-7 Kita-Aoyama, Minato-ku, Tokyo

In Aoyama you will find iconic Momotaro, where you can source jeans made in Okayama Prefecture, the centre of Japan's denim production. Aficionados can spot this high-craftmanship denim instantly, thanks to the two white stripes that are usually painted on one pocket. You can get your jeans hemmed for free in-house, which is done using an antique chain-stitch sewing machine.

KAPITAL LEGS

↘ 2-23-12 Ebisuminami, Shibuya City, Tokyo

Selling perhaps one of Japan's most cult denim brands, this little spot has plenty of original selvedge denim, the threads of which are indigo dyed using the labour-intensive skein-dyeing process. Besides jeans, the denim jackets here are particularly sought after. Be sure to ask about their Century Denim, jeans which are made with the goal of lasting 100 years. The scent you can detect in the shop is Japanese persimmon dye, which besides providing a beautiful layer of colour also has antiseptic and deodorising properties.

LEVI'S

↘ 3-29-12 Shinjuku, Shinjuku-ku, Tokyo

Some of the larger Levi's stores in Tokyo have only-in-Japan denim, and usually have larger and longer sizes as well. Stop by the branch in Shinjuku, which is one of only five Levi's shops in the world with a tailoring service, which includes personalisation via embroidery.

REMADE KIMONO & OBI

Kimono are absolutely gorgeous, but most people don't have much use for one in their everyday life. But no fear: creative minds have come up with many ways to reuse the gorgeous fabric and incorporate it into your lifestyle.

ASAKUSA TATSUMIYA

↘ 1-18-2 Asakusa, Taito-ku, Tokyo

One of the most intriguing options for remade kimono and obi is this shop, found along the Nakamise Dori approach to Sensoji Temple. They take top-class Nishijin-embroidered kimono and obi from Kyoto and transform them into one-of-a-kind tumblers, face masks, cushions and table runners. The prices reflect the quality, but they also have a range of hair accessories which are quite affordable.

TOKYO KIMONO SHOES

↘ 2-11-9 Hanakawado, Taito-ku, Tokyo

A short walk away from Tatsumiya, this friendly shop has true made-in-Japan craftmanship, creating beautiful sneakers made from silk kimono and genuine Japanese leather. Each pair is completely unique, as they all feature patterns from different kimono. They also have a selection of really snazzy bags.

TANSUYA

↘ Various locations

For a budget-friendly option, look for haori (light, hip-length jackets worn over kimono) at second-hand shops around the city. This omnipresent chain is one of the easiest to find via online search or map apps, with three shops in the Asakusa area alone. Haori often only cost a couple thousand yen but look incredible when worn over a simple shirt. These types of shops also often have cheap obi (perfect as table runners or wall hangings), small bags made from kimono fabric and other little treasures. If you want to wear a *yukata* (summer cotton kimono) to attend a festival, you can find well-priced sets there too.

変わった東京

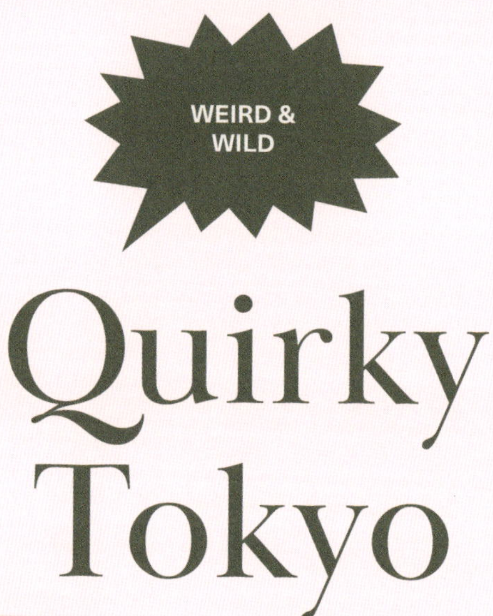

Quirky Tokyo

AFTER LIVING IN TOKYO for more than 10 years, I sometimes forget how incredible the city is. The hyper-punctual trains, clean streets and general safety become normal. No big deal.

Maybe it's this societal safety that lets so much oddity thrive. It's not uncommon to see older gentlemen dressed up in school uniforms, teenagers in outrageous fashions and people walking around in offbeat costumes, and no one blinks an eye. As long as you aren't causing others trouble, breaking the law or being aggressive, the chance of getting hassled is extremely low.

This chapter is all about Tokyo's outrageous sides. Whether you are interested in nerdy pursuits, more 'adult' entertainment, lesser-known bits of traditional Japanese culture or just want to experience the wackiest things possible, Tokyo will take you on a trip.

WEIRD & WACKY MUSEUMS

From creepy obsessions to geek-fabulous collections, there is absolutely no shortage of museums if you like taking a walk on the weird side.

INTERMEDIATHEQUE

This curious little outpost of the University of Tokyo's vast collection is found inside the KITTE building right by Tokyo Station. It feels like a gentleman's cabinet of curiosities on a grand scale, with lots of beguiling things (and lots of taxidermy) beautifully set up with minimal explanations. Entry is free. Don't miss the observatory on the seventh floor.

MEGURO PARASITOLOGICAL MUSEUM

A favourite of writers creating lists of weird things to see in Japan, this museum is about 10 minutes by foot from Meguro Station. It's still a working research facility, originally set up in 1953 by a doctor, but now has cult status among lovers of the creepy. From mind-bogglingly long tapeworms to skin-crawling specimens in jars, you may want to skip breakfast before stopping by.

KITE MUSEUM

This ode to one man's obsession with kites is just a few steps from Nihonbashi Station, on the fifth floor above Taimeiken, the 1931 restaurant renowned for its fluffy *omurice* (omelette rice). Look for the small metal sign post at the entrance of the building. The tiny museum is packed with over 3000 kites, from children's toys to large-scale replicas of aeroplanes and birds, combining Japanese kites from the Edo period with international versions from Asia, Europe and the United States.

OKUNO BUILDING

While not exactly a museum, this modernist building, constructed in the early Showa era (1926–1989), feels like a time capsule that you get to secretly explore. While it was formerly one of Ginza's high-class apartment buildings, the current tenants are mainly art galleries and workshops, antique shops and a few private offices. If it is open during your visit, check out slightly creepy Room 306, which hasn't been changed since its last tenant left.

Okuno Building ➧

WILD & WONDERFUL EXPERIENCES IN TOKYO

While immersing yourself in places like Harajuku or Akihabara can give you a taste of the more unusual sides of Japanese culture, sometimes you just need to jump into the weirder sides of Tokyo with both feet. From pretty tame immersive art experiences to adult-only bars, the capital does not disappoint in terms of left-field experiences.

(TOTALLY NOT) MARIO KART-ING

After several legal run-ins with Nintendo, the go-kart tours around Tokyo have resumed. Zip around the city at knee level, decked out in the wild costume of your choice and blasting tunes. All the drives are guided, so you don't have to think. You can just enjoy the feeling of being in a real-life video game!

Keep in mind that you can't just show up and expect to participate, as you need to check their website regarding driving licence requirements. The street karts are considered cars, so most visitors will need an international licence or provide a translation of their regular licence. Also, it may be best not to wear a Mario-related costume anymore, as it is a touchy point for the companies.

There are a number of businesses who offer go-karting, but Street Kart Tokyo Bay has the best reputation and safety record.

GHIBLI MUSEUM

An oldie but a goodie, this is a great option if you can't get to the larger Ghibli Park in Aichi Prefecture. While not exactly a museum, this fanciful building allows you to step into the mind of Hayao Miyazaki and the insanely detailed world his films create. You don't have to be a Ghibli fanatic to enjoy the art and, for ¥1000, it's quite reasonable.

Wend your way around the building, including the roof, where you can meet the robot from *Castle in the Sky*, and a booth on the ground floor, where Totoro grins out at you. The permanent exhibitions, including a recreation of Miyazaki's workshop, are supplemented by temporary exhibits. The short films shown in the Saturn Theatre feature mini gems of Ghibli magic that you can only see here.

Tickets are always in high demand, so make sure to book in advance (they go on sale on the 10th of the previous month).

BUDDHIST 'THEME PARK'

Fukagawa Fudodo Temple in the old-school Monzen-Nakacho area (and just a short walk from the station of the same name) combines the traditional and modern in a way I haven't seen anywhere else in the country. In the wooden temple building you can attend regular goma fire rituals every 2 hours between 9 am and 5 pm, which are accompanied by mesmerising taiko drumming. Up a flight of stairs by the ceremony area is a room filled with rows of hand-carved wooden statues of Fudo Myoo, the fierce deity for whom the ceremony is performed.

But it is the newer building that is dreamlike. It's a dramatic, modern temple covered in black, white and gold Sanskrit characters. Enter the building, pass through the narrow corridor lined with 10,000 small, glowing crystal pagodas (and giant prayer beads), then make your way to the second floor, where you can do the entire 1200 km (746 mile) Shikoku 88 Temple Pilgrimage in one go (complete with trippy audiovisual effects).

PEPPER PARLOR

Nope, this is not a restaurant where you test your mettle with ultra-spicy foods. This cafe, tucked away in the often-overlooked Tokyu Plaza Shibuya building, is run by a squadron of Peppers, the cute white robots created by one of Japan's major telecom providers. With their big, blinking eyes and soft, gesturing 'hands', the clever critters will take your order (English is okay) and will even recommend dishes based on your current mood. The food is quite good, if simple, with the creative waffles being particularly popular. Peppers will also stop at tables to chat, play digital games or tell your fortune. Dishes are brought to the table by serving tray robots, and you will probably spot a few other robotic friends around the place as well. The atmosphere is relaxed and low key, and actually not techy at all.

AVATAR ROBOT CAFE DAWN

For a more personal and connected experience, this fascinating cafe in Nihonbashi truly shows how technology can be used to create a more inclusive society. DAWN stands for Diverse Avatar Working Network, and the robots are avatars piloted remotely by people living with disabilities.

With their plain white faces and green glowing eyes, the OriHime bots look like something directly out of a sci-fi movie, but you get used to chatting with the pilot surprisingly quickly. Unlike more gimmicky cafes, the food is as good as the service, especially the gourmet burgers. If you want something lighter, the TeleBarista experience is fascinating, and you'll be pleasantly surprised at how good robot-made coffee can be. The OriHime bot will also help you select the perfect chocolate to match your coffee. Booking in advance is a good idea, as this cafe is rapidly gaining fame.

ROBOT RESTAURANT

The number one question I get asked about this famous show is: is it worth it? Well, if you're expecting a good meal, lavish Broadway-standard production values and a plot ... no. But if you're up for glow-in-the-dark costumes, over-the-top zaniness, an interior that looks like the manifestation of a psychedelic migraine and leaving a 'restaurant' thinking, 'what on earth just happened?', then go for it.

Elaborate floats, dancers in wild costumes, wacky mash-ups between Japanese traditions (on drugs) and pop culture references chase each other in a fever dream of 10-minute bursts, with breaks for getting drinks or visiting the garishly gold bathrooms. The atmosphere is festive and fun and aims to overwhelm. The space is small and the simple drinks available are a bit pricey, so having dinner and a few pre-show glasses of sake is the best bet to get the most out of this wild show while being kind to your wallet.

Two tips: book your tickets online via activity providers, as they will be far cheaper; and when you are offered free noise-reducing headphones, take 'em. Your eardrums will thank you.

VIBE BAR WILD ONE

Looking for a buzz of a different kind? Vibe Bar Wild One, on the third floor above a longstanding sex shop in Shibuya, is a vibrator bar that's still flying under the tourist radar. Enter through the genitalia-shaped door into a bar which is entirely covered with vibrators and sex toys. Touching is allowed and all the phallic fancies are available for sale. Note that this is not a sex club, just an unusual bar. Patrons must be 20 or over (20 is the legal drinking age in Japan). For safety reasons, only women, couples, and groups in which women outnumber men are allowed in.

Bookings are recommended and the ¥3000 cover charge includes 90 minutes of access and two drink tickets.

ANIMAL CRUELTY IS NOT QUIRKY

You've probably heard of the only-in-Japan animal cafes, where you can pay to handle owls, cats, capybaras, reptiles, rabbits, hedgehogs, puppies ... the list goes on. While we humans are often at our happiest sipping coffee in a cafe, it's absolutely no fun for these creatures to be crammed into tiny indoor cafes and constantly picked up, poked at and prodded by humans.

Animal protection laws in Japan are rarely enforced, so the neglect and stressful conditions these animals are put under for no good reason often result directly in the death of the animals or in them being shipped off to inhumane mills or resellers. Please make the ethical choice and do not support them.

There are a handful of truly ethical cat 'cafes', all of which are run by no-kill shelters and use their (usually very basic) cafe section as outreach for cats to get socialised and adopted into their forever families. Asakusa Neko-en, Necoma, Meeeow! (and, in case you pass by more remote Chofu, Hogoneko Rafu Space, where I was adopted by my own beloved kitty) fall into this category. The wellbeing of the cats comes first and, as such, the rules are strict, but you know that you are supporting a good cause and not perpetuating a cycle of abuse.

Akihabara Pop Culture Tech Walk

Tokyo's 'electric town' is one of the more unusual parts of the city, where electronics shops sit side-by-side with maid cafes. The whole area is a massive haven for *otaku* (people with all-consuming pop culture or tech obsessions), and you'll find countless shops dedicated to the full spectrum of interests, from major animation series to ultra-niche vintage cameras.

But Akiba, as it is known, was not always a centre of pop culture. Its history as a marketplace goes back more than a century, first as a large produce market then, after WWII, as a thriving black market. It was full of entrepreneurial souls who, over the course of a decade, transformed the neighbourhood into a more futuristic spot. Electronics stores started popping up in a boom of post-war prosperity, offering luxuries such as fridges, washing machines and audio equipment, before shifting their businesses in the 1980s to the then-rare computers.

Start your day on an unexpected note at M's Pop Life department store, right by Akihabara Station's Electric Town South Exit. Thought to be one of the largest sex shops in the world, it has seven storeys dedicated to all things considered (apparently) erotic. It's not at all seedy, as the sheer quantity and variety of apparel and apparatus make it feel more like a regular department store. From sexy costumes and SM gear to phallic objects that defy both the imagination and anatomy, window shopping here certainly isn't boring.

If that doesn't bamboozle you enough, fire up your map app, cross the Mansei Bridge and check out the bizarre collection of vending machines described later in this chapter. From here you should be able to see the red-brick facade of the retro mAAch ecute building along the Kanda River. This 1912 former train station built under a railway bridge now houses interesting shops within the lovely arched interior. Buy a cup of coffee and wander up to the observation deck, where you can sit on a terrace flanked by railway tracks and whooshing trains.

Once caffeinated, retrace your steps across the bridge and dive into the otaku side of Akihabara. Start at the Tokyo Radio department store, Japan's first 'mall' dedicated to electrical parts, which has stood for over 70 years. About 60 small shops are crowded together, allowing you to get a bit of a feel for what the neighbourhood must have been like during its 'electric town' heyday. Be sure to stop by Maywa Denki on the second floor to see the incredible musical inventions of the mad scientist–like president, who combines performance art, technology and sound in mind-bending ways.

If old-school games are your thing, relive your childhood just around the corner at Super Potato, a shop and arcade specialising in retro games and consoles, ranging from 8-bit era oldies to more recent PlayStation, Sega and Dreamcast creations. Head up to the fifth floor to play a few rounds of classic arcade games.

One important tip: if you're tempted to buy games or electronics to take home, make sure they work on non-Japanese systems, as many games are only coded for Japan.

Work in IT or find yourself plagued with computer issues? Make a pilgrimage to nearby Kanda Myojin Shrine, which offers special chip-shaped charms to protect your tech. As the shrine is also connected with a popular anime series called *Love Live*, check out the ema prayer plaques, which petitioners often decorate with drawings of their favourite characters.

When pondering lunch, a visit to a maid cafe is certainly a popular choice for people visiting Akihabara. It can be a wacky experience, but for some it might be a bit awkward, and even off-putting, if you're not familiar with this subculture of infantilised femininity. In my opinion, Little TGV offers a more relaxed experience. The staff at this railway-themed izakaya are in costume, but they aren't overly simpering. The decor is authentic, and the food is also pretty good, especially the cocktails inspired by various train lines.

Just a street away is Akihabara Gachapon Hall, where you'll find around 500 capsule toy machines squished together from floor to ceiling. The owner constantly rotates the selection, so you never know what tiny treasures you may find, from mini handmade art pieces to figurines from popular anime, animal-shaped coin purses and sushi-shaped keychains. Most gacha cost around ¥200, but some of the higher-end versions may be around ¥500.

End your visit to Akihabara on a creative note, by walking towards the train tracks, where, about halfway between Akihabara and Okachimachi stations, you'll find the entrance to 2k540 Aki-Oka Artisan Street, which stretches beneath the railway tracks for the entire 2.5 km (1½ mile) section between the two stations. The 50-odd shops here are dedicated to local creators and products. Close to the Akihabara end is Chabara, a large shop that sells thousands of regional specialties from all across Japan and is a fun spot to pick up unusual snacks and gifts.

CRANK UP THE STRANGE

Want the weirdest night out in Tokyo? Ask a Japanese-speaking friend or use a translation app to book tickets for the Kamen Joshi 'underground idol' performance at Akihabara P.A.R.M.S.

You can't miss the idol groups in Japan – those troupes of young performers who sing, dance and generally act chirpy and adorable. But the Kamen Joshi (and sister group, Steam Girls) put a very different spin on the genre by wearing hockey masks and wielding fake machetes or 'steam guns' in their energetic performances. Half the fun is watching the hardcore fans in the audience, who dance along and take turns doing specific 'calls' for their favourite performer. Get a feel for what you'll be in for on their website.

I CAN SEE YOU! TRANSPARENT TOILETS

Designed by architect Shigeru Ban, these slightly unnerving bathrooms are completely transparent until you lock the door, when the glass turns opaque. Although counterintuitive, the design is meant to promote safety and hygiene, as you can immediately see if it is clean or if someone is already inside. During the evening, they also light up, glowing like lanterns in the dark.

There are two of these ingenious glass-walled wonders: the yellow, pink and purple one is in Yoyogi Fukamachi Mini Park, just a few steps from Exit 3 of Yoyogi-koen Station, while the blue-green version is in Haru-no-Ogawa Park, a 6-minute walk from Yoyogi-Hachiman Station.

Interestingly, these aren't the only noteworthy toilets designed by famous architects and creative firms. You can see the full line-up of artistic public facilities at the Tokyo Toilet project website, in case you want to check out the rest.

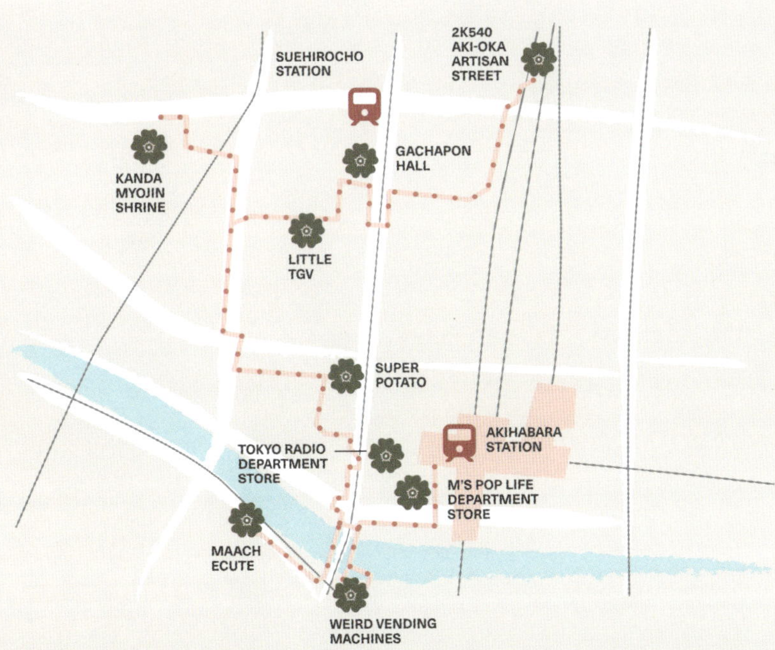

Quirky Shops in Tokyo

Tokyo is an absolute magnet for innovators and creators. The streets practically sprout unusual little shops, galleries and eateries before your eyes.

Every time I go for a walk, I find something new that piques my interest: a candy shop/tattoo parlour, a live house that specialises in traditional Japanese instrument performances, a pop-up event for corgi obsessives, a nail salon specialising in anime designs or a 'designer popcorn' shop in a housing development. You can easily miss these niche businesses, as they're often tucked out of sight, but they're worth tracking down for their distinctive offerings and passionate owners.

#FFFFFFT & #000T

↘ 2-3-5 Sendagaya, Shibuya-ku, Tokyo / 1-12-4 Kabukicho, Shinjuku-ku, Tokyo

No, my cat did not sit on my keyboard. This pair of shops, the former a 10-minute walk from Harajuku Station and the latter in the Kabukicho entertainment district of Shinjuku, specialises in monochromatic t-shirts.

#FFFFFFT exclusively stocks white shirts in over 60 varieties, and the expert staff can help you find the exact gram weight of the perfect shirt for you. The moodier #000T (which is only open from 6 pm to 12 am on weekdays) offers a selection of around 30 carefully selected black t-shirts. There's also a bar and small art gallery on the second floor. The owner's aim is to highlight the breadth of variation in the simplest of basics.

WALTZ

↘ 4-15-5 Nakameguro, Meguro-ku, Tokyo

Record stores are pretty common around Tokyo, but Waltz, in chic Nakameguro, takes a decidedly analog approach. This sleek shop stocks around 3000 new and used cassette tapes, along with a smaller selection of vinyl, VHS tapes and vintage cassette players. Not sure you're going to love your potential purchase? They'll let you play the tapes in-store first.

This is one for serious music collectors and the owner can get a bit tetchy if you're just looking around or there to take photos.

PIGMENT

↘ TERRADA Harbor One Bldg 1F, 2-5-5 Higashi-Shinagawa, Shinagawa-ku, Tokyo

Halfway between Shinagawa and Odaiba, the Tennozu Isle area is often overlooked, despite being home to a thriving artistic community, great contemporary galleries and permanent outdoor installations.

The array of colours at Pigment is completely mesmerising, with an entire bamboo-lined wall dedicated to thousands of pigments in every shade imaginable. They also sell a huge array of brushes, pastels, paints and supplies for traditional Japanese arts, like paper and ink stones. Architect Kengo Kuma designed the shop, which is simple, elegant and airy.

POCO A POCO & KQURIOUS

↘ Shibuya 109 3F, 2-29-1 Dogenzaka, Shibuya-ku, Tokyo / Noa Shibuya 4F, Udagawacho, Shibuya-ku, Tokyo

As taking your shoes off in private spaces and on tatami mats is still very common in Japan, there is a big market for interesting, conversation-starting socks. Poco a Poco is on the third floor of the famous Shibuya 109 building, the temple of women's youth fashion (which also houses a branch of Punyus, one of Japan's few cool plus-sized clothing brands). The footwear specialist has hundreds of wild and wonderful socks and tights in crazy patterns, with the shark socks that make your legs look like they're being eaten a particular favourite.

Less than 10 minutes away by foot is gender-neutral KQURIOUS, hidden on the fourth floor of an unassuming multi-purpose building. They stock over 150 different socks carefully selected from all across the world. It's more relaxed than Poco a Poco and, besides picking up a few one-of-a-kind socks, it's also a great place for a quiet coffee break before heading back out into the bustling streets of Shibuya.

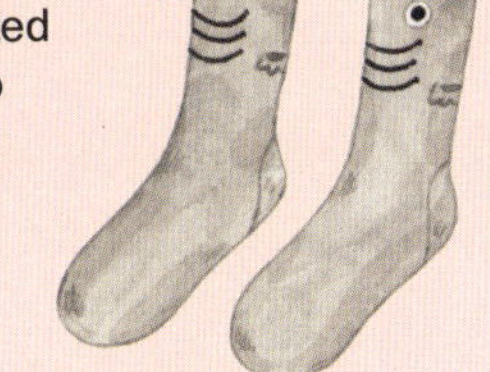

ALICE ON WEDNESDAY

↘ 6-28-3 Jingumae, Shibuya-ku, Tokyo

This three-storey shop, inspired by Alice's Wonderland adventures, turns the shopping experience into a topsy-turvy one of art and discovery. The decor is completely wacky and over-the-top, taking cues from the books and movies. Keep your eyes open for the keyholes that give you a peek at artistic tableaux and check out how the Cheshire Cat's eyes follow you around.

To get in, figure out which of the doors actually leads inside. You start in the White Room, where tempting treats and drinks await, including some 'Drink Me' bottles from Lewis Carroll's book. The Queen of Hearts Room on the second floor is ringed in cute, Wonderland-like accessories, and the top Mad Hatter floor is dedicated to Alice-themed clothing and merchandise. The store is a short walk from Meiji-jingumae Station (near Harajuku) and is best visited in the early afternoon on weekdays if you want to avoid a long wait.

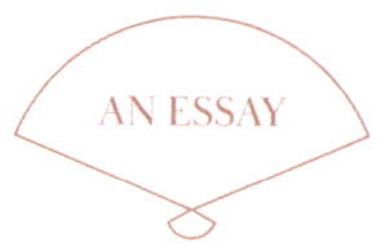

VENDING MACHINE MANIA

No question about it, Japan has the largest number of vending machines per capita in the world. Wherever you look, banks of these alluring, glittering boxes tempt you with all kinds of drinks and snacks, as well as more intriguing offerings. But why the obsession?

Japan has limited land that can be used for construction, which means high population density and real-estate prices in major cities. There's not much room to keep stock on hand, so companies turn to vending machines to meet demand. Add to this a shrinking workforce, limited vandalism and crime, and a longstanding fascination with automation, and you have a perfect environment for vending machines to flourish.

Besides the common drinks, ice cream and snack vending machines, there are also some that are a bit more unconventional. Since the pandemic, there has been an increase in machines that sell entire chilled or frozen meals (such as gyoza, curry and ramen).

While you are sure to come across a few bangers while exploring, here are just a few personal favourites.

—

SPICY

↘ Inokashira Park, by the concession stand in front of the Nanai Bridge

Are you a hot pepper and hot sauce fanatic? This small vending machine with hilarious English translations has a rotating stock of insanely spicy snacks, flavoured with mind-meltingly hot peppers like the revered California Reaper. If you can't take the heat, whip around the corner to where there are machines dispensing tamer options, like canned bread, unusual regional candies ... and munchies made with bugs like grasshoppers. In both cases, snack at your own risk!

WEIRD

↘ 2-19-11 Sudacho, Kanda, Chiyoda-ku, Tokyo

A 5-minute walk from Akihabara Station, there's a fairly rag-tag bunch of vending machines housed in what might have been a former shopfront. It's a favourite spot for Japanese YouTubers angling for attention. The options here range from regular drinks to cans of meat sauce, realistic plastic beetles, wrapped 'mystery packages' (which often turn out to be candy or boxes of chocolates), balls and whatever else the mastermind behind this curious spot finds to sell. Everything is properly packaged and sealed (this is Japan, after all), so everything is safe to eat or take home. Find out more about other spots to see nearby in the Akihabara walk on page 114.

SWEET

↘ Haneda Airport Terminal 2, 1F Arrivals Lobby

Dive into Japan's eccentricities the second you land, at the 'omusubi cake' vending machine near the main arrival lobby in Terminal 2. Inspired by and shaped like the ever-present triangular rice balls you see in every convenience store, the double portion of tasty cake may fool your eye, but not your palate! Skip the Sky Blue version and go straight for more Japanese flavours like matcha, chestnut or milk tea. It's the sweetest welcome to Tokyo.

If you're leaving from Haneda, check out the rank of 'local specialty' vending machines on the second floor of Terminal 2 (near Exit 2). Cities and prefectures around the country showcase their best eats and products (and adorable mascots), so pick up some perfect last-minute gifts like unusual, packaged ramen, cute Akita dog plushies and high-grade tea.

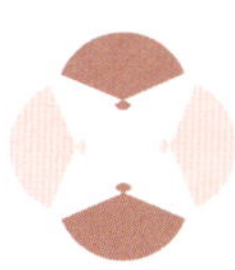

THIRSTY

↘ 5-25-4 Jingumae, Shibuya-ku, Tokyo

While wandering around fashionable Cat Street in Harajuku, keep your eyes peeled for a slimline white vending machine with a picture of a kingfisher on it. The little glass bottles within contain the delicious craft cola made by Iyoshi Cola, which has been around since 1954. The spices and refreshingly 'real' flavours make for an effervescent and truly local cola option.

An offshoot of the popularity of vending machines is the major presence of gachapon, coin-operated toy dispensers that usually range in price from ¥100 to ¥500. The tiny creations run the gamut from popular anime figures to miniature pieces of art, bags and even underwear, all enclosed in a plastic capsule. These can make excellent gifts, as they are compact and definitely have that only-in-Japan feel. Check out the following spots.

OVERWHELMING

↘ Sunshine City 3F, 3-1-3 Ikebukuro, Toshima-ku, Tokyo

Owned and operated by Bandai, this is the world's largest capsule toy store. Besides boasting 3000 different gachapon to (try to) choose from, it also contains exhibits that show the history of the toy vending machine, from its beginnings in 1977 in the US to the fancy, high-tech versions you see in Japan today.

ARTSY

↘ Shibuya Parco 1F, 15-1 Udagawacho, Shibuya-ku, Tokyo

The Discover Japan Lab craft store, housed within the super-fashionable Parco department store, usually has a couple of more artful gachapon machines, some only available for a limited time. They often feature traditional crafts or works by modern Japanese artists. During a recent visit, you could choose between hand-painted daruma doll charms, blown-glass mushrooms (for ¥2000 a pop) or the *Chim Chim Gods* by artist Ryota Aoki: tiny, strangely cute anthropomorphic penis figures ...

KIRIN
FIRE

東京の夜

Late-night Tokyo

TOKYO'S NIGHTLIFE is very much divided. In areas like Shibuya, Shinjuku and Roppongi, the neon lights never go out, with people drinking until daylight. But just a few neighbourhoods away, the shutters come down at 10 pm and you don't hear a peep on the streets.

You'll find this dichotomy timewise too, as people either wrap things up by 11 pm or plan to stay out until 5 am, to fit with the first and last train schedules of the day. Also, nightlife is not reserved for the weekends. While the pandemic did curtail post-work drinking culture to some extent, it's certainly not dead, so you will find izakaya pubs, karaoke boxes and bar hopping on weeknights as well. This chapter covers a wide variety of options for night owls, whether you want to dance until the break of dawn or just quietly walk around the lantern-lit side streets without having to deal with crowds.

WHERE TO GO AFTER DARK

While there are certainly plenty of clubs and dive bars, you don't have to be a massive party person to enjoy Tokyo's neon nights.

FOR THE GLAMOROUS PARTIER

There are a number of famous clubs in Tokyo, from the budget-friendly Atom in Shibuya (particularly good for weeknight parties) to popular newcomer WARP in Shinjuku and fancy 1 OAK in trendy Azabu Juban. But for the most only-in-Tokyo experience, I suggest splurging on a night out at RAISE, on the sixth floor of the Tokyu Plaza building in Ginza.

Even just walking to the club, along the broad avenue lined with glittering signs and high-end hostess clubs (along with many small bars where you can enjoy a craft cocktail), feels glamorous. Make sure you're well dressed, as the dress code is pretty strict. Once you're in, the massive windows offer fabulous views of the Ginza skyline and give it the feel of a church dedicated to great music, light shows and confetti cannons.

Keep in mind that the cost of entry to clubs in Japan is drastically cheaper for women, and RAISE is no exception. Entry (which includes two drink tickets) is usually around ¥4000 for men and ¥2500 for women. If you're partying during the week (Friday included) and you're all danced out, stumble over to nearby Hashigo Ginza for a bowl of ramen, which they serve until 5 am.

FOR THE QUIET WANDERER

Like the nightlife but don't like the crowds? Make your way to Asakusa and visit Sensoji Temple after dark. Admittedly, you won't be able to go into the temple or try much street food, but the shutter art along Nakamise Street and lit-up buildings have a magical atmosphere, and make for very pretty, moody photos.

Plus, if you visit in the evening, you can make a stop at Kamiya Bar, a short walk away from the Kaminarimon Gate. It's been around since 1880 and has been serving its mysterious Denki Bran cocktail to generations of writers and creative folks ever since. You can try this 'electric brandy', with its herby, floral and slightly sweet aroma, for only ¥300–¥400, served in a fluted shot glass. This acquired taste is also a mystery, as the recipe is still a total secret.

If you're feeling peckish, head to Hoppy Street, just behind the temple, which is lined with old-school izakayas with outdoor seating and cheerful lanterns. Drinks are plentiful (including the eponymous hoppy, a hop-filled, low-alcohol, beer-like drink that often gets mixed with shochu) and many joints serve bowls of delicious stew and other cheap, filling eats. Izakaya Koji, about halfway down, is always a good bet.

FOR THE SHOW LOVER

Tokyo has its fair share of musicals and stage shows but, as they're performed in Japanese, they might be a bit impenetrable if you don't speak the language. A better bet are the over-the-top extravaganzas at Roppongi Kingyo.

Calling itself a 'neo kabuki' theatre, Kingyo presents a polished combination of drag, burlesque, Japanese dance and high-energy choreographed ensembles. The 50-minute show is riveting, with the moving stage, wire acts and on-stage rain adding drama to the performances, which change regularly to include popular new songs from Japan and overseas. The show charge is ¥5500, and it's best to just order the required one food and drink order per guest, instead of the full-course meal option.

After the show, take a walk around the Roppongi Hills area to see Mori Tower (and the hulking Maman spider statue) glowing in the dark, then head for late-night dumplings at much beloved Chinese Cafe 8, known for its 24-hour service and somewhat erotic decor.

FOR THE NIGHT GRAZER

Travellers familiar with the fantastic night markets of South East Asia are often a bit disappointed to find out that this tradition hasn't really made it in Japan. While there are a few evening markets throughout the year, there are no regular ones where you can just pop by to check out the stalls. There is, however, an only-in-Japan equivalent ...

DRUNKEN ALLEYWAYS

If you are an adventurous eater with no allergies, diving into the many *nomiyagai* (narrow streets lined with bars and eateries) will guarantee you a memorable evening. Just do your best with gestures or a request for the chef's *osusume* (recommendations), and you'll have a night filled with amazing dishes and drinks you may never have heard of.

If this sounds right up your alley, then keep an eye out for the word *yokocho*. It literally means 'alleyway' but is usually associated with the afore-mentioned tiny nomiyagai. These are ideal if you want to go bar hopping and try a range of dishes, although sometimes the atmosphere of the first spot you try is so fun that you don't move for the rest of the evening ... serendipity is definitely the name of the game here.

Most tourists head to Shinjuku's Golden Gai, which has a lot of bars but only a few restaurants that are hidden up narrow, rickety stairs, so you can't be quite sure of the atmosphere within. For first timers diving into yokocho adventures, there are a few tips to help things go smoothly:

- **Size matters** – A lot of these bars and restaurants are very small, even by Tokyo standards, so showing up with a bunch of friends will likely get you turned away. A small group of two or three (or even by yourself) is the ideal number.
- **Travel light** – Don't bring in large bags or huge, puffy coats. Space is at a premium, and your stuff may get in the way of other patrons.
- **Wear comfy shoes** – Japan has a culture of *tachinomi* (stand-up bars) and enjoying a drink and a bite to eat while standing at a counter or around a small, tall table is pretty common, and these spots tend to be quite cheap, too.
- **Cash is king** – An increasing number of small eateries are starting to accept credit cards or payment apps like PayPay or LINE, but many of the more old-school ones only take cold hard cash. Smaller denominations and exact change are also appreciated.

Read on to discover a few good yokocho that are used to non-Japanese visitors but are still fun and authentic.

Traditional yokocho ◆

ラーメン
ひなどり

EBISU YOKOCHO

Just a couple of minutes' walk from the West Exit of Ebisu Station, this 'indoor alleyway' has 19 tiny eateries crammed in, with a wide variety of options. Two personal favourites are Kinoko, immediately recognisable by the cute mushroom-shaped stools which celebrate the main ingredient, and Denraku, which serves Kyoto-style oden hot pot.

HARMONICA YOKOCHO

You'll find the shops in this semi-covered alleyway opposite the East Exit of Kichijoji Station. The shops here are also open for lunch, ideal for those who aren't night owls. There are just a dozen bars in this teeny spot, with the yakitori at Tecchan and the international beers at Ahiru Beerhall both being excellent spots to kick off your night (or afternoon).

DAIICHI ICHIBA YOKOCHO

For those who want lots of choices and space to roam, artsy Kouenji, on the western side of Tokyo, seems like it is entirely made up of yokocho. Daiichi Ichiba is just a couple of minutes from the station's North Exit and is a former covered market that now has excellent Vietnamese, Japanese curry and yakitori spots.

Right underneath the tracks is Kouenji Street with its rows of eateries lining the narrow street along the tracks. Dive into the side streets around Central Road to find even more quirky bars and restaurants. The famous 'free gyoza' of Tachibana, where you get a free plate of perfectly fried potstickers when you order a drink, is a longstanding favourite for broke students, while those who enjoy vodka need to head to Tico, where they flavour the spirit with everything from pineapple to dried bonito!

NOMBEI YOKOCHO

So it's not exactly a hidden gem, being right by Shibuya Station, but the famously friendly owners and staff make Nombei an easy option for those who just want to dip a toe into the experience. With around 40 bars and eateries serving everything from Japanese to French and Indian-inspired fare, you'll be able to get a feel for the local drinking culture. Make a stop at Appre to try sake and shochu, and Tight is known for being particularly friendly to visitors.

QUEER TOKYO

Japan's relationship to the LGBTQIA+ community presents a dichotomy. On the one hand, it's perfectly safe and laws are definitely slanted against discrimination. On the other hand, Japan still doesn't recognise same-sex partnerships, and has some outdated legislation that poses major obstacles for the transgender community.

Nichome in Shinjuku is Tokyo's hub for queer nightlife, with over 100 little bars, clubs and other services aimed at the LGBTQIA+ community. But, as with any part of Japan's nightlife, many of these spots are closed off to casual visitors or are a bit wary of non-Japanese clientele. Also keep in mind that many are quite segregated by gender, and there have been issues with some places refusing entry to transgender customers.

The best place to start your night is at AiiRO, an open-air bar right on the corner of the main intersection. Just look for the rainbow-painted torii gate. AiiRO is a great place to chat, get your bearings and ask for recommendations of where to go next. Arty Farty is another favourite and usually has some dancing (which is not always a given at Japanese clubs), as does nearby Eagle Tokyo, which also hosts regular drag shows and bear parties. Both tend to attract a predominately male crowd.

Goldfinger is Nichome's most famous lesbian bar and, while it is usually open to anybody, Saturdays are just for women. They also host parties in collaboration with Club Aisotope, have regular holiday-themed events and, on Mondays, host a fun FTM Bois bar night.

Line your stomach for the drinking ahead and make some new friends at Dorobune, a casual teppan restaurant that welcomes men (as long as they are accompanied by a female friend), except on Saturdays, which, again, are female only. Then there's the ninja-starred Kamari. It might feel a bit unnerving to enter, but once you get through the door, the staff are welcoming and the atmosphere gives you a bit of a taste of Japan's 'snack bars' (which have a distinct lack of actual snacks, but plenty of hostesses entertaining and doting on salarymen instead).

Be sure to check out Tokyo Comedy Bar just a couple of stations away in Shibuya, which hosts regular LGBTQIA+ themed comedy shows in English.

Hotel Experiences for Night Owls

What if your hotel was an experience in itself? If your feet are just a bit too sore from sightseeing to tackle a night of bar hopping, these wonderfully quirky lodgings make staying in as much fun as going out.

BOOK AND BED SHINJUKU

Bookworms who routinely get lost in their latest novel and suddenly realise dawn is breaking will feel perfectly at home at this book-inspired hostel hideout in central Shinjuku. For the full experience, book the single dorm bunks that are recessed into the bookshelves, although they also have slightly more private double rooms available. With 4000 books, including a good selection of English titles, and their dramatic black lattes and hefty breakfast sandwiches, your book-stagram feed will find plenty of inspiration here.

BNA HOTELS

Support local artists by staying in the wildly creative rooms of this small boutique hotel chain. Each room is decorated by a different creator, varying in style from pop arty Japanesque designs to marvels of refracting light, ultra-minimalist hideouts and a shockingly colourful child's playroom. The Nihonbashi and Kouenji branches have small, informal bars, in case you feel like chatting with other guests and artists.

YUEN BETTEI DAITA

If you want to stay at a ryokan inn with hot springs but don't want to leave the city, then Yuen Bettei Daita is ideal. This little oasis of calm is right by Setagaya-Daita Station, only a 10–15-minute walk to trendy Shimokitazawa (and adjacent to the famous Shirohige Cream Puff Factory and its adorable Totoro-shaped choux creme puffs). Despite its traditional look, the architecture and design are brand new. Spend your evening with a restorative soak in the baths or a steam in the sauna.

Top tip: if the ¥30,000–¥50,000 price tag is a bit much, opt for one of the 'day plans' where you can enjoy the onsen and a green tea snack at the Saryo Tsukikage tearoom for a much more wallet-friendly price.

Tokyo Jazz Club Experiences

From big clubs hosting international jazz stars to smoky little jazz kissaten where the owners play their favourite albums on vinyl, Japan's love of jazz remains strong.

The genre first made a splash in the early 1920s and, to this day, there is a small but thriving community of jazz performers and aficionados who come together at the dozens of (often tiny) clubs scattered around the capital. The talent is usually first rate and the fees quite reasonable, so taking a dip into this part of the music scene can be great fun.

SOMETIME

This cosy club, tucked away in a basement just a couple of minutes from Kichijoji Station in Musashino-shi, has hosted a slew of Japanese and international performers since 1975. The musicians play in a circle in the middle of the room, with raised seating around them. The music fee is usually around ¥2500 and includes all sets, which is a great deal for music lovers on a budget.

ALFIE

The dim, warm lighting and perfectly polished bar counter give this classy jazz bar the feeling of a speakeasy. It's in the bustling nightlife centre of Roppongi, and it's been an important place for jazz musicians for over 40 years. They showcase different genres of jazz but tend to host more vocalists than other bars. The music fees are usually around ¥5000 per person.

COTTON CLUB

For the full glitz and glamour of the Golden Age of jazz, you can't go wrong with a night out at this top club (near Tokyo Station), which is a sister club to the venerable Blue Note. Inspired by the famous Cotton Club of 1920s New York, the golden chandeliers, gleaming wood and deep-red banquettes capture the era perfectly. Music fees range between ¥6000 and ¥10,000.

Majestic Night Walk Around Tokyo Station

For those who have travelled or lived in major cities across Europe, Australia and the US, the idea of wandering the neighbourhood around a major train station at night generally feels a bit scary. No worries here, though. The area around Tokyo Station is not only perfectly safe, but also absolutely gorgeous at night, with a combination of shimmering modern skyscrapers and Meiji period architecture that really encapsulates how the city has changed throughout the decades.

I do have one word of warning about Tokyo Station, though: it is absolutely huge and completely filled with temptations. Not only does it feel like there are countless train lines jostling for your attention, but the lower levels of the station are filled with intriguing restaurants, shops and *omiyage* (edible souvenirs) purveyors all attempting to distract you. (Ramen Street often wins this particular game.)

Follow the signs to either the Marunouchi North or South Exit, step out of the ticket gates and look up. The octagonal domed ceilings are magnificent, featuring eagles and eight animals from the Japanese zodiac. Exit the station and take a right so you can see the gorgeous brick facade all lit up and restored to how it looked when it opened in 1914.

Turn your back to the station and walk down the ginkgo and lamp-lined Gyoko Dori Avenue, which will lead you towards the Imperial Palace gardens. You should see a small section of the moat to the right. Cross over to that side of the street, and take a quick wander through Wadakura Fountain Park, which has some neat illuminated water features, along with a coffee shop that stays open until 9 pm. Check out the wooden Wadakura Bridge right behind it, which has a romantic view of the lights from the Palace Hotel reflecting on the water.

Walk back towards the Imperial Palace and cross the street so you are right by the moat. Take a left and keep following the moat through the Imperial Palace Outer Gardens (the Inner Gardens are closed to the public at night). On one side, you'll see the various thick wooden gates lit up while, on the other, towering office buildings and luxury hotels create a glittering skyline. Be careful not to get mowed down by runners, as the 5 km (3.1 mile) loop around the palace is a favourite of urban athletes.

About a 10-minute walk will take you to a photo spot par excellence: the Nijubashi Bridge. I think this spot is prettier at night than during the day, and the lights make the bridge's elegant double arch reflect in the water, giving the impression of glasses (or eyes). The elaborate ornamental lamps on the bridge and Fujimi Yagura watch tower in the background just add to the grandeur of the scene. From here, make a small detour to the dramatic equestrian statue of samurai Masashige Kusonoki, who is remembered for his fierce loyalty to his lord, dying in a doomed battle and supposedly uttering the famous (in Japan) words 'Would that I had seven lives to give for my country!'

Get on the main road that passes between the statue and Hibiya Park and head back towards the bright lights of the skyscrapers, aiming for the fancy Peninsula Hotel. Pass the hotel and keep going, until you see the sweetly old-fashioned Yuraku Concourse underpass. Turn left to follow the tracks and prepare to get a taste of Showa era Japan, as hundreds of little restaurants with lanterns and colourful signs line the area below.

One of the first you will come across is iconic Andy's Shin Hinomoto. Despite the very traditional look (keep an eye out for the white sign with red kanji characters), this fish-focused izakaya has been run by British expat Andy for almost 30 years. He's a pro at haggling over fish at Tsukiji Market, and this is a friendly joint for an unpretentious meal.

If seafood isn't your thing (or you're in the mood for something a little more romantic), keep following the tracks until you see the distinctly modern 'ship' cutting through the night sky on your left. This is the Tokyo International Forum, designed by Uruguayan architect Rafael Viñoly, and resembles what can only be described as a mammoth ark of glass and steel. Sneak through the inner courtyard, punctuated with large-scale works of modern art and, when you get out to the other side, look to the left.

The Mitsubishi Ichigokan Museum could not be any more different. This genteel, three-storey masterpiece of red brick was designed by Josiah Conder, originally built in 1894, and was the very first office building in Japan. The art gallery is closed in the evenings, but you can still get a quick drink at Cafe 1894, which was once a bank. The service can be a bit patchy, but just consider it the price to pay to enjoy a glass of wine under the high ceilings of intricately juxtaposed wood, elegant columns and gleaming brass lamps.

After your drink, pop around the corner to the pretty courtyard of the Ichigokan, with its fountain, flowers and outdoor sculpture, and the adjacent Brick Square building for dinner at one of the quality restaurants inside. There are often light-up events in the winter and outdoor dining in the summer, making it a particularly pleasant place for a meal.

The last stop is at the KITTE building, just a short walk away. Once a post office, it's now a shopping and retail space with some esoteric pockets like the curious Intermediatheque (see page 108), which houses pieces from the University of Tokyo's scientific and cultural heritage collections (open until 8 pm on Fridays and Saturdays). Zip up to the roof garden on the sixth floor (open daily until 11 pm and 10 pm on Sundays) for amazing views of Tokyo Station and its domed turrets.

This walk is especially beautiful from mid-November to mid-February, when Naka Dori street (which crosses with Gyoko Dori avenue) hosts evening illumination events, with 1.2 million fairy lights strung across the trees, special pop-ups and permanent outdoor statues to check out. Keep in mind that most restaurants and events finish at 11 pm (or around 10 pm on Sundays and public holidays) so people can catch a train home.

IMPERIAL PALACE
WADAKURA FOUNTAIN PARK
GYOKO DORI AVENUE
TOKYO STATION
IMPERIAL PALACE OUTER GARDENS
KITTE
BRICK SQUARE
NIJUBASHI VIEW POINT
MITSUBISHI ICHIGOKAN MUSEUM
STATUE OF MASASHIGE KUSONOKI
TOKYO INTERNATIONAL FORUM
ANDY'S SHIN HINOMOTO

Cocktail Hour

Start (or end) your night right, with a round or two at one of Tokyo's best cocktail bars (perhaps skipping the *Lost in Translation* pilgrimage to the somewhat overhyped New York Bar at the Park Hyatt in Shinjuku). Note that table charges of ¥500–¥1000 per person are the norm, and most bars are quite small.

TIR NA NOG

↘ Cheers Ginza B1F, 5-9-5 Ginza, Chuo-ku, Tokyo
11 am–4 am daily except Sunday 11 am–11 pm

If you love Alice in Wonderland and fairytales, this 'iron fairies'-inspired cafe/bar is just the ticket. Find your way through the neon lights of Ginza, open the heavy metal door and descend into the cosy bar, where keys drip from the ceiling and the walls are lined with apothecary bottles filled with pixie dust. The drinks are equally magical, particularly the Pink Tako, a deep-pink, fruity concoction decorated with squid tentacles.

THESE

↘ Quartet Bldg 1F, 2-15-12 Nishiazabu, Minato-ku, Tokyo
6 pm–3 am

The made-to-order fruit cocktails, where you can choose your ingredients from a bowl of seasonal produce, is one of the main draws of this intimate library lounge bar in Azabu, just a short walk from the Aoyama Cemetery.

The atmosphere is quiet and distinctly bookish, with books lining the walls and piled on tables. Their escargot and curry are also top-notch, making this an interesting option for a light meal and cocktails, enjoyed on couches in the romantic dim light. Table charge is ¥500.

GINZA MUSIC BAR

↘ Brown Place 4F, 7-8-13 Ginza, Chuo-ku, Tokyo
7 pm–4 am, closed Sunday and Monday

If you want a night out with good tunes, this international bar hidden on the fourth floor of one of Ginza's cinematic side streets is perfect, with more than 3000 vinyl records handpicked by the fabulous DJ.

The royal-blue interior and velvet seats set a luxurious scene for sipping your Espresso Saketini or New Tokyo Sour. Since it's a music bar, it can be hard to have a conversation when it gets busy, so go early if you're feeling chatty.

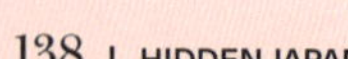

BEN FIDDICH

↘ Yamatoya Bldg 9F, 1-13-7, Nishishinjuku, Shinjuku-ku, Tokyo
6 pm–1 am, closed Sundays

Finding this pocket-sized bar is definitely a challenge, but it's worth it. The farmer/bartender behind this multi-award-winning venue creates custom, apothecary-style cocktails, using ingredients grown on his family farm in nearby Saitama.

There's no menu. Instead, have a chat with the bartenders and let them craft you a bespoke libation from their extensive collection of vintage liqueurs, whiskies, absinthes, herbs and spices. No surprises, with a name like Ben Fiddich, that this bar has a distinctly old, Scottish vibe, which is wonderfully warm and restful. The prices (about ¥2000 per cocktail) are also pretty reasonable, considering the quality. If you can't get in, head down to the second floor and try B&F, their sister bar, which specialises in fruit brandies.

HOST & HOSTESS CLUB EXPERIENCE

The modern equivalent of hiring a geisha to entertain you and your party guests, the culture of hostesses (and more recently, male hosts) is one of the peculiarities of Japan's nightlife.

Considered completely normal (and lucrative, if you have a knack for it), these clubs provide guests with entertaining conversation and company. There are no illicit services involved, so be sure to keep your hands to yourself.

If you want to experience this side of the local culture for yourself, a little online research is in order, as most clubs don't have English-speaking staff. It's hard to make concrete recommendations, as hosts and hostesses tend to have short careers, and the clubs themselves change quite often, but the Zen group, which operates a number of stylish hostess bars in Ginza, is open to non-Japanese visitors, has some English-speakers in its line-up and makes its fees very clear on the website. For those more interested in host bars, the Smappa! group has a more international approach than most, with some hosts who can speak English, Chinese or Thai.

As always, make sure the fees are clear upfront, and don't follow any touts. Budget at least ¥7000–¥10,000 per person and be careful about what drinks you order for yourself and your host/hostess, as the fees go up sharply.

TOKYO FESTIVALS & EVENTS

Edokko (the children of Edo) loved nothing more than a chance to let their hair down and throw a good festival. Thanks to this fun-loving tradition, there's pretty much a festival, either historic or more recent, every month of the year.

—

JANUARY – Thousands brave the cold for the Setagaya Boroichi Market, a more than 400-year-old 'rag market' held on 15–16 January (and 15–16 December). You'll find everything from truly bizarre second-hand items to antiques, crafts, a huge assortment of foodstuffs and stalls selling street eats. The market takes over the length of Boroichi Dori street, which runs between Kamimachi and Setagaya stations.

FEBRUARY – This is the month of Setsubun, a spring-welcoming festival that dates back to the Heian period (794–1185 AD). The exact date varies according to the lunar calendar, usually falling around early February. An entertaining part of traditional celebrations is *mamemaki* (bean throwing). At home, children will throw beans at a parent wearing an oni demon mask to symbolise warding off evil spirits. You can experience a grander version at Zojoji Temple's Mamemaki Festival, where people in kimono throw packets of beans from a raised stage under the shadow of Tokyo Tower.

MARCH – Head out of central Tokyo to the Chofu area and visit Jindaiji Temple for the Daruma Doll Fair on 3–4 March. Daruma are hollow, rounded figures representing Bodhidharma, the founder of Zen Buddhism. They're usually red, but you'll see daruma of all colours, shapes and sizes at the 300 stalls surrounding the temple. Once you find the perfect one, take it to the Daruma Kaigansho, or 'eye opener booth', where one of the priests will write the character that stands for the 'O' of Om, the sacred syllable, on it. This is a unique practice of this temple, so it's worth the wait. At 2 pm the priests parade down the main street, playing ritual instruments.

APRIL – As the weather warms and the cherry blossoms begin to bloom, Tokyo's events calendar starts to get busy. Check out the Nature Tokyo chapter of this guide for ideas on where to do *hanami* (cherry blossom viewing).

The Kanamara Festival, held in Kawasaki in early April, is worth the half-day trip to experience, with its raucous procession of sacred phallus figures and tons of penis-related foods and goods. During the old days, sex workers from the area's tea houses visited Kanayama Shrine to pray for protection against sexually transmitted diseases, and the modern festival raises money for HIV research. With drag queens and penis-shaped snacks galore, how can this not be a good time?

MAY – Two of Tokyo's major festivals take place in May – the Kanda Matsuri and the Sanja Matsuri.

The Kanda Matsuri only takes place in odd-numbered years and is at its most boisterous on the weekend closest to 15 May. On Saturday, a procession crosses a large part of the city, starting at Kanda Myojin Shrine and going around Nihonbashi, Otemachi and Akihabara. Expect to see samurai on horseback, festival floats with elaborate designs inspired by folktales (and pop culture), dancers and more. Sunday is dedicated to a procession of *mikoshi* (portable shrines) that make their way to Kanda Myojin Shrine, with plenty of energetic calls and flashing gold.

On the third weekend of the month, the excitement moves to Asakusa for the Sanja Matsuri, which celebrates the three men who founded Sensoji Temple. Expect 100 mikoshi, ranging from three enormous ones from Asakusa Shrine to tiny versions carried by overexcited neighbourhood children. Try to go on Friday and watch the elegant parade towards Asakusa Shrine, featuring Buddhist priests, geisha and others dressed up in Edo period garb, and musicians playing flutes and drums on elaborate floats.

JUNE – The weather can be wet, but that doesn't dampen the spirit of the Sanno Matsuri, which is held on even-numbered years so as not to compete with the Kanda Matsuri. The festival is associated with Hie Shrine in Akasaka (not Asakusa, an easy mistake to make!). It is one of the capital's biggest festivals, lasting 10 days from about 7 June and featuring parades of around 500 people decked out in traditional costumes, processions of portable mikoshi shrines and exhibitions of drummers and kagura sacred dances.

JULY – The Hozuki Market at Sensoji Temple in Asakusa gives you a taste of old Edo, as vendors line the streets to sell hozuki, or lantern plants. The papery reddish-orange covering of the fruit is not only considered an auspicious colour but was also once believed to be a powerful medicinal remedy. The event runs on 9–10 July but, according to traditional belief, offering a prayer at Sensoji Temple on 10 July will bring you 46,000 days (or 126 years!) of good luck.

Another photogenic event is the Shitamachi Tanabata Festival in Kappabashi, the cookware district halfway between Asakusa and Ueno. This star festival takes place on the seventh day of the seventh month, the only day when the (literally) star-crossed lovers Altair and Vega can meet across the Milky Way. The festival usually runs from 4–8 July, with parades on the weekend, while the long, elaborately decorated paper streamers and tall stalks of bamboo (to which you can tie a colourful piece of paper with your wish written on it) stay up for the duration.

AUGUST – Tanabata is celebrated all over Japan, but dates vary by region. The Asagaya Tanabata Festival timing, usually running for about one week around the first weekend of August, matches up with that of the city of Sendai, in northern Miyagi Prefecture, which is renowned for its ginormous paper streamers. The covered Pearl Centre shopping street right by Asagaya Station is fantastically decked out, not only with hundreds of large, fancy paper streamers but also with dozens of huge, creative papier-mâché figures, ranging from the adorable to snarky political commentary. They're created by the local shop owners themselves, a tradition that has continued for over 60 years.

Just a station away in Kouenji, the energetic Awa Odori dance festival takes over the neighbourhood streets from around 5 pm to 8 pm on the last weekend in August. This colourful team dance hails from Tokushima in the southern island of Shikoku, and has a history that spans over 400 years. Each team is divided into those who perform the men's and women's dances, with the latter being particularly striking thanks to their elegant prancing on tiptoe in wooden sandals and the large, straw, taco-shaped hats they wear.

SEPTEMBER – A slight cooling of the weather in September brings a number of unusual events. The Tokyo University of the Arts Festival (known as Geisai) takes place on the first weekend of the month, and is a great spot to see really unusual mikoshi made by the students, along with performances, exhibitions and their traditional samba dance party. Speaking of the pulse-pounding dance spectacles, on a Sunday in mid-September you can catch the Asakusa Samba Carnival, where 18 teams of performers in over-the-top headdresses and tiny costumes show off their moves, celebrating the strong connection between Brazil and Japan.

OCTOBER – This is a great time to visit Tokyo, as the intense summer heat finally dissipates. One spicy event is the Bettara Pickle Market held by Takarada Ebisu Shrine in Nihonbashi. On 19–20 October, 400–500 stalls, mainly selling bettara-zuke pickled daikon radish, take over the entire street. The lanterns, non-pickle-related street foods and calls of the vendors all give a great Edo vibe.

And of course, don't forget Halloween, which has become quite the production in Tokyo. Check out all the crazy costumes in Shibuya or around Roppongi, where the nightclubs have lots of special events.

NOVEMBER – The Tori no Ichi market on the outskirts of Asakusa is a personal favourite, but exact dates depend on 'rooster days' based on the Chinese zodiac and lunar calendar. The approach to Otori Shrine near Iriya Station is lined with hundreds of vendors selling kumade, gloriously decorated rakes that are said to 'rake in' wealth and prosperity. Whenever they make a sale, the vendors do a clapping ritual with their customer. The street behind the shrine is covered with hundreds of street food stalls, so arrive hungry. Hanazono Shrine in Shinjuku also has a famous Tori no Ichi market.

DECEMBER – Early December in Tokyo is hard to beat. The days are clear and crisp, and the autumn colours start to appear. It's also the beginning of illumination season, with many areas around Tokyo brightening up the evenings with sparkling displays of festive lights.

From 17–19 December, check out the Toshi no Ichi Fair at Sensoji Temple, where you may spot geisha and kabuki actors meandering through the many stalls to find the perfect hagoita good-luck charm. These ornamental racquets are based on those used in a traditional New Year's game similar to badminton. Over the years, they've become intensely embellished, featuring elaborate fabric recreations of famous kabuki actors, along with popular cartoons and characters. You'll even see people having fun haggling over the prices (a rarity in Japan) and may be astonished by how expensive they can be.

東京日帰り旅

Day Trips from Tokyo

IF YOU'RE TIGHT ON TIME AND MONEY, exploring other cities and rural areas in Japan might be out of the question, but don't worry. Tokyo's fantastic rail and bus connections give you access to plenty of affordable and fascinating day trips, all within 2 hours of the capital.

There are already a couple of recommendations in the Nature Tokyo chapter of this guide for those who want outdoorsy adventures, so here are just a few of my own personal recommendations, which cover everything from vintage vibe seekers to serious hiking enthusiasts and foodies looking for the perfect bowl of noodles. These day trips are great for visitors who are short on time or dealing with a strict budget, as many of these easy, affordable destinations give you a taste of a different side of the country.

Pretty Kamakura has a similar feel to the temple and wooden house–lined areas of Kyoto, while Yokohama has a little of the port city energy of Osaka. Mount Oyama feels far more remote than its actual distance from Tokyo, and Kawagoe will keep foodies of all ages very happy.

EDO VIBES IN KAWAGOE

This is one of my favourite day trips for anyone who wants to see a more traditional side of Japan, as getting to Kawagoe takes less than an hour from Tokyo. Known as Koedo (or Little Edo), the city still has several buildings dating back to that period, along with plenty of other experiences that make it an easy, stress-free and charming day-trip destination.

Once you get off the train, grab a free map from the tourist information centre and head to Kitain Temple, where you can see the only buildings that remain of Edo Castle and visit the 540 rakan, expressive carved stone statues of the disciples of Buddha. Heading towards the main road that leads to the preserved districts, be sure to stop at Koedo Kurari, housed in a former sake brewery. Within the building, you'll find Kikizakedokoro Showagura, where you can try sake from the prefecture's 35 breweries using a cool 'vending machine'. Exchange ¥500 for four coins that let you buy four sample cups of sake. There are descriptions in English available, and staff are happy to help you pick.

Keep walking down the street, passing through the wonderfully nostalgic Taisho Roman Yume Dori street, until you reach the Kurazukuri area, home to about 200 Edo storehouses lining both sides of the main road. In the side streets, you'll find the 16 metre (52 foot) wooden Toki no Kane belltower, lots of tiny temples and shrines, and Kashiya Yokocho, the 'penny candy lane', where they still sell traditional candy and treats, including the arm-length sticks of *fugashi* (puffed wheat gluten flavoured with black sugar).

Kawagoe is known for its sweet potatoes, so many eateries feature the beloved tuber, with some even creating elaborate *gozen* (set meals) with sweet potato in almost every dish. Torocco, hidden inside a pottery shop, is particularly good.

Wander over to Honmaru Goten, on the grounds of the former Kawagoe Castle. This is the only surviving building and was the private quarters of the castle's lord. About an 8-minute walk away is Kawagoe Hikawa Shrine, where people go to wish for luck in love. Enter the gargantuan orange torii gate, then try your luck at catching an omikuji fortune shaped like a tiny red snapper fish by using a mini fishing rod. Pose in the photogenic tunnel of *ema* (wooden prayer plaques).

In summer, you'll find a pretty wind chime tunnel, and if you go during cherry blossom season, follow the cherry tree–lined riverside behind the shrine.

The most direct way to Kawagoe is on the Tobu Tojo Line, leaving from Ikebukuro Station, which takes just 30 minutes. From most other stations in the city, your best bet is to take another line to Ikebukuro and go from there. Alternatively, take the direct train from Seibu Shinjuku Station, which takes about an hour. Seibu Railways offer a special discounted day-pass for foreign passport holders, which can help save a few hundred yen that you can spend on snacks instead. Note that Kawagoe has three stations: Kawagoe Station, Kawagoe-shi Station and Hon-Kawagoe Station. The last is the closest to the main sights.

RETRO RETREAT IN KARUIZAWA

This elegant resort town in the foothills of Mount Asama in Nagano Prefecture has been a favourite retreat since the 1910s, when Japan's first expats, such as diplomats, professors and missionaries, began flocking here in the summer to escape the Tokyo heat. It quickly became popular with the rich and famous, including members of the imperial family, as a place to buy a holiday home. Although the first 'discoverers' of the area came here to enjoy the cooler summer temperatures, I think that it is at its most beautiful from late October to early November, when the autumn colours take over.

There are three main areas to explore (not counting the excellent hiking trails and ski slopes): Kyu-Karuizawa, Naka Karuizawa and Shiozawako.

The *Kyu* (old) Karuizawa area is where most visitors start their explorations, as many sights are just off the main Ginza shopping street, which used to be part of the ancient Nakasendo Highway. The street is lined with retro shops and eateries, including Mikado Coffee, which serves delicious mocha ice cream. Unusually for Japan, there's a couple of churches here – the wooden Shaw Memorial Church and striking Saint Paul's Catholic Church, designed by Antonin Raymond in 1935. You can also stop for coffee or lunch at the glorious, old-school Manpei Hotel, built in 1894, and where John Lennon spent several summers.

If you can't make it to the Shiozawako area, at least stop by the Kumobaike Pond, about a 15-minute walk from the shopping street, which is beautiful in autumn. Alternatively, catch a bus from the stop on Mikasa Dori street, close to where it forks with the Ginza shopping street, and go see Shiraito Falls, a 70 metre (230 foot) wide waterfall made up of countless little white streams, that truly deserves its name, 'waterfall of white threads'.

Another short bus ride starting from the same spot (or Karuizawa Station) will take you over to Naka Karuizawa, specifically the elm-surrounded Harunire Terrace, part of an area overseen by the luxury Hoshino Resorts. Maruyama Coffee, one of my favourite small roasteries (which started in Karuizawa) has a branch here, and having coffee on the wooden deck is extremely pleasant. Cross the road and enter one of the side roads to find the magical little Kogen Church, which resembles a mountain chalet and has candlelit light-ups in summer and Christmas illuminations in winter. A short walk away is the Uchimura Kanzo Memorial Stone Church, a mind-bending yet serene example of organic architecture which, despite being quite new, has the deep spiritual feel of a holy site. Keep in mind that both are functioning churches, so may be closed to the public for weddings or mass.

About a 15-minute walk away is Picchio, the visitors' centre for the Karuizawa Wild Bird Sanctuary. This is one of Japan's four wild bird forests, and great care is taken to protect the 80 species of birds and 40 species of mammals (including the adorable giant flying squirrel) that live in this open park. There are well-maintained trails snaking through the forest and the 90-minute trail leads to a fantastic lookout to Mount Asama.

The Shiozawako area is around 3 km (1.9 miles) from Nakakaruizawa Station. You can either take a quick taxi ride or catch the Seibu bus, which has around six departures a day from Karuizawa Station. It'll drop you right by Taliesin, a park and museum area surrounding Lake Shiozawa. Often overlooked by international visitors, this garden is stunning in the autumn, when the leaves reflect on the water and frame six buildings constructed in the 1930s and '40s, most of which used to belong to famous local writers. Skip the restaurants inside the park, and instead have an afternoon treat at the woodsy, book-lined Hitofusa no Budou cafe just a couple of minutes away from the entrance gate. Extend your exploration in the Forest of Muse nearby, which is free to enter and has a picture book and toy museum (note that the museums are closed from January to March).

From Tokyo Station, Karuizawa is 70–80 minutes by bullet train. The route is included in the JR Rail Pass.

RAMEN DAY IN YOKOHAMA

No ramen enthusiast worth their salt can come to Japan and not make a pilgrimage to Yokohama, one of the great ramen centres. Thanks to its ports, the city has a history of welcoming influences from around the globe. This relates directly to ramen, which arrived from China sometime after Yokohama became the first port town to open to foreign trade in 1859. To this day, the city boasts the largest Chinatown in the country.

Skip breakfast and take the train straight to Shin-Yokohama Station for the first stop on your ramen-centric day trip: the Shin-Yokohama Ramen Museum. This delightfully kitschy attraction is the world's first amusement park dedicated to the beloved noodle dish. While there is a museum dedicated to the history of ramen, an old-time cafe and a *dagashiya* (traditional penny candy store), the main focus here is the ramen food court. Seven shops from around Japan serve up their signature ramens in a space made to resemble a Japanese shopping street in 1958 (the year the first instant ramen was invented), complete with painted clouds and lighting effects. The shops offer small bowls so you can try several varieties, and there are even two vegan options. The museum opens at 11 am on weekdays and 10.30 am on weekends and holidays.

A 15-minute ride on the JR Yokohama line to Sakuragicho Station then either a 10-minute walk or a short ride on the new Yokohama Air Cabin gondola will get you to the Cup Noodles Museum. Don't be deceived by the plain exterior. This pop arty temple to instant ramen shares the uplifting story of Momofuku Ando, who invented cup noodles in 1958, along with other appealing exhibits. My personal favourite is the History Cube, a room lined with all the varieties of instant noodles his company, Nissin, ever made. You can create your own personalised cup as a souvenir and, if you're still hungry, you can check out the Asian bazaar and food court, where you can try some of the international noodle dishes that inspired the inventor.

After all these delicious carbs, a walk to digest is in order, and there is plenty to see along Yokohama's waterfront. Wander down to the nearby

Akarenga Soko, two majestic red-brick warehouses built in the early 1910s that now house a variety of shops, coffee houses and restaurants. Continue on through Zou no Hana Park, which was the site of Yokohama's original port and still has a good view of the elegant Yohokama Customs building, a mosque-like beauty from 1934 that has a very niche little museum dedicated to the work of customs officers. To the left is the Osanbashi cruise terminal, a neat bit of architecture with sinuous, curved wooden walkways.

Straight ahead is Yamashita Park, where you get a real feel for how the port must have looked a century ago. Walk through the pretty rose garden and check out the *Hikawa Maru*, a passenger ship from the 1930s. It's now a museum (with a small entrance fee), as it is the only remaining pre-WWII cargo-passenger liner built in Japan in the world. On the opposite side is the New Grand Hotel, a lovely building from 1927 that has played host to General MacArthur, Charlie Chaplin and many other international and local historic figures. The 1960s Yokohama Marine Tower gazes down on the park as well. On a more modern note, Gundam fans will want to check out the giant *mecha* (robot) about a 10-minute walk away.

Take a left just before the hotel and go straight until you see the elaborate gate that welcomes you to Chinatown, a colourful warren of restaurants, food stalls and curious little shops centred around the bright and elaborate Kanteibyo Temple. The temple was built in 1873 by the area's first Chinese residents and is dedicated to the god of business and prosperity. From here, you can walk over to the fancy Motomachi area, where you will find an elegant shopping street and the hilltop Yamate area, which has gardens with port views, the pretty Western-style homes of some of Yokohama's first international residents and the fascinating Foreign General Cemetery.

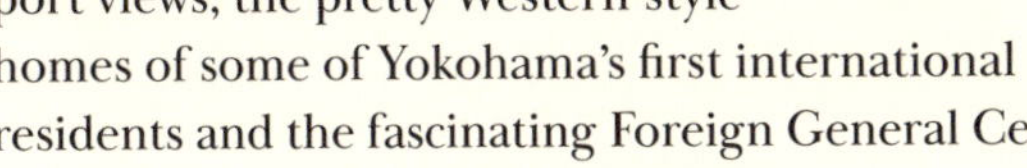

Alternatively, catch a bus near Motomachi-Chukagai Station and head to the majestic Sankeien Garden. Although the bus ride takes about 20 minutes (followed by a short walk, depending on which bus you take), there's a lot to see at this huge garden, which was created by a prosperous silk merchant and opened to the public in 1906. Within the grounds, there are 17 traditional buildings that were moved here from Kyoto and Kamakura, including a three-storey pagoda. There are a range of flowers and trees that bloom throughout the year and regular seasonal events.

At this point, you've probably worked up an appetite for one last bowl of ramen. Take the 45-minute bus ride to the major train hub of Yokohama Station. About a 7-minute walk down Pal Nerd Street, which starts just outside the station's Southwest Exit, is Yoshimuraya, the iconic originator of Yokohama's famous iekei-style ramen.

Back in 1974, Yoshimuraya created a whole new genre by combining broths based on *tonkotsu* (pork bone) and *shoyu* (soy sauce), and topping this new blend with spinach, a few sheets of dried seaweed and an egg. The style spread like wildfire, and there are dozens of iekei ramen shops all around Yokohama now. Don't worry about the line, as the chefs move fast, serving groups of 10 at a time. Buy your colour-coded plastic tickets in advance and place them before you once you are shown to your seat. This is a must-try experience for ramen aficionados, and the salty yet creamy soup is usually a big hit!

A lot of people confuse Shin-Yokohama with Yokohama Station, which can be problematic because they are 5 km (3.1 miles) apart! For Shin-Yokohama, it takes about 45 minutes from Shinjuku Station (and you can even use your JR Rail Pass, as the bullet train stops there). Yokohama Station takes 35–50 minutes, depending on which trains you catch.

HIKING & SIGHTSEEING IN KAMAKURA

When you first see this relaxed little seaside city, it's hard to imagine that, from 1185 to 1333, Kamakura was the ruling capital of Japan and a stronghold of the samurai warrior class. Evidence of this former glory is found in the huge number of temples and shrines in the lanes and on the hillsides, many of which have the minimal, stark beauty that the military-based government preferred. Sometimes nicknamed the 'Kyoto of the East', Kamakura definitely still retains the flavour of old Japan.

Most people start their explorations at Kamakura Station, meandering through the Komachi Dori shopping street towards Tsuruoka Hachimangu Shrine. However, I prefer to step off one station earlier at Kita-Kamakura and combine sightseeing with a light hike along the Daibutsu Trail, passing through the hills that surround the city on three sides.

But before getting on the trail, make a quick detour to nearby Meigetsuin Temple, also known as the 'hydrangea temple', as its steep steps are surrounded by masses of the blue-ish flowers that bloom profusely in June. Take a left from the East Exit, and walk until you reach a little river; follow the river by turning left again and proceeding down attractive Meigetsuin Street. The main hall has a circular window that perfectly frames the inner gardens, which are only open during the peak of iris season in the summer and autumn foliage. Look for bunny motifs throughout, inspired by the 'bright moon' of the temple's name and the mochi-pounding rabbit who, according to legend, lives here.

Retrace your steps and head towards Jochiji, one of Kamakura's five major Zen temples. You'll find the start of the trail along the side and towards the back of the temple. From here, simply follow the marked trail (sturdy walking shoes are highly recommended, as some sections can be a bit muddy), stopping by Kuzuharaoka Shrine to throw a few plates for good luck, Genjiyama Park and Zeniarai Benzaiten Shrine, where you can wash your money in the hope that it will multiply.

If you're tired or strapped for time, follow Genjiyama Park down to Jufukuji Temple (which has a very photogenic gate and pathway, although the temple itself is often not open to the public), then cross at the train track and keep going straight until you reach Komachi Dori, where you can either check out Tsuruoka Hachimangu Shrine or head to the station.

If not, continue the hike following the signs to Kotokuin, the temple that houses the Great Buddha. The final section (about 20 minutes) follows a suburban road, but eventually reaches the temple and the 11 metre (36 foot) bronze Buddha. A short walk away is Hasedera, one of my favourite temples in Kamakura. Not only is the 10 metre (32 foot) gilded Kannon statue enshrined within an incredible piece of religious art, but it also has a hill covered with hydrangeas in June, great views of the coast, fluffy steamed buns for sale and the moody Benten Cave, where you can stoop to see 17 hand-carved stone figures lit up by candles.

There are a lot of restaurants and cafes around this area, including a few that offer the most famous local dish, shirasudon, a bowl of rice topped with tiny whitebait, either served raw or kettle-boiled, along with a bit of ginger.

From Hase Station you can catch the adorably retro Enoden train back towards Kamakura Station, or extend your visit to nearby Enoshima, a little island just off the coast. It's home to Enoshima Shrine, dedicated to the goddess of good fortune, music and knowledge, along with caves, beaches, an observatory and a rather nice spa where you can soak your tired legs in the hot springs.

Both Kamakura and Kita-Kamakura stations are on the Shonan Shinjuku Line, which are both 1 hour from Shinjuku Station.

SPIRITUALITY & HIKING AT MOUNT OYAMA

This hike was once one of the most popular pilgrimage destinations for cool Edokko (citizens of Edo). The climb from the lower shrine to the upper shrine at the top of the 1252 metre (41,000 foot) peak is not too long, usually taking a competent hiker about 90 minutes; however, it is very steep. No plateaus here, just a straight up and down course, so best taken on only if you've got good hiking boots and are ready for a serious workout.

After taking the train and bus to the bottom of the cable car area, you're already in for a short climb. To reach the cable car, you must first climb up the steps of one of the most unusual and vertical *shotengai* (shopping streets) I have seen. The retro Koma Sando approach has 362 steps and is lined with restaurants and shops selling interesting edible souvenirs and wooden crafts, in particular the *koma* (spinning tops) the street is named after. This is a good place to pick up a few things to munch on at the top of the mountain. Also check out the 27 landings, where ceramic tiles decorated with images of tops let you know how far you have to go until you reach the cable car.

You could start your hike here, with the onnazaka and otokozaka (slightly less steep but longer 'women's trail' and shorter but tougher 'men's trail'), to see the lovely temple halfway up, but I recommend doing this on the way down or using the cable car to save your strength.

Take the cable car all the way to the top, where you will find Oyama Afuri Shrine, dedicated to the three rain- and water-related gods who are associated with this (often misty) sacred mountain. One is said to be the father of Mount Fuji's deity, Konohanasakuya-hime, and the two mountains have been connected since the Edo period, when it became a 'substitute pilgrimage' for

Mount Fuji. At the time, the shogunate strictly restricted travel, and travelling to Mount Fuji required a special permit. Associations, guilds and local neighbourhood groups in Edo would make the pilgrimage to Oyama instead, as it was closer and didn't require any special permissions.

When you enter the shrine, you'll see the long wooden swords that pilgrims would carry all the way from Tokyo to present to the gods of the shrine. You can still see Edo period swords displayed today, with the longest measuring 6 metres (19½ feet).

Now it's time to start hiking to the upper shrine. Find the path that starts a bit behind and to the left of the shrine building. While it is a tough trail, it's well marked and easy to follow, and the views of Sagami Bay and (on clear days) Mount Fuji are incredible. There is a tiny food vendor at the top as well, so you can enjoy a warm drink or bowl of noodles as you gaze down. The steep 45–60-minute trail down passes by the Niju waterfall and shrine towards the end, which is also a good viewing point for Mount Mitsumine. (If you don't feel like clambering all the way to the top, you can do a shorter trek by taking the route to the right of the stone stairway to the shrine, and just walking to the viewpoint instead.)

Take the cable car down to the stop by Oyamadera Temple, to see the staircase lined on both sides by metal statues of the fierce Fudo Myoo guardians, with a line of stone lanterns going straight down the middle. It's particularly magical in autumn, as the blood-red maples frame the staircase perfectly. The temple itself dates back to the 8th century AD, with elaborate wood carvings and three Buddhist figures cast in iron, which is unusual.

By this point, you're probably starving, so head back down to Koma Sando and look for a hot pot restaurant serving one of two local specialties: the smoothest tofu you will ever taste or locally caught wild boar. This is a pleasant area for an overnight trip as well, and the historic, 400-year-old Tougakubou ryokan is a welcoming spot. The young chef's brother runs the tofu shop across the street, so the meals feature plenty of his freshest product, and he can accommodate vegans and vegetarians. The outdoor hot springs are also perfect after a tough hike.

It takes just under 2 hours to get to the start of the cable car. From Shinjuku, take a rapid-express Odakyu Line train towards Odawara, get off at Isehara Station and switch to the number 10 bus towards Oyama Cable Car.

WHAT TO EXPECT AT A RYOKAN

These traditional inns are found all across Japan, particularly in areas known for their *onsen* (hot springs). Many people are drawn to the experience of staying at a ryokan, with their pretty tatami rooms, hot spring baths, the delicate, elaborate meals often served in your private room and that attentive, thoughtful Japanese hospitality.

Like hotels, ryokan range from budget-friendly spots to the extremely exclusive with year-long waiting lists. But, unlike regular hotels, there are a few specific things you need to know before you go, especially when it comes to the sleeping arrangements. Here are my hard-earned tips so you know what to expect.

—

TIMING & MEALS – Check-in is usually 3 pm and check-out is 10 am and, although not common, some ryokan still have curfews. While the reason is understandable (the staff have a right to sleep too), it can feel a bit limiting, so be sure to check when booking.

Dinner is usually served around 6 pm to 7.30 pm and breakfast is exclusively served between 7 am and 8 am (8.30 am at the latest). If you're not an early bird, see if you can just book the room plus dinner, and skip breakfast.

A word of warning for coffee lovers: there are still ryokan that only serve green tea at breakfast. Depending on your level of dependency on the bean, this may be an issue, so pick up a packet of single-serve pour-over filter coffees to make in your room. They're easily available at most konbini.

SLEEPING ARRANGEMENTS – This is the big one. If you're used to sleeping on a big, bouncy hotel mattress, that's not the way of the ryokan. You'll be sleeping on a futon on the tatami-covered floor, which can be a shock to the system, as futons are often quite thin (even at very high-end ryokan) and it can feel like you are sleeping directly on the floor, particularly if you tend to sleep on your side. You can check in the cupboards of your room to see if they have extra futon mats for more cushioning, or you can ask the staff to bring you one (which may potentially cause a bit of confusion).

Traditional Japanese pillows are often stuffed with buckwheat husks or beans, which creates a bit of rustling noise. They can take some getting used to, but if you're really struggling, some ryokan have a stash of down pillows that you can request. And pack an eye mask if you're sensitive to light (or have a streetlight outside your room), as the paper screens don't really block it out.

PRIVACY – In terms of bathrooms, moderately priced ryokan have shared bathrooms, while the higher-end ones have private bathrooms for each room.

Oh, and one final thing to keep in mind: the walls and floors of old-school ryokan are thin. You can certainly hear your neighbours and they you, so choosing to stay in one on your honeymoon may not be ideal.

& BEYOND

WELCOME TO KANSAI

After Tokyo, the Kansai region is the most visited area in Japan. This is where you'll find popular cities like Kyoto, Nara and Osaka, and the lesser-known prefectures of Hyogo, Wakayama and Shiga.

Often considered the cradle of Japanese culture, much of Kansai feels like it is mainly covered in shrines, temples, burial mounds and other reminders of Japan's long history, including the largest collection of national treasures.

There is a fascinating east–west divide between Kansai and the Kanto area, focused around Tokyo. This is partly due to old grudges about the capital being moved from Kyoto to Tokyo in 1868, as the emperor's residence had been based in Kyoto since 794 AD. As such, Kyoto still considers itself the preserver and protector of Japanese tradition, in comparison to the capital.

You will also find a distinct difference in Osaka, as, during the Edo period, it was a city of rich (but looked-down-upon) merchants, with just 1 per cent of the population being of the samurai class, a shocking difference from the military-based society in Edo.

Small cultural differences will hit you as soon as you leave your chosen station, as people line up on escalators on the opposite side from Tokyo! Even the spoken language differs, with variations of Kansai dialect popping up to test your ears.

京都

Kyoto

WHEN EMPEROR KAMMU decided to make Kyoto his capital in 794 AD, he had the city designed to match the rectangular layout and gridded streets of Xian, the then capital of China. Although there have been changes throughout the centuries, this clear grid of streets makes finding your way around relatively easy.

Kyoto remained the capital of Japan for over 1000 years, until the dramatic changes and modernisation of the Meiji period, when Tokyo became the capital in 1868. But this long stint definitely left its mark and, even now, the 'old capital' is the centre of traditional culture and crafts (in particular silk dyeing and weaving) and a major historic centre of Buddhism ... although certainly Shinto is also very prevalent, sometimes leading Kyoto to be called the 'City of 10,000 Shrines'.

Sadly, many parts of the city suffered due to fires or the push for modernisation, with countless *machiya* (traditional wooden houses) being destroyed to make way for the hulking Kyoto Station or in preference for less draughty accommodation. Fortunately, this trend has since abated, and the parts of the city that escaped the axe are truly stunning in their understated elegance.

Of course, this means that Kyoto is (understandably) an incredibly popular tourist destination, both domestically and internationally. Visitor numbers can be mind-boggling, especially during the peak spring and autumn seasons. Do your best to be a good visitor and be respectful of the Kyotoites who need to go about their daily lives while surrounded by literally millions of tourists. Don't mob the maiko and geisha for that perfect Instagram shot or take photos in areas where you are requested not to do so, and don't block entrances to private homes. Aim to patronise local businesses instead of chains, and remember that temples and shrines are sacred sites, not just sightseeing destinations.

THE BIG SIGHTS (& HOW TO SEE THEM BEST)

Although I definitely feel for my fellow night owls, the secret to a peaceful visit to Kyoto is to aim for weekdays and to get up early ... really early. The must-see sights below are famous for good reason and can get incredibly busy at peak times. This is particularly true for the 'big three' of Kyoto: Kinkakuji Temple (also known as the Golden Pavilion); Fushimi Inari Taisha Shrine; and Kiyomizudera Temple.

There are so many things to see in Kyoto that it can become a bit overwhelming, and getting around by bus and train can get confusing and tiring. Choosing one area per day and focusing on a few of the major sights, then wandering the lanes to find more hidden gems, is likely to be a more peaceful and meaningful experience. The city is very walkable, and all that movement will make sure you are always ready to try the many tempting foods (and especially desserts) the former capital has to offer.

KINKAKUJI TEMPLE

The image of Kyoto's Golden Pavilion has graced thousands of travel guides, magazines and social media feeds. Views of this gold leaf–covered structure reflected in the adjacent pond have a grandeur that is hard to match, which is unsurprising, as the grounds were set out by a mid-14th-century shogun to feel like heaven on earth. Note that the current building is a more recent recreation, as the previous structure was set ablaze by a fanatical monk in 1950! Be sure to get there when they open at 9 am, as it gets very busy.

Kinkakuji and Ginkakuji are actually sub-temples of the massive and powerful Shokokuji Temple, despite all being located in different parts of the city. Shokokuji has a fantastic museum filled with artistic treasures, lots of sub-temples to explore (if Rinkoin is open during your visit, pop in to see the really sweet ink-screen painting of a tiger by contemporary artist Yusen Fujii) and far fewer crowds.

The Golden Pavilion is on the western side of the city, accessible using the 101, 102, 204 or 205 bus. Afterwards, you can easily check out nearby temples, such as Daitokuji, Ryoanji and Ninnaji, and Kitano Tenmangu Shrine.

FUSHIMI INARI TAISHA SHRINE

This shrine has been considered a sacred spot since well before Kyoto became the capital, and is dedicated to Inari, the god of the rice harvest and commerce. The fox statues you will see all around are messengers of the god. They're sometimes shown with a key in their mouth, representing the keys to the rice storehouses of yore. According to legend, if you look closely enough, you will find a fox that resembles you!

The main temple and lower sections of the trails tend to be crowded (especially the part where the row of torii gates splits in two) but be sure to check out Higashimaru Shrine (near the dance stage) to see the thousands of strands of origami cranes, folded by students praying that they will pass their exams.

The higher sections of the trail are much more peaceful, as most people don't realise that this amazing shrine, with more than 10,000 bright-orange torii gates, actually snakes up a 233 metre (764 foot) 'mountain'. The trails crisscross and can be a bit confusing, so give yourself at least 3 hours (and pick up a map at the lowest shrine) to complete your explorations.

Getting to the temple is easy, with regular trains from central Kyoto dropping you off at either Keihan Fushimi-Inari Station or JR Inari Station.

KIYOMIZUDERA TEMPLE

Climb up one of the hilly paths lined with souvenir and street food shops to the entrance of Kiyomizudera Temple, which holds a lofty position over Higashiyama, one of Kyoto's areas with the highest density of sights. It was founded in 780 AD on the location of the sacred Otowa Waterfall, which you can still drink from to this day. Choose from one of the three streams, said to give longevity, scholastic success or luck in love, but don't drink from all three, as it is likely to displease the gods! Take in the majestic city views from the wooden terrace, ringed with maple and cherry trees, which display their colours in autumn and spring respectively. According to legend, people used to jump off this lofty perch in the belief that, if they survived, their wish would be granted.

Look for the dark doorway in the Zuigu Hall to try the Tainai Meguri, a walk through a dark corridor that represents the womb of a Bodhisattva. You use a rope to find your way until you reach a stone said to grant every wish, before being 'reborn' as you step back out into the light.

Although there are buses from Kyoto Station, you can also walk from Gion-Shijo or Kiyomizu-Gojo Station. There are tons of sights nearby, such as the geisha district of Gion, Kodaiji Temple, Yasaka Shrine, Chionin Temple and Maruyama Park. The temple opens at 6 am.

SANJUSANGENDO

The hall of this temple is the longest in Japan. It's filled with 1000 golden statues of Kannon, the goddess of mercy, surrounding a 3.3 metre (11 foot) 'thousand-armed Kannon' with crystal eyes, carved in 1254. You may notice that the statues actually only have 42 'extra' arms ... you simply can't see the remaining 958 because they are said to be on the other 25 planes of existence.

This marvellous temple is just across from the Kyoto National Museum, a lovely Meiji period red-brick building. The closest station is Shichijo. Chishakuin Temple is just a short walk away, and has fantastic gardens, even by Kyoto standards.

DAITOKUJI

This huge walled temple complex is one of my favourite places in Kyoto, as its size and sheer number of sub-temples dotted around means you can find a quiet spot to sit and reflect. This was once a major centre for tea ceremonies associated with venerable tea master Sen no Rikyu.

While many of the temples are not open to the public, those that are have excellent rock gardens that exemplify the spirit of Zen. Daisenin Temple's garden resembles a Chinese painting, while Ryogenin has five different examples, including one that represents the universe itself. Kotoin is my personal favourite, with a long approach lined with lush moss and bamboo groves, while those with a keen eye may spot the Christian imagery at Zuihoin.

Stop for a lunch of *shojin-ryori* (Buddhist cuisine) at Izusen, right by the Daijiin sub-temple or, for a real taste of history, head to the beautiful Imamiya Shrine nearby and the two shops that serve grilled abura mochi. Kazariya has been making these sweet treats since 1656, while Ichiwa has done so since 1002!

Daitokuji is about a 15-minute walk from Kinkakuji Temple, and a short bus ride on the 204 or 205 bus from Kyoto Gyoen National Garden and the former Imperial Palace.

NISHIKI MARKET

If you want to get a taste of local Kyoto flavours, this five-block, covered shopping street is where to do it. Sample pickles, matcha-flavoured treats, senbei rice crackers, freshly grilled skewers or *tako tamago* (candied baby octopus stuffed with a quail egg). Be aware that eating while walking is considered impolite in Japan and, while the rules here are a little looser, just be considerate of not blocking others, as locals also shop here.

Keep an eye out for Nishiki Tenmangu Shrine, with its adorable plum-shaped amulets hanging from the trees, and the side streets off the market with troves of interesting shops, antique sellers, cool restaurants and bars. The market is a short walk from both Karasuma and Kyoto-Kawaramachi stations and is close to the Pontocho alleyway. This cinematic narrow street has tons of interesting restaurants, and you might also see a *geiko* (the Kyoto term for a geisha) or *maiko* (trainee geiko) on her way to work.

GION

Gion is Kyoto's largest entertainment and geiko district. The streets lined with restaurants, bars and traditional machiya are centred around the main Hanamikoji Lane. At dusk, you can spot maiko and their older 'sisters' making their way to their evening appointments at traditional restaurants and tea houses, where they dance, play party games and chat with attendees. The area is pretty in the daytime, but really striking after dark, with lanterns and streetlights reflecting on the stone pavement. If you do spot a maiko or geiko, respect their space and just admire them from afar. Some visitors pay to get dressed up as a maiko, but you can tell them from the real deal as they're the ones clutching phones or cameras and wobbling in their high sandals.

Don't miss the Shirakawa area, where wooden houses and weeping willows line the canal, leading you to little Tatsumi Shrine, which sits right where two lanes fork, very close to Gion Komori, a traditional sweets and tea house that makes fantastic matcha-based parfaits.

ARASHIYAMA

Home to the photogenic Sagano Bamboo Grove, the Arashiyama area is perhaps only second to temple-filled Higashiyama in terms of popularity.

It's crowded and touristy on the main road and around the Togetsukyo Bridge, so just head straight into the temple area. If you want to get shots of the bamboo grove without hordes of people, get there well before 9 am. Nearby, you'll find the north gate of Tenryuji Temple, which has gardens that incorporate the mountains into the design. In the Dharma Hall, there's a dramatic painting of a massive dragon in swirling clouds, and its eyes follow you around the room.

The Okochi Sanso Villa tends to get skipped, as the construction is more recent, but the gardens with views over Kyoto (and the fact that the entrance fee includes a bowl of matcha and a traditional sweet) allow you to combine sightseeing with a scenic rest. Check out little Gioji Temple, a marvel of moss, and follow the Saga Toriimoto Preserved Street on your way to touching Adashino Nenbutsuji Temple, an 8th-century temple with some 8000 stone markers and small pagodas to remember people who passed on without kin to bury them in family graves.

Saga-Arashiyama Station is only 17 minutes by train on the San-In Line from Kyoto Station, and there are also regular buses.

Hanamikoji Lane ▸

Early Morning Reflection Walk

It bears repeating that getting up early is one of the best ways to experience Kyoto at its most peaceful. Even if you are not a morning person, this walk alone is worth the early alarm to follow in the literal steps of a philosopher.

Take the subway to Keage Station to begin this 3 km (1.9 mile) walk. Climb up the Keage Incline, where you can walk along the tracks of a defunct railway that was created in 1890 to allow boats to be moved between two reservoirs. This spot is particularly gorgeous in spring, when the morning light shimmers through the blossoms of the cherry trees.

Keep going until just before the reservoir (with its brass statue), take the stairs on your right back up to the street level, then take the road that gently goes left between the stone pillar and little hut. This will lead you to gorgeous Nanzenji Temple, which opens at 8.40 am. The Hojo Hall has a rock garden which represents tigers and their cubs crossing the river, but the most unusual sight on the grounds is an incongruous section of an elegant, Meiji period brick aqueduct that used to connect Kyoto and far away Lake Biwa.

From the majestic Sanmon Gate, take a right and then another immediate right to get onto tiny Shishigadani Dori street and follow it for about 5 minutes until you reach scenic Eikando Temple, which is considered one of the top autumn foliage spots in the city. It opens at 9 am and you can easily spend an hour exploring the expansive grounds, with elegant, covered walkways that connect the buildings, majestic Tahoto pagoda overlooking the city and the Hojo Pond, where an arching bridge connects to a little island with a tiny shrine, all framed by foliage.

The Philosopher's Path starts very close to the temple, just down the first side street to the right if you leave via the Central Gate. This pleasant, cherry tree–lined riverside stroll is the most scenic way to walk the 2 km (1.2 miles) towards Ginkakuji Temple. It got its name from being the daily commute of Nishida Kitaro, one of Japan's most famous philosophers, who would practise walking meditation while taking this path on his way to teach at Kyoto University.

At the second bridge, take a right and follow the stone-paved road to nearby Otoyo Shrine, dedicated to the god of matchmaking and watched over by two adorable mouse guardians.

Returning to the Philosopher's Path, keep strolling and peeking into the tiny temples and shrines that regularly pop up along the route. As you get close to the Ginkakuji Bridge, keep an eye to your right for the charming second-floor cafe Brown Eyes Coffee, which opens at the relatively early (by Kyoto standards) hour of 10.30 am.

Take a right at the Ginkakuji Bridge and follow the signs to this famous temple, also known as the Silver Pavilion. Unlike its Golden Pavilion 'sister', the building here is not covered in silver leaf; however, it is far older, having survived centuries of fires and earthquakes. The Sea of Silver Sand garden is one of the most unusual examples of the dry garden style, featuring a huge sand cone called the Moon Viewing Platform.

If you're hungry, retrace your steps and follow broad Imadegawa Dori road to Ikazuchi Udon. It's popular with locals for its chewy noodles and modern, minimalist decor. It opens at 11.30 am and there are often lines.

If you want a longer, more solitary walk, Yoshidayama Park is just a couple of streets behind Ikazuchi. It's overgrown and wild and feels far more remote than it is. At one end is Yoshida Shrine and the rest of the park is sprinkled with little temples, moss-covered stone staircases and an inari shrine with a row of torii gates. Use your map app to find Yoshida Kaguraoka Old Town, a tiny street that looks like it hasn't changed in hundreds of years.

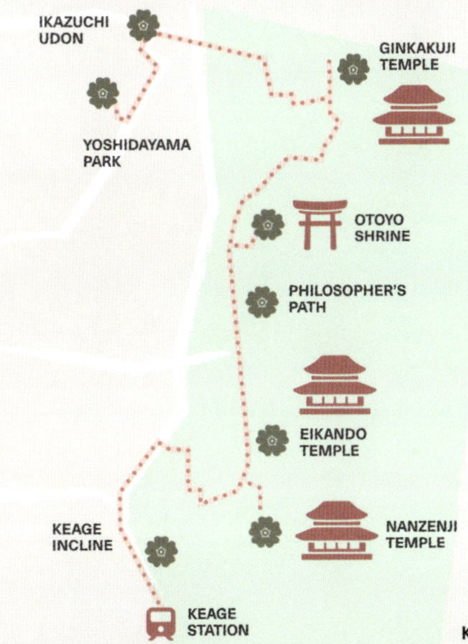

WHAT TO EAT IN KYOTO

The temptations in Kyoto are constant, particularly in tourist-heavy areas, from candied strawberries and skewers of mochi to pickles, freshly fried croquettes and tea-laced drinks.

As long as you avoid the obvious tourist traps (overly shiny signs mainly in English or Chinese), it's pretty hard to go wrong. While you should try a little bit of everything that tickles your fancy, there are five foods you shouldn't leave Kyoto without trying.

TOFU & YUBA

Tofu in Japan is on a different level and, in Kyoto, you'll see just how delicious it can be, along with *yuba* (tofu skin). Made fresh every day, it varies from silky smooth cubes to sturdy slabs that get grilled and covered in savoury dengaku miso sauce.

Try the local cold-season speciality of yudofu, squares of tofu boiled in a clay pot, along with a number of side dishes featuring the same ingredient, at 370-year-old Okutan, a restaurant on the grounds of Nanzenji Temple and the oldest operating yudofu restaurant in Japan. For quality yuba at a decent price, Yubasen on Gojozaka (one of the roads approaching Kiyomizudera Temple) has tasty set meals, including a delicious yubadon, in which the hand-lifted sheets of tofu skin are served on a bowl of rice, covered in savoury sauce.

UDON

The broth used for noodles differs between the Kanto and Kansai regions. In Kyoto, it's got a sweeter, rounder flavour prized by locals, and what better way to sample it than with a steamy bowl of chewy udon noodles. If you really want to eat like a Kyotoite, opt for a bowl of kitsune udon. Literally meaning 'fox udon', it's inspired by what is said to be the favourite food of the messengers of Fushimi Inari Shrine, featuring a huge sheet of fried, sweetened tofu. Ask for an extra topping of kujo negi, a spring onion (scallion) prominent in Kyoto's cuisine.

One of my favourite udon spots is Mannaka Tsururu, just across the street from the Ryokan Kinoe and right between Gion, Yasui Konpiragu Shrine and Kodaiji Shrine. The broth is made from natural ingredients with no additives, and the noodles are made from 100 per cent Japanese flour. In addition to the bowls of hot, freshly made noodles, they also have a good selection of sides and Kyoto sake, so you may be tempted to linger.

Another favourite, Mimikou, which is only a 10-minute walk from Mannaka Tsururu and right by Yasaka Shrine, has been around since 1969 and is justly famous for its curry udon. They also have vegan-friendly options.

OBANZAI

This longstanding tradition in Kyoto is perhaps one of the most charming, in which the cooks make large batches of robust, hearty dishes (where at least half of the ingredients are produced or processed in Kyoto) and display them in deep bowls on the counter. This makes ordering easy, as you can just point at the dish you want a portion from. Most obanzai joints are not fancy, so you get a real taste of local homestyle cooking. The dishes tend to feature a lot of vegetables; however, vegetarian options are slim, as fish and meat are used as flavouring.

There are some contemporary versions of obanzai around, but for an authentic, homely experience, head to Pontocho and look for the slightly shabby building along the Takase River that houses Aoi on the first floor. The owner is a ray of sunshine, and she has a great selection of sake to match all the delights she and her assistant have lined up on the counter. Another great option in the hotel-filled Shijo area is Kitchen Yoshida. You can expect a friendly welcome and well over a dozen different dishes to try ... but go early, as this welcoming spot has a lot of regular patrons.

KAISEKI

At the other end of the formality scale, you have kaiseki. The elegant course cuisine originated as simple, light meals served to guests during tea ceremonies, but has evolved over the centuries into a far more rarefied (and multi-course) experience. The ingredients are always strictly seasonal and presented like works of edible art. Although each portion is small, you can expect to be served anywhere between seven and 12 courses.

As this is Japan's haute cuisine, with many of the best restaurants boasting Michelin stars, you can expect the bill to match. Still, it's an exceptional dining experience. Try the renowned 'living museum' of Kikunoi by Kodaiji Temple, run by third-generation owner-chef Murata, who is considered one of the country's greatest experts on the secret of dashi. They accept online reservations in English, but booking in advance is a must. Courses range from ¥30,000 to over ¥70,000 per person.

Manshige is both more affordable (around ¥10,000 to ¥20,000 per person) and a bit more old-school, with one of its specialties being sea bream simmered so long it is almost candied. Situated in the Nishijin textiles area (not far from Kyoto Gyoen National Garden), it is just far enough off the tourist path that customers are mainly Japanese. Manshige does have an online booking request form in English, which makes it easier to get a table.

My favourite restaurant is, unfortunately, also the hardest to book, as they only accept reservations by phone. Soujiki Nakahigashi, near Ginkakuji Temple, has two very much deserved Michelin stars. The chef's self-described 'herbivorous cuisine' and 'garden to table' ethos, his constant puns (mainly in Japanese), along with the fact that he will accommodate vegan and other dietary requirements, makes this the friendliest kaiseki restaurant I have been to. Expect to pay about ¥8000 for lunch and a minimum of ¥22,000 for dinner. Book as early as possible for the best chance of getting one of the coveted seats at the counter.

MATCHA DESSERTS

One thing you will notice when walking around Kyoto is the matcha-flavoured ... everything. From ice cream to soba noodles, mochi to pancakes, it seems like everything is tinted green! This is no surprise, as the city is right next door to Uji, one of the great green tea–producing areas of Japan (which also makes a fun half-day trip). But not all matcha is created equal, and you definitely get what you pay for. Lower-grade matcha has a bitter aftertaste, with none of the fresh, grassy, slightly sweet flavour of the finer grades.

Ditch the ubiquitous matcha lattes found in the tourist areas and experience the real deal at Gion Komori, housed in a former tea house right along the Shirakawa Canal. It's most famous for its matcha powder–covered *warabi mochi* (a jelly-like sweet made from bracken starch), but I go for the matcha bavarois parfait (usually for breakfast, as it gets super busy later in the day). For something a little more modern, just a couple of minutes from Yasaka Shrine is Jouvencelle, home of the rather unique 'matcha fondue' dessert set. Once you're done dipping, ask the staff to pour hot milk into the bowl to create a decadent matcha latte.

If you are interested in the tea itself, then head towards Toji Temple and find nearby MA, where a visit feels like you have gained entry to a secret world. From the topsy-turvy architecture to the craftsmanship behind every single cup of tea, piece of ceramic and deceptively simple-looking dessert, the experience is magical.

TOP 10 HIDDEN GEMS OF KYOTO

Like any city used to high tourist numbers, Kyoto guards its secrets well. The practice of *ichigensan okotowari* (no entry without introduction) is most famously connected to the world of geiko and maiko, but the ethos can also be found in some restaurants, cafes, bars and even temples.

Practising good etiquette and being a considerate guest are even more important here than in other parts of Japan, as the local patience for mistakes is much lower due to the onslaught of tourists who (sometimes) act as if the entire city is just a backdrop for their selfies.

On the flip side, if you enjoy meditative travel, I find Kyoto to be one of the best destinations in Japan for solo travellers. There is definitely a magic to the city which reveals itself to those who enjoy the quiet, more contemplative side of things.

KYOTO'S TWO IMPERIAL VILLAS

Katsura and Shugakuin are both a little out of the way, but worth the effort for the wonderful architecture and garden design.

The prince who commissioned the Katsura Imperial Villa in the early 1600s was enamoured by *The Tale of Genji*, and several views recreate scenes from the book. The mossy tea houses reflecting in calm ponds and the wabi sabi aesthetic are said to have inspired many architects and artists.

A 15-minute walk from Katsura Station on the Hankyu Kyoto Line will get you to the Katsura Imperial Villa. On the way, try the traditional sweets (and summer specialty, kakigori, a refreshing shaved ice with homemade syrup) at nearby Nakamuraken, which has been serving sweet-toothed folks since 1883.

The Shugakuin Imperial Villa is the largest and perhaps the finest of the four imperial properties in the city. The three areas showcase gardens and buildings of the traditional imperial style from the mid-1700s, and the views are particularly idyllic, as the surrounding farmlands were bought by the Imperial Household Agency and rented out to farmers.

The temple entrance is a 10-minute walk from Shugakuin Station on the Eizan Railway Line. Make a stop at nearby Manshuin Temple (particularly in autumn) for its famous screen paintings and rock gardens.

As both temples are under the protection of the Imperial Household Office, the only way to visit is on a pre-scheduled group tour and you must apply for permission in advance from their office in Kyoto Imperial Palace Park. You just need to fill out a basic form and show your passport.

MOSS TEMPLE

Also known as Kokedera (or, correctly, as Saihoji Temple) this Zen temple is a bower of green, with 120 different varieties of moss covering the deeply serene grounds. Walk through this fairytale-worthy world, the design of which dates back to 1339. The Moss Temple is at its best in the rainy season (June to early July), as the moisture makes the moss even fluffier than usual. (Note that the garden is closed in January and February.)

Visiting this mystical temple requires advance planning, as you need to send a request via email up to two months before your desired visit. Entry is ¥3000 and you must copy a Buddhist sutra before touring the garden. Head to their website for full instructions. The temple is a 20-minute walk from Matsuo Taisha Station on the Hankyu Arashiyama Line and is a few stations away from the Katsura Imperial Villa.

OKAZAKI SHRINE

This historic spot was one of the four shrines Emperor Kammu built when he established his new capital in Kyoto in 794 AD. But what makes it such a fun place to visit are all the images of rabbits. They're considered the messengers of the gods enshrined here, as well as representing fertility and wishes for a safe pregnancy. Instead of the usual *komainu* (the lion-dog statues you find in front of most shrines) there are two bunnies, who you can pet for luck in love. The theme is repeated around the grounds in carvings, lanterns, statues and rows of tiny porcelain rabbit charms perched on the railings!

Okazaki Shrine is about 10 minutes by foot from both Heian Shrine and Eikando Temple, best known for its phenomenal autumn foliage (and evening light-ups of the same).

TANUKIDANISAN FUDOIN TEMPLE

In Japan, you'll spot figures of *tanuki* (raccoon dogs) in front of restaurants and peeking out of private gardens. While they are real animals, they are also important trickster characters from folklore, with wide grins and a weakness for sake, and on the climb up to the main building of Tanukidanisan Fudoin Temple you'll be cheered on by more than 200 of these adorable statues. The temple has a projecting wooden balcony to take in the views, but if you want to skip the temple itself (entrance is ¥500), look for the steps marked by a tanuki statue just before the entrance which will take you on a mini 20-minute trek to 36 smaller shrines, which is quite peaceful and usually deserted.

It is a bit of a hike to the temple, which is about 25 minutes by foot from Ichijo Station on the Eizan Main Line. You can combine a visit with the nearby Shisendo Temple (the retreat of a particularly scholarly samurai, with lovely gardens and a collection of portraits of Chinese poets) or the more famous Enkoji Temple.

ISHIBEKOJI ALLEY

For a little taste of what Kyoto used to look like, explore this scenic alley between Yasaka Shrine and Kodaiji Temple. Elegant wooden ryokans, fancy restaurants and moody (expensive) bars peek out from behind wooden gates along this twisting, turning lane.

The entrance near Kodaiji Temple on Nene no Michi Street is the easiest to find. If you're coming from the direction of Yazaka Shrine, look for the little entry way on your left when following Shimokawaracho Street. Obey the 'no photography' signs and be respectful, as there are many private homes along the beautiful alley.

YANAGIKOJI ALLEY

This is another insanely photogenic, hard-to-find little alleyway, right near the major Kyoto-Kawarachi Station on the Hankyu Line. Just 60 metres (197 feet) long and so narrow two people can't walk side by side, it's still graced by a few of its namesakes (weeping willows) and hides fabulous little restaurants, bars and new shops, which have brought it back to life after being mostly forgotten for a couple of decades. Want your own 'lost in Kyoto' photo? This is where to take it.

Finding the alley can be tough, so using a map app to find Yanagi Koji TAKA (a beloved yakitori restaurant) is the best way to get there.

CAFE & GALLERY RIHOU

This lovely cafe that fronts the Shirakawa River is a short walk from Kyoto University's campus and far enough off the tourist trail to remain an oasis of calm. From the wooden front and ironwork door to the handmade furniture and crockery, every element shows a level of craftsmanship that is no longer common, even in Kyoto. The owner has a great collection of art books to flick through, and the coffee is great.

CRAFT CLUB

Just a couple of minutes by foot from both Yasaka Shrine and the geisha-spotting hub of Hanamikoji, this little cocktail bar is hidden down a quiet alley and housed in a refurbished *machiya* (traditional wooden townhouse) filled with gleaming dark wood. The atmosphere is much friendlier than other bars I have visited in Kyoto, with the head bartender and staff doing their best to explain things to non-Japanese speakers. If you're lucky, you may get seated at the table overlooking the little garden. Cocktails might feature less standard ingredients like green tea and shiso (perilla) leaves. Ask if they have their famous chocolates when you visit.

L'ESCAMOTEUR

The side streets around Kyoto-Kawaramachi Station are filled with interesting bars, to the point that it can be hard to choose where to go! But out of all of them, my feet point towards this magical drinkery where steampunk, alchemy and sleight of hand come together under the guidance of the French bartender. The (literally) Smoky Old Fashioned is perhaps their most famous drink, but all the mysterious ingredients of the craft cocktails perfectly match the feeling of being in a witch's cottage. If you can't get a seat, other excellent options nearby are Bee's Knees and Bar Rocking Chair.

KYOTO ISHUU TRAIL

This 84 km (52 mile) trail, which runs along the sides of the mountains that encircle Kyoto is still largely unknown to most visitors, although many do unknowingly walk a part of it when they visit Fushimi Inari Temple. The trails are well marked with little signposts in both English and Japanese; however, the distances can be a bit confusing, so it is worth buying a map of the trail you plan to walk (available at all major bookstores and some tourism information booths). There are four main trails: Higashiyama, Kitayama Toubu, Kitayama Nishibu and Nishiyama.

While walking the entirety of each course is a bit much, the section between signposts 30 and 52 of the Higashiyama course perfectly combines easy access, hiking, a few major sights (and a couple of uncrowded ones) and the essence of the Kyoto of yore. You can see the Keage Incline and Nanzenji Temple, climb Mount Daimonji, stop by Honenin Temple (which is both attractively mossy and free to enter) and end near Ginkakuji (the Silver Pavilion), all within a few hours.

You can also find extremely detailed (if a bit old-school) directions on the English webpage.

QUICK WHISKY TRIP TIP!

Whisky fans should take a short side trip to the Suntory Yamazaki Distillery, just a 15-minute train ride from Kyoto Station on the JR Tokaido Line and then a 10-minute walk from Yamazaki Station. It's also within easy reach of Osaka, if you're coming from the other direction.

The 80-minute tour costs ¥1000 and ends with a tasting of their single malt and all the whiskies (which can only be tried here, as they are not available for sale) that are blended to create it. Advance bookings are required and can be made on their English website. Afterwards, stop at the tasting counter to try some of their rarer varieties, and other whiskies from around the world, for an additional fee.

Day Trips from Kyoto

The most common day-trip choice from Kyoto tends to be to neighbouring Osaka and Nara, but these two cities have so much to see that they warrant their own detailed guides. There's also nearby Uji, a fun destination for green tea–obsessed foodies who also want to check out Byodoin Temple, whose Phoenix Hall graces the ¥10 coin.

However, one part of Kyoto most folks don't get to see is the more rural side of this ancient area. Here are two options that combine traditional landscapes with cultural highlights, all wrapped up in a nice walk (or hike).

KURAMA–KIBUNE HIKE

This relatively easy 4 km (2.5 mile) hike takes you from the pretty village of Kurama to the equally attractive Kibune (or vice versa, although I recommend this order to avoid an extra climb). It only takes 30 minutes to get to Kurama Station on the Eizan Line train from Demachiyanagi Station, which is close to Kyoto Gyoen National Garden.

Once you step out of Kurama Station, you'll be welcomed by a huge, bright-red tengu, the mythical messenger of the gods. Hang left and start climbing up the main street – you should soon see Kuramadera Temple and its lovely lantern-lined stairway, which is particularly attractive during the autumn colours or in early summer when the maples glow in fresh green. Enter the temple and follow the path that continues up into the Kitayama mountains. You'll soon pass a towering sacred cryptomeria tree before arriving at Yuki Shrine, where you can stop to say a prayer for a safe hike.

Keep going, passing the rather odd Inochi statue (supposed to represent the three precepts of Buddhism) and after a wooden gate you take several flights of lantern-lined stairs – which make a great backdrop for photos – until you reach the main hall of Kuramadera Temple, surrounded by cherry trees. To get to the trailhead follow the path to the left of the hall (and perhaps ring the giant bell once), then climb the steps to get to the ridgeline. Follow the ridge heading away from the rock encircled by a fence, passing through an area with prominent tree roots.

The trail is straightforward, but the only spot to be careful is at the wooden Osugi Gongen structure, where (when facing it) you will want to take a right. The forest trail slopes gently downwards towards Kibune, until you reach the bridge over the Kibune River. The main street is lined with old-school ryokan and restaurants, with Hirobun being a particularly good bet. During summer you can eat on kawadoko, platforms set over the river, to enjoy the cool breeze, or try the fun nagashi somen, where you catch the noodles as they flow down a bamboo shoot.

To return to Kyoto, walk 2 km (1.2 miles) down to Kibune-guchi Station on the Eizan Line.

OHARA WALK

If you prefer your adventures to be on flatter terrain, then the quiet agricultural area of Ohara may be a better fit. There are regular buses that run directly between Kyoto Station and the Ohara bus station, usually taking between 60 and 90 minutes, depending on traffic.

This little village nestled in the valley between the Hira and Kitayama mountains definitely feels suspended in time, and strolling among the traditional wooden houses, rice fields and quaint private gardens is deeply relaxing. The main two sights are in opposite directions, and I recommend going to Jakkoin Temple first, as the 15-minute walk takes you right through the lovely village, with shops, tea houses, photogenic bridges and even a 'foot-bath cafe' on the way. Jakkoin has been a Buddhist nunnery since 1186, but the buildings are quite recent, as the original temple sadly burned down in 2000. Fortunately, the gardens have retained their beauty, with plenty of mossy steps and seasonal foliage.

Retrace your steps to the bus stop, then follow the signs to Sanzenin Temple, the jewel of Ohara and, some might say, the whole of Kyoto. While spending your entire visit sitting on the wooden verandah overlooking the Ghibli-esque Shuhekien Garden is tempting, the golden figures of the Amida Buddha, Kannon and Fudo Myoo in the Shinden hall are quite striking. From here you can also get the iconic view of the Ojo Gokuraku-in Hall framed by maple and cedar trees.

Don't overlook nearby Hosenin, as the entrance fee includes a bowl of matcha and sweet to enjoy while overlooking the garden ... under a ceiling made from the floorboards of Fushimi Castle, still splashed with the blood of the loyal samurai who committed ritual suicide in 1600 when they realised the battle was lost.

Osaka

AS JAPAN'S SECOND-LARGEST METROPOLIS, Osaka has a brighter, more in-your-face charm that might take a little time to get used to. Although it became the very first capital of Japan for a brief period starting in 645 AD, it is really the mercantile history of the city that has had the greatest influence.

This powerhouse of the Kansai region has been a major trading port for at least 1400 years as, during the 5th century, Naniwa (the city's former name) was one of the main doorways to Japan for ships from other Asian countries. This constant exchange of knowledge and technology made it an important centre for crafts like pottery and metal forging and, to this day, it remains one of the busiest transport hubs in Japan.

Although it is harder for non-Japanese speakers to tell, the city is also a major centre for comedy, with a long history of producing outstanding *rakugo* (traditional storytellers) and *manzai* (comedy duos who perform skits). It's such an integral part of the culture that being told you're not funny in Osaka is a major burn. You'll probably notice that the locals are louder, more flamboyant, friendlier and more likely to try to joke with you. The general vibe of the city is more relaxed than Kyoto and much more boisterous than quiet Nara.

Having been razed to the ground twice, Osaka has a distinctly urban look. Many of the sights tend to be more modern, dating from the Meiji period onwards, but there are reminders of the city's history and its connection to the spread of Buddhism across Japan.

Osakans love good food, and the city is sometimes known as 'the nation's kitchen'. Foodies will want to spend at least one day in the city, trying all the cheap and tasty street food, checking out the markets and diving into the alleys of bars and tiny restaurants.

THE BIG SIGHTS (& HOW TO SEE THEM BEST)

The highly developed public transport system in Osaka makes getting around very easy and, as many of the city's attractions are a bit more modern, they're able to handle large numbers of visitors, so getting up early to avoid the crowds isn't as much of a concern here as it is in Kyoto.

Perhaps due to it being a centre of commerce and trade for so long, cafes and eateries in Osaka tend to open earlier than those in other Kansai cities, which makes finding a spot for breakfast or an early lunch much easier.

One tip to really stretch your budget is to get an Osaka Amazing Pass, which covers entry to a huge range of sightseeing spots, as well as public transport (if you're using a Rail Pass, almost none of the top sights in the city are along the JR train lines, so getting an Osaka Amazing Pass makes a lot of sense). It's ¥2800 for a one-day pass, and ¥3600 for a two-day pass. Take a river cruise, visit the Umeda Sky Garden or Tsutenkaku Tower, maybe a couple of other places, and it more than pays for itself.

Unlike other cities where I tend to recommend specific sights, in Osaka I prefer to suggest entire areas to wander around, as taking in the atmosphere is key to understanding its particular charms.

OSAKA CASTLE

This important spot (particularly during plum or cherry blossom season) rises high above a massive moat surrounded by gardens and walking paths. The original building was ordered in 1583 by Toyotomi Hideyoshi, one of the three daimyo lords who worked to unify Japan. He planned to rule from Osaka but, unfortunately, shortly after his death the powerful lord Tokugawa Ieyasu wrested power from the Toyotomi family and established a new capital in Edo (now Tokyo). The castle was destroyed and rebuilt twice, with the current version dating back to 1931.

It remains a symbol of the city and a poignant reminder of how, if things had gone differently, Osaka might be the capital of Japan. The grounds and Nishinomaru Garden (which requires a small fee to enter) are covered in cherry trees and, when they're in bloom, if you look from a distance it looks like the castle is floating on a frothy, pink cloud.

The best way to see the castle is via the Otemon Gate, a short walk away from Tanimachi Yonchome Station.

NAKANOSHIMA

This 3 km (1.9 mile) island between two rivers combines old and new, while giving a feel for just how prosperous Osaka was during the Meiji period. The island boasts an impressive rose garden, along with interesting buildings and museums. Two striking examples are the Osaka City Public Hall, an elegant brick building from 1918 designed by the same architect who envisioned Tokyo Station, and the 1904 Osaka Prefectural Nakanoshima Library, with its grand entrance and dome.

The brand new Nakanoshima Museum of Art has a great collection of modern Japanese and international art, with the uncanny Ship's Cat (*Muse*) statue outside. You can also visit the Museum of Oriental Ceramics, National Museum of Art, Osaka, or pose with the giant apple by the Nakanoshima Children's Book Forest.

There are a couple of ways to get to Nakanoshima, but I recommend walking from Kitahama Station (on the Sakaisuji or Keihan Line) because you'll pass a number of attractive Meiji buildings, including the 1922 Arai Building, which houses the excellent Gokan patisserie and tea salon, which is a timeless treat.

DOTONBORI

This shopping and dining street is known for its Blade Runner–esque flashing neon and huge, vaulting storefronts with signage that ranges from kraken-sized octopi to giant mechanical crabs. Do not eat before you go, because it's such a frenzy of food stalls and sizzling smells that you will want to try *all the things*.

While interesting during the day, Dotonbori is particularly festive at night, when the signs glow against the dark sky, the lights reflect off the canals and people pose on Ebisu Bridge with the famous Glico running man sign. You can take a river cruise down the canal, which will give you a great view of the unusual buildings without the crowds.

The street is easily accessed from Namba Station but consider making a 15-minute detour to Namba Yasaka Shrine to pose in front of the building shaped like a huge lion head.

KUROMON MARKET & SENNICHIMAE DOGUYASUJI STREET

Kuromon Market, where chefs and locals go to pick up ingredients and kitchen gear, has been catering to the needs of Osakans since the Edo period. There are currently around 150 shops selling fresh fish and veggies, along with sweets and pre-prepared foods and treats. Many of the shops offer bite-sized portions of their wares (especially the fish and fruit vendors) so you can try whatever is in season, right on the spot. As with Nishiki Market in Kyoto, do your best not to get in anyone's way and dispose of any garbage properly.

Many visitors end their trip to this corner of Osaka here, when really it is best paired with a wander through nearby Sennichimae Doguyasuji, a smaller, but equally fascinating, version of Tokyo's Kappabashi cookware street. It's more of an alley than a street, but it's filled with stores selling ceramics, knives, chopsticks ... if you love cooking, this is your treasure trove.

The two markets are both in the proximity of Namba Station, with the latter being very close to Exit E9.

Dotonbori ▸

glira
LOTTER
グリカ
ビール
くくる

NATIONAL BUNRAKU THEATRE

This form of traditional Japanese puppet theatre has a deep association with Osaka, but it's pretty hard to see live, even in Japan. Bunraku gained great popularity in the Edo period, as it was one of the few performing arts, along with kabuki, that was available to commoners instead of just the noble class. Three fully visible puppeteers each deftly operate a large puppet and, accompanied by a narrator and a shamisen player, bring historical events and love stories to life.

Performances are usually held in January, April, June, August and November, and run for about three weeks at a time. Tickets can be booked online on their English website, and they provide a synopsis (and sometimes subtitles or earphones) in English so you can follow along with the action. The plays can be quite long, but you can get tickets for a single act at some performances, just enough to get a feel for the puppeteers' impressive, emotive ability.

The theatre is close to Kuromon Market and Nippombashi Station on the Sennichimae and Tanimachi lines.

SUMIYOSHI TAISHA GRAND SHRINE

After exploring all the thrills of the shotengai shopping streets and entertainment districts of Osaka, a visit to the vast grounds of this venerable shrine, with its saturated orange hue, makes a nice change of pace.

Founded in 211 AD, this is not only one of the oldest shrines in Japan but is also one of the few that is built in a style that predates any Chinese influence. The straight lines, gates and layout feel a bit unusual due to this, despite being a purely 'Japanese-style' shrine. The god enshrined within is said to protect travellers, fishermen and sailors, which explains why this and all the other Sumiyoshi shrines around the country tend to be close to harbours.

The tree-filled lanes, highly arched Sorihashi Bridge, sacred rice paddy and many smaller sub-shrines around the extensive grounds make it feel peaceful and somehow far away from the big city, despite only being a 10-minute train ride from Namba, at Sumiyoshi Taisha Station on the Nankai Main Line.

EXPO '70 COMMEMORATIVE PARK & TOWER OF THE SUN

This humongous park was the site of the very first Japan World Exposition in 1970. The towering work of artist Taro Okamoto is what brings most folks to the park, as photos do not do justice to the sheer magnitude and presence of the 70 metre (230 foot) Tower of the Sun. Although a bit timeworn, this only seems to add to its uncanny charm.

However, the most interesting thing is the inside of the tower, which was reopened in 2018 for the first time in 48 years. The Sun of the Underworld and various masks and statues suggestively lit up are fascinating, but the highlight is the Dr Suess–like Tree of Life, where you can see everything from amoebas to a massive brontosaurus, celebrating the evolution of life on Earth. They still play the same music that was selected in 1970, which just adds to the surreal feeling. Book your tickets well in advance via their website.

Besides the tower, the park also boasts 5000 cherry trees, the Dream Pond (where you can rent a boat and paddle around sculptures poking out of the water), a lovely Japanese garden, fields of flowers like tulips and sunflowers, and an area covered with red kochia bushes in autumn.

It takes about 40–50 minutes to get to the park from central areas like Namba or Umeda. The closest station is Bampaku-kinen-koen Station on the Osaka Monorail Line.

AMERIKAMURA & 'URA-DOTONBORI'

When facing the giant Glico sign on the Ebisu Bridge, the part of the city I call 'ura-Dotonbori', or backstreet Dotonbori, stretches out behind you. If you take one of the stairways down to the walking paths along the river and follow it, you'll find an area dedicated to street artists, who turn the walls into elaborate canvases. Use a map app to find the nearby Dotonbori Hotel, known for the giant faces that grace its front pillars. At the second bridge (the Daikoku Bridge) you should take a right, going straight until you end up in the heart of Amerikamura, Osaka's equivalent of Harajuku.

Back in the '70s, fashion lovers would head to the warehouses here to get their hands on jeans, American clothes, second-hand records and other treasures, mainly from around California. Ever since, it has been a hub for youth and subculture fashion, attracting artists and business owners who enjoy putting their unique spin on things. You'll find all kinds of hidden gems in this area, so go for a wander and check out all the street art, people-shaped streetlights and wild fashions.

UMEDA SKY BUILDING & KUTCHU TEIEN OBSERVATORY

When arriving by bullet train or riding the subways across the bridges, you may notice this distinctive building. The two towers rise up to 173 metres (568 feet) and are topped with a circular platform, which houses the Kutchu Teien or 'Floating Garden Observatory' on the 39th floor. The views over the city are stunning, and it is quite romantic at night thanks to the little phosphorescent stones inlaid in the path, which make it feel like you are walking on stars. One of the most thrilling parts of the experience is taking the glass elevator that's suspended between the 35th and the top floor ... definitely not for those afraid of heights!

Detour via the 27th floor of the West Tower to check out the trippy Koji Kinutani Tenku Art Museum, where mixed media, VR and Japanese legends combine to create an immersive art experience. (The museum and observatory are covered by the Osaka Amazing Pass.) The Takimi Koji restaurant alley in the basement is worth a look for its 1920s streetscape decor, and the New Satoyama garden around the building is very attractive and peaceful.

The building is a 15-minute walk from Osaka and Umeda stations.

OSAKA FESTIVALS

There are three festivals held throughout the year at Osaka Tenmangu Shrine. The first, Tenjin Matsuri, is Osaka's biggest festival, celebrated on 24–25 July, when the god is paraded around the Tenma neighbourhood in a *mikoshi* (portable shrine). There are religious rituals on the first day while, on the second, you can expect to see dance teams, marching bands, fireworks and the iconic boat procession that attracts over a million people to the banks of the Okawa River to watch the elaborate vessels passing by.

A lesser-known event is the two-day Ebisu Festival in early January. It's a smaller version of the same event held at Imamiya Ebisu Shrine, with 20 *fukumusume* (lucky women) dressed in pink and gold Heian period–inspired costumes paraded down the streets around the shrine.

Finally, if you're around on 8 February, you can catch the 'needle funeral', where tailors and avid sewers bring their blunt needles and lay them to rest in giant blocks of *konnyaku* (a grey, jelly-like food made from potato starch).

Tenma Retro Charm & Bar-hopping Walk

The inbound tourism boom and constant push to redevelop and modernise popular areas of Osaka means that the city is constantly changing. Fortunately, there are still areas that have successfully resisted the push of developers – places where you can still get a feel for the cluttered but comforting nature of the city. One such area is the hidden (for now) gem of Nakazakicho, and another is the gloriously old-school and labyrinthine market- and eatery-filled Tenma. During the day, the main shopping street is a hub of independent shops and market stalls. When evening falls, it's time to hit the backstreets, with their countless bars and eateries.

Start your visit at Osakatemmangu Station, taking Exit 7 and walking the short distance to Osaka Tenmangu Shrine. The shrine was founded in 949 AD to honour the deity of scholarship, former poet and scholar Sugawara Michizane, who was deified after his death.

Retrace your steps back towards the station and look for the entrance to Tenjinbashisuji which, at 2.6 km (1.6 miles), is the longest *shotengai* (shopping street) in Japan. The independently owned shops and more traditional goods on sale are pure, old Osaka, and more interesting and authentic than the tourist gloss of Shinsaibashi.

At the opposite end of the shotengai, by Tenjimbashi 6-chome Station, is the Osaka Museum of Housing and Living. This is a great place to see how the city changed from the Meiji (1868–1912) to the post-war period, portrayed effectively with finessed scale models. The best part is the recreated Edo streetscape, where you can wander freely among houses and shops, which are always decorated to fit the season and have lights that change between night and day. It's great value at just ¥600.

Once the sun starts to set, head back along the shopping street and, about halfway down, choose one of the many little side streets to your left, taking you into the Ura-Tenma or 'backstreet Tenma' area. Hundreds of lantern-lit eateries and bars come alive as locals head to their favourite haunts to eat, drink and make merry. Wander down Chouchin Street, a little covered enclave near the Pulala wet market, where the ceiling is covered with dozens of cheerful beer bottle–shaped lanterns.

If you can't decide where to eat, you really can't go wrong here. This area is still quite local, and Osakans are very serious about the quality of their food, so places that are sub-par don't last.

My tried and true favourites include Sake no Okuda, a cheap standing bar that's usually my first stop of the night. Line up with the salarymen and construction workers, order a pint (or one of their overflowing glasses of sake), a couple of kushikatsu skewers or a few selections from the giant bowl of oden hot pot they have in the winter. There is no English menu, so check out what others are ordering and ask for the same. Next up is Okonomiyaki Tsuruya, a decades-old local favourite that serves its pancakes with a great homemade sauce, along with favourites like grilled squid and yakisoba stir-fried noodles. Try the modanyaki, where the okonomiyaki is topped with thick noodles. Or for something a bit different, head to Motsu to Kyabetsu, which blends equal parts 1980s American diner, stainless steel and neon lights with a menu that specialises in *motsu* (tripe) and cheap cocktails. This nutty new addition to the area attracts a younger crowd, a change from the clientele of the traditional bars. They don't advertise in English, so use the address: 4-11-22 Tenjinbashi, Kita-ku, Osaka; however, it stands out so much you might just come across it while wandering about. Happy hopping!

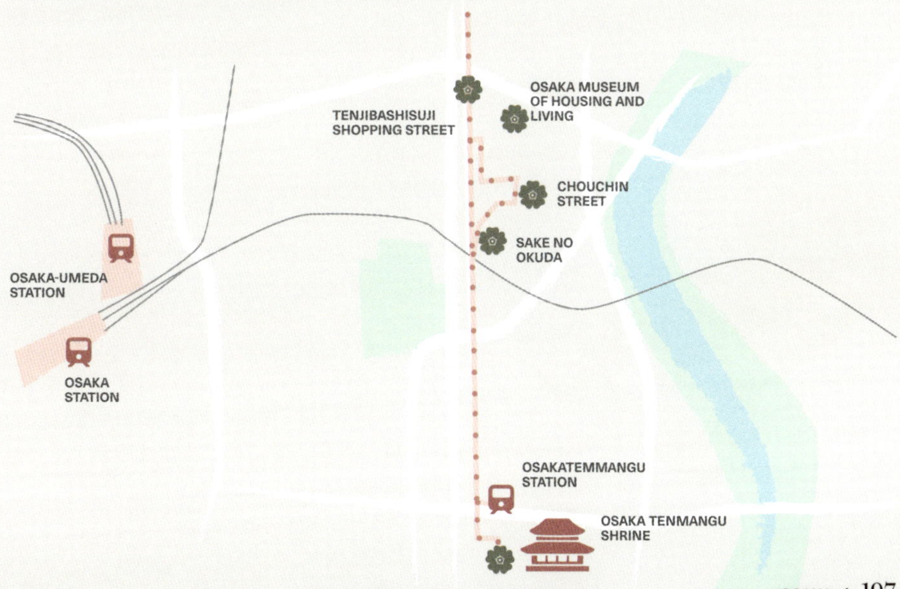

What to Eat in Osaka

As a city famously obsessed with food, it seems easier to ask, 'what isn't there to eat in Osaka?' When sampling the most iconic specialties of this merchant city, you will quickly realise that most have something in common: they all include wheat flour, a seemingly odd ingredient in a country famous for its love of rice.

While wheat has been part of the Japanese diet for centuries, it started becoming deeply associated with Osaka around the 17th century. The city was flourishing as a centre of trade and commerce, and this attracted lots of busy merchants, porters and traders. The elite did business over lavish meals, spurring innovation that trickled down to the more common folk. As a generally thrifty and creative bunch, cooks in Osaka looked for ways to make the most of every ingredient, resulting in a thriving culture of cheap, fast street foods that use simple batter to bulk up the star ingredients.

TAKOYAKI

If you don't try this famous street food, have you even been to Osaka? All over the city, you'll see stalls where nimble cooks toil over cast-iron hot plates, filling the ball-shaped indents with a batter spiked with octopus, *tenkasu* (crunchy tempura bits), pickled ginger and spring onions (scallions). They're sizzled until they're glistening golden brown on the outside and soft and melty on the inside. (You can ask for no octopus in your batch if you're not into it.) A regular serve is eight pieces, usually doused in savoury sauce, bonito flakes and *aonori* (powdered seaweed).

If you really want to dive into the history of takoyaki, then you need to make the trip to Aizuya, near Tamade Station (and just a couple of stops away from Sumiyoshi Taisha Grand Shrine). This is where takoyaki was invented in 1935, and their version is served without any condiments so you can really taste the dashi. Even better, you can try rajioyaki, the beef-filled predecessor of the octopus version, which is now very rare. If you don't want to make the trip, stop by Juhachiban when exploring Dotonbori instead, as their creamy, milk-filled batter and generous use of tenkasu give their takoyaki great texture. Get the ohako sampler, so you can try them in a variety of sauces.

OKONOMIYAKI

These thick, savoury pancakes consist of a batter mixed with cabbage and your choice of additional ingredients added in or on top, then finished off with tangy sauce, aonori, bonito flakes and Japanese mayonnaise. They are cooked on an iron griddle and sometimes served directly on it as well, so you use a small metal spatula to cut off chunks and move them to your plate. Like takoyaki, its current form first appeared around the 1930s, but similar crepe-like foods have been around since the 16th century. The ability to customise the dish (the name literally means 'as you like it') is one of the greatest charms of okonomiyaki, and I have seen quite picky children fall under its spell.

There are countless okonomiyaki joints in the city, but my favourite is Chitose, which combines an old-school heart with a modern outlook. It's a 10-minute walk from the Shin-Sekai entertainment area, and down a side street of the very authentic (and slightly rundown) Dobutsuenmae Ichibangai shopping street. The tiny restaurant doesn't take bookings and there's often a line, as they are known for happily accommodating vegans and vegetarians, plus they use a special ingredient that elevates their pancakes: a hint of pineapple. Alternatively, the friendly atmosphere, cheap drinks and vegan and gluten-free okonomiyaki options at OKO, a 10-minute walk from Dotonbori, all make for a fun evening.

KUSHIKATSU

Love anything crumbed and deep-fried? These skewers give that golden, crunchy treatment to a wide range of fish, meat, vegetables and more unusual things like shiso-wrapped cheese or mochi. Kushikatsu is a post-war creation that's a real rib-sticker and still a big favourite with locals, who sit around the counter munching the free cabbage (the traditional accompaniment) and downing beers. For a real only-in-Osaka flavour, try the beni shoga skewer, featuring thick chunks of bright-red pickled ginger. (Oh, and no double-dipping into the communal sauce!)

Kushikatsu was invented in Shin-Sekai, a delightful time warp of an area, with old-school restaurants and the Tsutenkaku Tower. There are plenty of restaurants here, but Tengu is particularly good if you're on a budget (look for the bright-red, long-nosed demon mask). However, I find it pays to go a little fancier with kushikatsu, as better-quality oil can be gentler on the stomach. Right by Umeda Station (and just a couple of minutes from the red HEP 5 ferris wheel) is Akatombo, where they serve a good mix of standard and more inventive skewers, all fried with a light touch. Look for the red sign and dragonfly decor.

For something really special, book a table at Beignet, where they marry French cuisine with this Osaka soul food.

UDON SUKI

This lesser-known hot pot dish is a mash-up of udon and *sukiyaki* (hot pot). It's loaded with vegetables, meat, fish and local chewy udon noodles, and cooked in a fragrant dashi broth right at your table. The dish was invented at a 250-year-old *ryotei* (traditional high-end restaurant) called Mimiu in the neighbouring city of Sakai. Fortunately, they have branches in Osaka, and the loveliest is the elegant Honten (main branch), which is a short walk from Yodoyabashi Station. The dashi broth, made fresh every day, is the star here, and a warming bowl of this dish makes a pleasant change from a pile of fried street snacks.

DOJIMA ROLL

This cake, which has been made by the Mon Cher patisserie since 2003, has captured the hearts of Japanese dessert lovers. It's a seemingly simple roll cake filled with fresh cream, but the secret to the light and pure flavour appears to be something very Japanese: just-in-time production. The company has almost as many kitchens as shops, so the cakes are made and delivered fresh regularly and to suit demand.

They have about two dozen shops around Japan and Korea, but the most pleasant branch is the Salon de Mon Cher, right near Shinsaibashi Station. The decor is a chintzy grandma-chic, down to the little pink rosettes on the sugar cubes. You can combine different options for your dessert plate, and there are a number of seasonal rolls, so keep an eye out for those.

TOP 10 HIDDEN GEMS OF OSAKA

Osaka is densely urban and, unlike the incredible historical glamour of neighbouring Kyoto, much of its appeal lies under the surface. Hopefully, these secret spots will give you a little more insight into just how hospitable (and funny!) people in Osaka can be, and make you feel like a local yourself.

KAMIGATA UKIYO-E MUSEUM

This small, off-the-radar museum is only a couple of minutes by foot from the iconic Glico sign and Hozenji Temple with its mossy sacred statue. Look for the building with the kabuki manekineko cat on it. This is the only museum in the world that specialises in woodblock prints made in Kamigata (the former appellation of the Kansai region), which have a more realistic style compared to those made in Edo. Most of the prints are related to kabuki and, during the Edo period, the prints functioned very much like movie posters today.

The entrance fee is only ¥500 and, if you book in advance, you can try doing some simple woodblock printing yourself. Check out the gift shop, as the printed tenugui cotton towels make particularly pretty, useful and light souvenirs.

NAKAZAKICHO

If you are wondering what most of Osaka used to look like before the urban development craze hit, this 'lost neighbourhood', hidden a quick 10-minute walk from the shopping and office hub of Umeda, is worth checking out. Pass through the tunnel entrance painted bright orange (right by Noon cafe and nightclub), and enter a world of low, wooden houses, tons of cafes bursting with personality, artsy enclaves, curious shops and lots of tiny alleyways that beg to be explored. While wandering around and making your own discoveries is a huge part of the fun, I do recommend Cafe Kaya and its phenomenal tofu-based tiramisu, and the animal-themed adorableness of Only Planet. Give yourself at least an hour to ramble about, and more if you plan to grab a bite to eat.

If you wander all the way to Nakazakicho Station, you will find yourself near the Tengo Nakazaki Dori shopping street (sometimes known as Oideyasu Dori), a much more authentic experience with lots of mom-and-pop shops, especially compared to the fast fashion and international brand–lined Shinsaibashi street featured in most guides.

TEAMLAB BOTANICAL GARDEN

Only open for 2½–3 hours per evening (depending on the season), the parklands with their colourful installations, projection mapping and seasonal blooms make this one of the most pleasant of the permanent teamLab installations to visit. Forests of glowing, singing ovoids, interactive musical walks and, perhaps most stunning of all, bright calligraphy being written by an invisible hand against a backdrop of trees and branches all make you feel like you are wandering in a whimsical dreamworld. As with all of the collective's endeavours, it is best to book your tickets online in advance.

The garden also happens to be one of the least expensive of the artistic group's creations, costing half of their other installations in Tokyo. Nagai Station on the Midosuji Line is the closest station, and it is also a 15-minute bus ride from Sumiyoshi Taisha Grand Shrine.

MOTO COFFEE

This cafe's enviable position is part of its charm, as it is located just across from the island of Nakanoshima, right by the lion and lamp post–topped Naniwa Bridge. On a warm day, try to snag one of the terrace seats for a view of the elegant Osaka City Public Hall across the water. The clean aesthetic, excellent blended coffees (try the French roast) and hearty open-faced toasts and desserts make it a lovely stop when exploring the art museums and interesting buildings of Nakanoshima.

NEU CAT CAFE

If you are searching for an ethical cat cafe in Osaka, this is the place to go! This small shelter and vegan cafe lovingly fosters cats and kittens looking for their forever homes, and the small fee also helps

the operation continue its important TNR (Trap, Neuter and Release) operations around the city. The kitties are clearly happy and treated with respect, which is also demanded of visitors. The small, cosy cafe is upstairs in a separate area from the cats and offers simple and well-priced vegan lunch sets.

It's a 5-minute walk from Matsuyamachi Station and just a couple of stops away from Osaka Castle. It's tucked away in a covered alleyway, so you may have to search for it, but just look for the wooden gate.

RAILWAY CAT CAFE

Another truly kitty-centric and ethical spot for cat lovers is this quirky spot which goes by a couple of different names, including Diorama Restaurant and Tetsudoukan Cafe and Rest Bar. The restaurant used to be dedicated to the owner's love of model trains and dioramas, which suddenly got a distinctly feline twist when he rescued a mama cat and her kittens. Diners were entranced by the kitties lounging on the dioramas and playing Godzilla with the trains, leading the owner to start a small shelter to help other cats.

Booking is required via railway-cats.com, as entry times and the number of guests are strictly limited to avoid stressing the cats. The ticket includes either a lunch or sweets set, depending on the time you choose. The cafe is near Teradacho Station, just a couple of stops away from Shinsekai.

CRAFT CAFE YU

Much like the Railway Cat Cafe, this cute cafe is probably not better known due to it having many names, including Ka cafe E Yu and Cafe Yu. It's hidden in a side street just behind Osaka-Umeda Station and the Hankyu Sanban Gai underground shopping mall, so look for the leafy trees and displays of pottery outside. The interior feels like a cosy home with highly polished wood furniture and white-washed walls, and you get to choose your favourite handmade cup (all created at their pottery atelier).

The menu options are mainly light meals, such as hot-pressed sandwiches, along with cakes and parfaits, all served on rustic handmade plates and bowls. Despite being in one of the busiest parts of the city, the hustle and bustle feels far away. They have plenty of their creations for sale as well, making it a great stop for lovers of ceramics and interior design.

PC & RETRO BAR SPACE STATION

Gamers and those in search of a bit of childhood nostalgia should head to this expat-owned bar, where you can enjoy vintage games to your heart's content. The atmosphere is welcoming, with inexpensive drinks, no cover charge and tons of consoles, arcade games and even old-school PC adventures to play for free. This is a great spot for solo travellers or small groups to start the night, as the owner, who has been based in Amerikamura since 2011, will give you tips on fun games to try, as well as offbeat sightseeing spots and restaurants to try in the area. Look for the incredible 8-bit illuminated stairway and order a drink or two based on your favourite game characters.

BAR SHINKA

Ever wanted to spend an evening in a steampunk-inspired submarine that would make Captain Nemo proud? You'll feel right at home at this tiny bar with a dozen seats, whose official name is Deepening Submarine Bar Shinka. The IPA and cocktail menu is pretty standard, although the gin and tonic is pretty darn good, and is quite affordable compared to similar bars that make more fanciful cocktails. Check out the details and fixtures from a real 1930s submarine and try to chat with some of the eccentric (but friendly) loyal patrons.

Bar Shinka can be a challenge to find. It's a short walk from Tanimachi 6-chome Station (and not far from Osaka Castle). Look for the building with the modern white facade, and the tiny, forbidding covered alleyway to its right. Gather your courage and walk through and you'll see the submarine door at the other end. Avoid going with a large group, as space is limited and you may get turned away.

SEXY GACHAPON

You will find Japan's (supposedly) sexiest *gacha* (capsule toys) in a corner of Zarigani, a video game arcade in the Shinsekai area, just behind the Tsutenkaku Tower. Look for the gachapons with a black front and large pink writing. You can choose from the men's, women's, couples' and plain 'erotic' gacha ... if you dare.

Day Trips from Osaka

Osaka has convenient connections to a whole host of day-trip destinations, but there are two I especially recommend because they give you a completely different experience from the city.

The Minoo-Katsuoji Temple duo is the closest of the two and gives a good hit of nature and peaceful scenery after the frenzy of the city. Koyasan can be done as a day trip, but the atmosphere in the evening (especially in the Okunoin Cemetery) is so otherworldly and spiritual that it is absolutely worth opting for an overnight trip, staying in shukubo temple lodgings.

MINOO & KATSUOJI TEMPLE HIKE

This is a beautiful hike from magical, daruma-filled Katsuoji Temple to Minoo Park, especially if you visit in autumn or spring/early summer, as you'll see plenty of momiji maples in their seasonal colours (red and gold in autumn, and fresh green in summer).

Most guides start this course in Minoo but, due to the limited number of 30-minute bus rides to Katsuoji Temple from Senri-Chuo Station (which is a 15-minute train ride on the Midosuji Line from Umeda Station), I find it is best to start at the temple. Take the 29 Hankyu bus at 9.10 am, 11.15 am or 2.15 pm, and get off right in front of the 'temple that helps you triumph'.

Katsuoji is best known for the thousands of red daruma charms of all sizes deposited in every corner of the grounds. People come here to pray for success in their endeavours by writing their wish on the bottom of one of the charms (available for sale on-site) and leaving it at the temple. You'll notice that some daruma have both eyes filled out (rather than just one): this shows that the petitioner's wish came true as, traditionally, you fill in the right eye when making a wish, then add the left when it is fulfilled. The grounds are particularly beautiful in autumn, but also have cherry trees, azaleas and hydrangeas that brighten the gardens in other seasons.

The trailhead for the Tokai Long Distance Nature Trail starts behind the main hall and will take you to the Minoo Waterfall area in about an hour. The trail is pretty clear and, along the way, you will pass the tomb of 8th-century monk Kaijo, a massive topographic map made from copper and a bridge that passes over a small regional highway. About halfway along, the trail will fork and, while both trails eventually lead to the Minoo Waterfall, the one to the right is quicker and easier.

Once you get to the Minoo Visitor's Centre, follow the river to get to the famed 33 metre (108 foot) waterfall, which is framed by a curved red bridge (and great foliage in autumn). The paved route slopes gently downwards, so the 40-minute walk back to the station is pleasant, with lots of temples, elegant restaurants, unusual rock formations and even an incongruous hot spring (with a somewhat ridiculous elevator) where you can relax post-hike. An interesting fact is that, at under 10 sq km (3.9 sq miles), Minoo Park is the smallest national park in Japan!

Towards the end of the walking route to the station, you'll find shops selling bites to eat. You should definitely try the momiji tempura, a sweet, deep-fried Minoo maple leaf! Take the Hankyu Minoo Line to Ishibashi Handai Mae Station, then switch to the Takarazuka Line, which will drop you off at convenient Osaka-Umeda Station.

MOUNT KOYA

This serene temple town feels far removed from the busy world below. The main temple of Kongobuji is the heart of Shingon Buddhism and was established in 805 AD by Kobo Daishi, one of Japan's most revered religious figures and the founder of the Shikoku 88 Temple Pilgrimage.

There is a lot to see in the town, such as the Danjo Garan temple complex with its massive orange pagoda, the Tokugawa family's mausoleum, the Nyonindo (a 'women's hall', used back when women were not allowed to enter the temple grounds), treasure-filled Reihoukan Museum and small side streets lined with over 100 smaller temples.

But the absolute highlight is vast Okunoin, home to the graves of many historical figures and Kobo Daishi's mausoleum, where he is said to be in 'eternal meditation' and is still served meals by the monks. The 2 km (1.2 mile) path is lined with over 200,000 tombstones, many gloriously covered in moss and some featuring creative sculptures, jizo statues clothed in hats and bibs, and stone lanterns.

I highly recommend splurging a little and staying overnight in *shukobo* (temple lodgings), where you can experience a slice of the monastic lifestyle, try *shojin ryori* (Buddhist cuisine) and start your day by attending the early morning prayer service. This will also allow you to see the Torodo Hall (Hall of Lamps) in Okunoin lit up after dark, which is a truly magical experience.

Getting to Mount Koya takes a bit of time, but it's easy. From Namba Station, there is a direct Nankai Koya Line train, which takes between 1 hour and 20 minutes and 1 hour and 40 minutes, depending on whether you catch the express or local train. Get off at Gokurakubashi, and switch to the quick cable car ride up the mountain. Koyasan-World Heritage Tickets, available for sale at the station, can help you save some money on transport and admission fees.

However, if you want to really experience what it was like for the pilgrims of yore, you could also walk part of the way on the Choishi Michi trail, which is lined with stone markers in the shape of pagodas, making it very easy to follow. The entire trail is around 24 km (15 miles) and takes at least 7 hours, but you can do a shorter section in 3 hours by getting off at Kii-Hosokawa Station and taking an alternative trailhead that includes a stop at the Yadate tea house. The route is not overly taxing and passes entirely through peaceful forests.

Nara

DESPITE BEING AN EASY TRAIN JOURNEY from Kyoto and Osaka, this ancient cradle of Japanese civilisation feels far more remote and has an atmosphere of quiet grandeur. Perhaps this is due to the city's illustrious history as, after centuries of changing the location of the capital each time an emperor died, Nara became Japan's first permanent capital.

Although it lasted less than 90 years, the Nara period (710–794 AD) managed to pack in a lot of culturally significant events, from the writing of important political and historical chronicles (the Kojiki and Nihon Shoki) to the development of Japanese poetry separate from Chinese influence and the establishment of Buddhism in the country.

Nara's main sights are built on a grand scale. Huge temples tower over everything in the vicinity, set apart in a way that clearly indicates the powerful cultural influence of Chinese architecture and landscaping during the Nara period. In contrast, the cityscape is much lower than nearby Kyoto and Osaka and feels a teensy bit more rural, in a good way.

Nara Prefecture has a lot of interesting towns and sights to explore, but getting around can be tough as public transport is a bit limited. During cherry blossom season, it is worth the 90-minute journey to Yoshino, the country's most famous cherry blossom destination, with 30,000 cherry trees that turn the mountainside pink and white, framing historic Kinpusenji Temple.

Due to it being a common day-trip destination for visitors, Nara is most crowded from late morning to mid-afternoon. My tip is to arrive around 3 pm, catch a few of the major sights, then stay overnight and get an early start. You will have the city to yourself, you can say hello to the deer tranquilly eating grass, have a lunch featuring the fabulous local narazuke pickles, then head off to your next destination. As there are far fewer hotels than in Kyoto, evenings in Nara are quiet.

THE BIG SIGHTS (& HOW TO SEE THEM BEST)

The reason Nara makes such a great day trip is that most of the major sights are congregated in the Nara Park area, so you can walk between them while regularly getting accosted by the sacred (and extremely pushy) deer the city is best known for.

Unlike the temples and shrines in Kyoto, many of the sights in Nara are built to stand in rather splendid isolation, so they don't offer a lot of shade. This is important in the summer, as the glaring sun can be quite strong ... another reason to do your sightseeing early in the morning, or after 3 pm. On the same point, be careful about closing times, as Nara's sights tend to shut around 5 pm, which is a bit earlier than in other cities.

KOFUKUJI TEMPLE

Established in 710 AD, this was once the family temple of the Fujiwaras, who controlled Japan's government for most of the Nara and Heian periods through craftily intermarrying with the imperial family and holding important political offices throughout the country. Although still impressively large, it has become far more manageable compared to the peak of the Fujiwara family's power, when the sprawling grounds contained around 150 buildings!

There are currently 11 buildings to see, including the towering five-storey pagoda which is considered the symbol of the city, along with a smaller three-storeyed version. The grounds are open 24 hours and are free to enter, and only three buildings require admission fees: the Central Golden Hall, Eastern Golden Hall and National Treasure Museum. The last is worth the ¥700 fee, as it holds the world's finest collection of Japanese Buddhist sculptures. Be sure to check out the Okuya (Great Bathhouse), as temples like this were where Japan's culture of public baths and onsen started, equating cleanliness with spiritual purity.

Kofukuji is a 15-minute walk from Kasuga Taisha Shrine and is the closest major sight to JR Nara Station.

TODAIJI TEMPLE

Believe it or not, when this hulking temple was constructed in 752 AD, it was even bigger than the current structure from 1692, which is only two-thirds its original size. This is even more impressive if you consider that the entire structure was built without using a single nail. The structure was meant to inspire awe, as it was the head temple of all of Japan's provincial temples ... something which worked far too well, as it eventually became so influential that the capital was moved to Kyoto to keep the powerful priests from messing with governmental business.

Until recently, the Daibutsuden (Big Buddha Hall), which houses a serene 15 metre (49 foot) bronze statue of the Buddha, was the world's largest wooden building. See if you can find the quirky Buddha's Nostril, a square hole in the base of one of the temple's great wooden pillars. If you can fit through it, you will be granted enlightenment in your next life. There are other buildings on the grounds, with the Nigatsudo Hall being perhaps the most interesting (and free), thanks to the view of the city from the terrace and its attractive stone-walled and paved approach.

Todaiji is a 30-minute walk from Kintetsu Nara Station or a 45-minute walk from JR Nara Station. It makes sense to take one of the regular buses from the station to the Todaiji Daibutsuden bus stop, and then see the other main sights by working your way back to the station.

KASUGA TAISHA SHRINE

Founded in 768 AD, this sprawling shrine lies at the foot of sacred Mount Wakakusa, a gateway to the ancient forest beyond. The bright-orange buildings and cloisters look particularly striking against the deep green of the forest and are further livened by drapes of purple wisteria in spring. All around the grounds you will see the city's famous deer, who are sacred to Takemikazuchi-no-mikoto, one of four gods enshrined here.

The shrine has the largest number of lanterns in Japan, with 2000 stone and 1000 hanging lanterns. All were donated in the hope of wishes being fulfilled, and some of the moss-covered stone lanterns are over 800 years old. In February and August, during the Mantoro Festival, all 3000 lanterns are lit, glowing ethereally in the dark.

The shrine is a 15-minute walk from Todaiji Temple and is open until 6 pm from April to September. It opens at 6 am, if you want a peaceful, solitary time with only sweeping Shinto priests for company.

YOSHIKIEN & ISUIEN GARDENS

Yoshikien is one of the lesser-known gems of the city and a lovely spot to take a break and enjoy the greenery. The gardens are divided into three sections: the pond area, moss garden and tea ceremony garden. During autumn, the russet foliage and deep-green moss are picture perfect.

If you're a Japanese garden fanatic, check out Isuien and the attached Neiraku Museum of Art (entry is ¥1200 for both), with lots of seasonal flowers, fun stepping stones across the pond and the elegant use of Mount Wakakusa and the Nandaimon Gate of Todaiji Temple as borrowed scenery.

These gardens are right across from each other and right in the middle of the three major sights listed on the previous pages, so making a quick detour is easy.

GANGOJI TEMPLE

Gangoji was one of the first Buddhist temples built in Japan and, despite being one of the city's UNESCO World Heritage sites, tends to get skipped in favour of the main three sights. Its 2500 statues of jizo (a Bodhisattva that protects children) and stone pagodas are rather marvellous, as is the little five-storey pagoda, thought to have been a scale model for carpenters building the many pagodas you see across Nara. Also, see if you can find all five oni demons on the grounds!

Gangoji is located in the Naramachi area. Just follow the signposts.

Nara Park ◆

NARA DEER ETIQUETTE

It should go without saying, but be respectful of the deer in Nara. Besides the fact that they are believed to be the sacred messengers of the god of Kasuga Taisha Shrine, they are also strong and can hurt you (or themselves) if frightened or angered. Be especially considerate with the fauns, as their herd can react unpredictably if they feel a baby is in danger.

If you wish to court their attention, buy a pack of the omnipresent deer biscuits: you will soon be surrounded by a mob of demanding four-footed friends. Once they do their adorable little trademark bow, give them their treat immediately.

Be careful about what you keep in your pockets and be sure to keep any bags zipped. There have been cases of deer getting sick from eating plastic bags, pamphlets and other purloined inedibles, so do your part to keep the cute (but occasionally dim) critters safe.

If they get a bit pushy with you, raise your palms to show them you aren't holding anything, and they will drift off in search of a different target. Some of the clever ones do seem to have learned the common phrase *mou nai yo* (all gone, sorry) as well!

NARAMACHI

You'll find Naramachi about a 10-minute walk from Kintetsu Nara Station via the Mochiidono Centre Gai shopping street. This warren of streets was a thriving merchant district during the Edo period, and still has many traditional wooden homes lining the streets, some of which have been transformed into restaurants, shops, hostels and museums. Many houses have a string of migawari-zaru by the front door, which are red cloth monkey charms said to protect the occupants from harm.

Make a stop at Koshi-no-ie, a well-preserved, Nara-style *machiya* (traditional wooden townhouse), which gives you a feel for the lifestyle of the merchants, from the kamado stove to the courtyard garden and the intriguing 'box staircase'. Entrance is free, as it is for the attractive Hosokawa and Mori residences. It's fun to just aimlessly meander the streets here. To see it at its best and without crowds of tourists, try to visit early in the morning or at night, when the lanterns of the many fancy restaurants and bars give it a moody feeling, similar to what it must have been like during the Edo period.

NAKATANIDOU

Possibly the most famous mochi shop in the world, as their high-speed pounding of the glutinous rice to make their dumplings has been featured on TV, YouTube and all over social media. They make fresh batches of mochi around 10–15 times a day, depending on demand, so the chance of catching a glimpse of this high-octane display is relatively good.

Try the yomogi mochi, with a mugwort-scented casing and a red bean paste filling. (Note that it's cash only here.) The shop is on Sanjo Dori street, the main thoroughfare that connects JR Nara Station to the sights in Nara Park, just before Kofukuji Temple.

WHAT TO EAT IN NARA

Many of Nara's most famous foods have ancient roots, often having been invented around the same time the city flourished as the first capital of Japan. They tend to have a lighter flavour profile, as there were far fewer condiments and spices available at the time than you'd find in a modern kitchen. Here are some of my favourite places that really showcase the area's delicate cuisine.

MIWA SOMEN & NYUMEN

Thought to be one of the oldest noodles in Japan, created thanks to exchanges with China around 1200 years ago, somen are ultra-thin and light. They were invented in the Miwa area, not far from the capital, and are particularly popular in the summer, served cold with a savoury dipping sauce and vegetables. Nyumen is simply the warm version, served as a soothing bowl of noodles in a fragrant broth.

Although the nearby city of Sakurai is considered the best place to try somen, just a couple of minutes from the Naramachi Museum is charming and inventive Somen Dokoro Surusuru, housed in a refurbished machiya. The chefs offer both warm and cold somen, ranging from very simple bowls to those with an added kick, such as a tomato-based soup or curry. It's pretty popular, so go early on weekdays (when reservations are not required), as they close once they have run out of their homemade dashi stock.

NARAZUKE

Walking along the shopping streets of Nara, you can't miss the many shops offering packages of these pickles, whose history dates back to the foundation of the city itself. Once luxury items only available to nobility, they are now an indispensable part of any meal in Nara. Ingredients like gourd, cucumber, watermelon, ginger and other vegetables are pickled multiple times in sake lees and sweetened with mirin, turning them a dark-amber colour. The result is both pleasantly sweet and salty.

Ashibi Honten, across the road from the rather wordily named Nara City Museum of Historical Resources in Naramachi, makes these renowned local pickles and has been supplying the kitchens of Japan since the Edo period. At their handsome shop/restaurant, they offer a ¥1600 lunch set where you can sample a wide variety of their creations, either at the long polished-wood sunken tables or in the pleasant garden that overlooks a wedding chapel.

KAKINOHA SUSHI

Although its origins are unknown, this unusual sushi is clearly a type of narezushi, an ancient technique where the fish is pickled or fermented in order to preserve it. These days most shops rely on vinegar to give their products that unique flavour without too much fishiness, but there are still a few that use the really old-school ways. You may not be able to figure out what this dish is at first glance, since each individual piece is wrapped in a persimmon leaf. This is another ancient preservation method, using the tannin in the leaves to keep the sushi fresh for several days and giving it a distinct aroma. The fish used is usually mackerel, salmon or red snapper.

If you are planning to catch a bullet train to your next destination, buy a pack of kakinoha sushi from one of the many vendors near the train stations (and perhaps a small bottle of sake) and enjoy it as many Japanese visitors do. If you are curious, but not sure you want a full meal of this pickled sushi, then head to Hiraso, just a few minutes' walk from Kofukuji Temple. They have been serving Nara specialties for over 150 years, including dishes like kakinoha sushi, grilled sweetfish sushi (which include the head!) and savoury chagayu tea rice porridge, along with options like udon and tempura for less adventurous eaters.

TOP 7 HIDDEN GEMS IN NARA

Since Nara is a fraction of the size of other cities in this guide, there simply aren't as many quirky businesses and sights to discover ... But there are certainly plenty more than most day trippers know.

This more provincial feel is part of the charm of Nara, but it does mean that outside the main tourist areas, information and signs in English drop dramatically.

HANNYAJI TEMPLE

If you're in Nara in June or October through November, you will want to visit this quaint spot, sometimes called the 'cosmos temple'. During these two blooming seasons, the grounds are covered in a carpet of pink and white cosmos flowers, which greatly enhance the views of the main hall and the 13-layer stone pagoda. Nearby, you will also find the Former Nara Prison, a surprisingly beautiful building with a whimsical turreted gate of Meiji brickwork, which is set to become (of all things) a luxury hotel.

From JR Nara Station or the Kenchomae bus stop across the street from Kofukuji Temple, take the 118 or 153 bus for about a 10-minute ride. This is another spot worth hitting up right when it opens at 9 am, to avoid the tour buses that stop by later in the day.

HORYUJI TEMPLE

Horyuji is definitely a half-day trip destination. Most international visitors seem to skip this temple, so it has an interestingly nostalgic feel of what sightseeing in Japan was like before the travel boom. Horyuji was actually the very first UNESCO World Heritage site in Japan, thanks to its stately Chinese- and Korean-influenced architecture, a pagoda that is the oldest wooden building in the world and more than 300 of the country's most precious Buddhist carvings. There is a distinct sense of grandeur, with long stone-flagged approaches and around a dozen buildings with gardens to explore. Walk the side streets around the temple, which are lined with nicely kept traditional houses.

While walking to the temple is possible, the surroundings are not terribly inspiring, so I recommend taking the 72 bus that regularly departs from Horyuji Station and saving your energy for exploring the grounds and alleyways around them.

SHIGISAN CHOGOSONSHIJI TEMPLE

Although it's not in Nara City, the relatively easy access and striking nature of this mountain temple make it one of my favourite sights, with a similar vibe to more famous Mount Koya.

Upon arrival, you'll be welcomed by the world's largest papier-mache tiger. You will find tigers all over the grounds, as Prince Shotoku had this temple built after he prayed for victory to the god of war at the hour of the tiger on the day of the tiger in the year of the tiger ... Obviously, he won, and Chogosonshiji has been affiliated with the noble feline ever since. Don't miss the chance to pass through the tiger-shaped tunnel, said to bring good luck to those who make it through the dark passage.

As you climb higher, you'll find the dozens of temples and shrines that make up this little 'town', with pagodas, large statues of the Buddha and other buildings peeking out. The view from the Bishamontendo Hall is particularly lovely, with the taller structures framed by the forested mountainsides. If you are up for a hike, the path leading to the temple at the top is lined with lanterns, torii gates and several pavilions. Three temples offer accommodation if you want to spend the night and see the lanterns illuminated after dark.

It takes about an hour to get to the temple from JR Nara Station, taking the regular Yamatoji Line (which also passes by Horyuji Temple) to Oji Station, where you switch to the 42 or 43 bus, getting off at the Shigiohashi bus stop.

ANY B&B+COFFEE

Nara locals are clearly not morning people and finding somewhere to get your morning coffee fix can be tough. ANY is a quick 6-minute walk from Kintetsu Nara Station (take Konishi Sakura Dori street; it is prettier) and is open from 8 am. The friendly owners lived in Australia and make possibly the best cup of coffee in Nara, using their signature roasts. They also have vegan and gluten-free menu options, bilingual menus and a cheery hello for all customers. The big windows and relaxed vibe are the perfect way to start the morning, and the sights of the Naramachi area are just across the road.

They also run a B&B directly above the shop, a rather fun and unusual proposition as the bathroom and shower are downstairs in the cafe, which closes at 5 pm. A stay includes breakfast and coffee, and the location is hard to beat.

LAMP BAR

Another highlight on Konishi Sakura Dori street, right by Kintetsu Nara Station, this bar adds some much needed nightlife to the generally quiet evenings in Nara. This three-room bar, run by multi-award-winning bartender Kaneko, feels like a cross between a classy speakeasy and an alchemist's den, which is fitting as most of the cocktails he creates are customised to guests' tastes and whims.

Many of the drinks have a distinctly local twist, featuring homemade bitters made with Nara cypress, vermouth created from sake from a nearby brewery and green tea from the hills outside the prefectural capital. As there is not much competition in town, it is best to go early to snag a seat before it gets too busy.

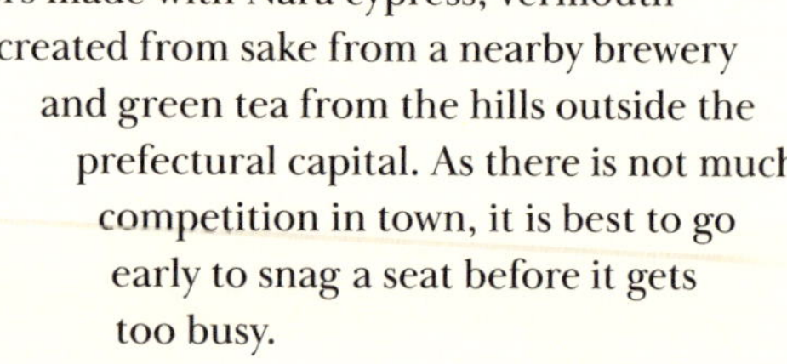

HARUSHIKA BREWERY

This beloved Narachi institution has been brewing sake since 1884, and produces some of the best-known sake in Nara, which is often thought to be the birthplace of this iconic drink. The setting is lovely, for the house was once the home of a senior priest of Kofukuji Temple before being passed to the Imanishi brewing family in 1924. Head directly to the shop next door, where the friendly staff hold sake tastings all day until 5 pm, featuring five different seasonal varieties for the bargain price of ¥500, including a little cup you get to keep.

The brewery is towards the furthest end of Naramachi, so a map app will be helpful – search for the address: 24-1 Fukuchiincho, Nara.

CONFECTION ARTISANAL BREAD & SWEETS

If you start your explorations of Nara early in the morning, this delightful bakery and cafe opens at 8 am (closed Wednesdays). Stop in for coffee and a large variety of luscious breads and sandwiches, with the cheese and narazuke pickle ciabatta being a favourite. Get provisions here then walk for 15 minutes to the Ukimido, a hexagonal pavilion that appears to float in the middle of the Sagiike Pond in Nara Park. Enjoy your breakfast (and deer spotting) in peaceful splendour.

Confection is just a minute away from the entrance to Gangoji Temple, on the major Naramachi Odori street that leads towards the luxurious Nara Hotel.

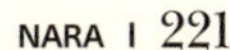

Walk the Yagyu Kaido Trail

This historic road with cobblestone footpaths is still basically unknown to most visitors to Nara. Besides being an easy half-day adventure, it is deeply culturally important, as this was once the route for samurai in training to get from Nara's courts to the village of Yagyu, known for its legendary swordsmen. It passes through forest, quiet valleys and rice paddy–filled countryside, and you can find free maps at tourist information centres in Nara or online.

There are three sections to the trail but the easiest section, transportation-wise, is the first part, called Takisaka no Michi. It's around 9 km (5.6 miles) if you start the trail near Kasuga Taisha Shrine (rather than Nara Station), and takes about 3–4 hours to complete at a leisurely pace. It's mostly quite gentle, with small shrines, temples, jizo statues and even a tea house on the way.

Note that a lot of the signs are only in Japanese, so get familiar with the kanji for Enjoji Temple (円城寺) and for Yagyu (柳生) to help keep you on track. Also, be sure to take plenty of water, snacks and a fully charged smartphone/portable WiFi.

The prettiest way to start the trek is from around the Ni no Torii gate of Kasuga Taisha Shrine, using the official map to find your way to the main trail. The first section passes through a somewhat suburban area, but once you get past that it becomes distinctly more scenic. If you worry about taking a wrong turn, use a map app to get to Oyarokujizoson (a tiny collection of jizo statues that marks the official start of the Yagyu Kaido) and continue straight down that path.

Keep on going straight for about 3 km (1.9 miles) along the historic cobbled road until you reach the Kubikiri Jizo, the 'cut neck' jizo said to have been used to test the sharpness of the blade of one of the master swordsmen of Yagyu. Take the path to the left and, shortly after, there will be an intersection; both routes eventually lead to the same point. The one marked 0.3 km is a shortcut, which takes you past a small shrine and then to a police box, where you turn right to get back on trail. The 1.3 km (0.8 mile) trail takes you by the Stone Cave Buddha, adding about an extra 25 minutes.

Keep following the trail until you get to a regular paved road and turn right. A sign will point you to Enjoji, so follow that and keep to the left as you continue on straight. After about 1 km (0.6 miles) you will come across the Toge no Chaya tea house, which has been serving tea and mochi to travellers since the Edo period.

The road continues through a secluded valley, eventually turning into a tarmacked forestry road. Where it splits, take the path back into the forest (keeping left whenever it splits) and, about 2.7 km (1.7 miles) later, you will be at peaceful Enjoji Temple, which has a rare Heian period 'paradise garden'. Right near the entrance you will also find Shokujidokoro Sato, a rather lovely eatery that serves seasonal specialties until 2 pm.

To get back into the city, there are three buses a day (at 12.05 pm, 1.35 pm and 4.07 pm) from the Ninnikusen bus stop a couple of minutes from the temple, which drop you at JR Nara Station. As bus schedules can change, double check before setting out. If you are worried about time, you can always do the hike in reverse too!

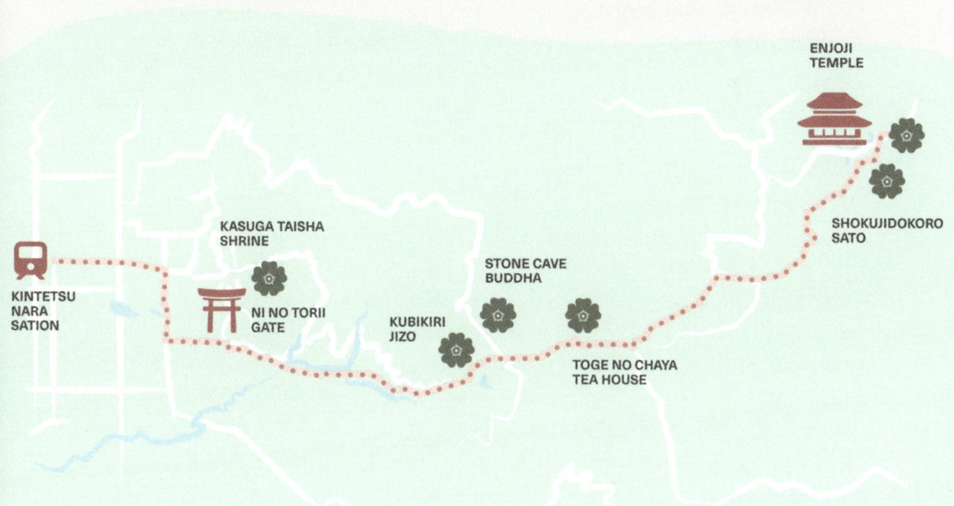

Day Trips from Nara

As Nara itself is usually considered a day-trip destination, heading out to these even more rural spots will mean you basically have the place to yourself for most of the year. Outside of the capital, most of the prefecture is still quite agricultural, with cute villages and farmland.

If the options I've chosen feel a bit too strenuous, you can instead take a 45-minute train ride from Kintetsu Nara Station to Yaginishiguchi Station and explore the photogenic and well-preserved merchant town of Imaicho. Most preserved districts in Japan are quite small, but here you can walk around the many alleys of an entire town. Be sure to stop by the Kawai sake brewery!

YAMANOBE NO MICHI

Due to the area's historical importance, many roads used to lead to Nara ... and you can still walk some of them. The Yamanobe no Michi is the oldest road mentioned in Japanese records, and you can follow in the footsteps of the travellers of yore while passing through attractive rural landscapes, with a number of shrines, temples and other sights.

There are a few ways of completing it, but the most pleasant option is the 14 km (8.7 mile) section from Miwa Station to Tenri Station. This part has lots of signs in various languages and is almost entirely flat, with bathrooms and even unmanned stalls selling snacks and fresh produce.

Omiwa Shrine is a 10-minute walk from Miwa Station. It is thought to be the oldest shrine in Japan, and is dedicated to Mount Miwa, the sacred mountain behind it. Don't miss the rare triple torii gate behind the main prayer hall. (Also, if you arrive around 10 am, you can have a late breakfast of somen noodles at venerable Morisho, close to the approach.)

The trail starts on the shrine grounds (look for the characters 山の辺の道) and then proceeds more or less straight until the end, so you won't get lost. You will pass by sights like Hibara Shrine, the kofun funerary mound of Emperor Suijn, Nenbutsuji Temple and Yatogi Shrine, but a lot of the joy of this trail is just soaking up the rural views. Isonokami Shrine is the end point of the route, before you head to Tenri Station. It is a truly fitting end to a journey along the ancient road, thanks to the dramatic architecture (which enshrines three swords said to be possessed by gods) and the chickens that strut freely across the grounds.

Tenri itself is a rather fascinating place, since it is the headquarters of Tenri-kyo, a 'new religion' and, walking down the covered shopping street towards the station, you'll see shops dedicated to the rather elaborate robes the followers wear.

Miwa Station is just 25 minutes on the Sakurai Line from Nara Station. Tenri is also on the same line. Another bonus is that the trail runs parallel to the train line, so if you get tired partway through, you have options for cutting the walk short. You could also do the walk in reverse, but Tenri has a lot more food and shopping options.

ASUKA

If you are visiting from mid to late September, I highly recommend a visit to Asuka, which was (yet another) of Japan's capitals over 1400 years ago. The protected landscapes make this a pleasant and peaceful village, with farming lanes passing through rice paddies against a backdrop of emerald hills and ancient burial mounds. Also in early autumn, the Inabuchi terraced rice field area becomes the site of a scarecrow contest. This marvel of creative folk art sees dozens of impressive entries, from the traditional to the avant-garde, lining the lanes.

Pick up a map and rent a bicycle near the station, and cycle for about 20 minutes to get to the rice paddy area, then enjoy a nice long wander. Asuka does not really have any major sights, but it's the atmosphere of the place that makes it feel so special, with rural views that look like they haven't changed in centuries.

There are a handful of cafes in the area, with Kotodama and Sanpo being particularly popular. Cafe Matsuyama, a short walk from the station, does good coffee and a daily set plate featuring local ingredients.

While it only takes about an hour to get to Asuka from Kintetsu Nara Station, you will need to change trains twice, once at Yamato-Saidaiji Station, where you will switch to the Kintetsu-Kashihara Line, and then again at Kashiharajingu-Mae Station, to the Kintetsu-Yoshino Line. Catching express trains drastically cuts down on travel time, so check your map app the evening before to figure out the departure time you need to make the connections.

冒険者の旅

Off-the-beaten-track Adventures

THERE ARE MANY OTHER CITIES, such as Kobe, Himeji, Hiroshima or Nikko, that also make excellent day-trip destinations from major cities. Information about them is plentiful, and planning a visit would not be complicated. If they pique your interest, by all means, go!

But, after more than a decade of travelling around Japan, my requirements for truly unique, authentic experiences are much stricter. There are so many interesting corners of this long, thin country, from remote port towns in the northern wilds of Hokkaido to the hidden beaches and sacred groves of Okinawa, that you could spend a lifetime exploring them all.

I want you to have the very best adventures in Japan, skipping any places that are 'meh' or, as is relatively common, have a few awesome sights but are surrounded by urban sprawl. It is also important that you can really see them, without fighting crowds of other visitors, and that there is plenty to do and see, to make sure the travel time is worth it. Finally, many of these are places where you can get a chance to communicate and interact with locals, as these connections are often what makes a journey special.

For ease of planning and navigation, my curated selection of unforgettable places is organised by the most convenient city to depart from (although this doesn't mean it's the only way, especially for places on the main island of Honshu). I've then subdivided these recommendations into one of three categories – old Japan, outdoor Japan and offbeat Japan – so you can choose your own off-the-beaten-track adventure.

DEPARTING FROM TOKYO

As the main hub for all bullet trains, Tokyo is an ideal launchpad for exploring areas in the northern or western areas of Japan. Checking out these less congested areas will give you a much deeper view into the regional differences around the country, and how strongly the influence of the former domains and their lords impacted local culture and aesthetics.

OLD JAPAN

KANAZAWA

If you love the romance of Kyoto, you can't go wrong with the attractive city of Kanazawa in Ishikawa Prefecture. One of the reasons that it has a great resemblance to the ancient capital is that it was also spared from the destructive bombings that flattened Tokyo and Osaka.

During the Edo period, Kanazawa was an immensely rich region, as the Maeda family who ruled over what was then the Kaga domain were only second to the Tokugawa rulers in terms of territory, rice production and trade. As such, there was plenty of cash going around to entice artisans, musicians and geisha to settle in the region and bolster a rich cultural life.

The two main geisha districts where you can still see the artists (locally known as 'geigi') perform are definitely highlights of a visit to Kanazawa. The Higashi Chaya District is the largest, with well-preserved streets lined with elegant tea houses (definitely visit Kaikaro, the most over-the-top, where entrance includes traditional sweets), restaurants and stores selling gold-leaf crafts. Hakuza, just across from Kaikaro, is worth a quick visit to see the gold leaf–covered tearoom, and look for soft-serve ice cream covered in the precious metal.

The Teramachi temple district, and smaller Nishi Chaya tea house area, are very close, and definitely have that Kyoto-esque feel, with clusters of temples and old buildings. Ninjadera Temple is particularly interesting, as it was basically a small fort disguised as a temple. The Nagamachi samurai district is a popular spot to take photos in kimono, and there are a few former samurai and merchant houses open to the public, which give a fascinating look into the very different lifestyles of these two ranks of society.

Other spots not to miss are Oyama Shrine (with a gate like no other I have seen in Japan), bustling Omicho Market and Kenrokuen, considered the finest of all the traditional gardens in the country. All this Edo period finery is balanced out with contemporary museums like the 21st Century Museum of Contemporary Art, best known for the *Swimming Pool* installation that makes visitors look like they are underwater. A quirkier option is the D.T. Suzuki Museum, a contemplative space dedicated to a Buddhist philosopher, where the architecture is meant to convey his world view and thoughts.

Most of the sights are within close proximity to the central hub that is Kanazawa Castle Park, making it easy to see everything by foot, bike or, if you prefer, the useful Kanazawa Loop bus.

Hop on a Hokuriku Shinkansen bullet train from Tokyo Station and, 2½ hours later, you'll be at Kanazawa Station, with its wonderful modern torii gate of twisted wooden beams. From Kanazawa Station, you can also catch regular Nohi and Hokutetsu buses to the thatched-roof village of Shirakawago and the post town of Hida Takayama.

MATSUMOTO

If I were to move to a smaller city in Japan, this would be my first choice. Matsumoto in Nagano Prefecture has access to the Japanese Alps, a thriving artistic and music scene, old-school streets, craft workshops and stylish coffee shops, all within easy reach of Tokyo.

The city's most iconic sight is Matsumoto Castle, dating back to the 16th century and one of the oldest surviving castles in the country. Known as the 'crow castle' due to its striking black hue, the main tower rises five storeys high and is surrounded by a moat and pretty red bridges. You can go inside to see the original wooden interiors and exhibits of medieval weaponry, and get a fantastic view of the city and mountains.

Most of the city's main sights are within walking distance. Going past the castle will take you to the Former Kaichi School, a late-19th-century elementary school which was the first one open to children of all backgrounds. Nagano is known as a prefecture deeply invested in education, and this school is a shining example, as locals donated 70 per cent of the funds. Despite the florid, Western-inspired look, its construction is quite Japanese, with ceilings made of paper, pillars taken from an abandoned temple, and walls made of mud and bamboo.

If you retrace your steps back towards the central area, you'll find Nawate Dori, a shopping alley dating back to the Edo period full of vendors selling tempting street food, little crafts and (for some reason) frog knick-knacks. In the larger and more elegant Nakamachi area, the main street is lined with perfectly maintained kura storehouses and other attractive buildings, many of which house the workshops and galleries of expert craftspeople. There are also coffee shops and restaurants that fit with the craftsman-chic vibe.

The Matsumoto City Museum of Art is a must-see, with permanent exhibits dedicated to Matsumoto-born artist Yayoi Kusama's polka-dotted works, along with the creations of other Nagano artists. A 5-minute walk from the museum is the Ishii miso brewery, a business started in 1868 and one of the few miso makers in Japan still producing the essential paste with traditional methods, using wooden barrels and fermenting it for three years (rather than the few months of most mass-produced miso). They offer free tours throughout the day, and a very tasty and affordable lunch set.

Wandering around, you will come across numerous water springs and wells, usually with drinking fountains or pumps. It is common to see locals filling up a couple of bottles from a favourite spring to take home, so feel free to do the same. Finally, if you have time when making your way back to the train station, take a detour to Kasamori Inari Shrine, a nice, hidden spot with a slightly comical fox statue.

Hikers (and skiers) may also want to look into spending a day in nearby Norikura, which has several notable peaks, or the gorgeous mountain resort of Kamikochi, just a bus ride away.

There are regular Azusa Limited Express trains from Shinjuku to Matsumoto Station, which take about 2½ hours. This is covered by the JR Rail Pass, but don't forget to go to the ticket counter to book a seat.

NAKASENDO TRAIL

During the Edo period, the Nakasendo Way stretched all the way from Tokyo to Kyoto. Then, over time, much of it was adapted into highways and train lines. However, thanks to the remote nature of the Kiso Valley stretching across parts of Nagano and Gifu prefectures, parts have been left intact, with ancient cobblestone sections, peaceful nature trails and historic post towns. The prettiest part is definitely the Magome to Tsumago trail but, if you have time, adding on the Yabuhara to Narai/Kiso Hirasawa section is also highly enjoyable.

I recommend departing Tokyo in the later afternoon and booking a night at the friendly Magomechaya Minshuku, so you can start the trail bright and early the next day. Don't forget to grab your caffeine fix at Hillbilly Coffee, before wandering up through the town, lined with traditional inns, colourful wildflowers and water wheels, all framed by the Central Alps.

Once you get to the more natural part of the trail, little markers and bear bells spring up every so often to keep you on track for the 9 km (5.6 mile) hike, crossing little hamlets, wooden bridges and bright-green rice fields filled with choruses of frogs. The trail is quite gentle, so it's suitable for beginners. There are a couple of huts which serve drinks and nibbles along the way, although it might be better to stock up in town.

Tsumago is thought to be one of the best preserved postal towns in Japan, and residents have gone to great lengths to ensure the feel of the town is not disrupted, such as burying electricity cables. They also maintain a honjin and waki-honjin, the former being the principal inn that was used by government officials and other elite travellers, and the latter being accommodation for those of lower status.

From here, an additional 3.5 km (2.2 mile) walk will take you to Nagiso Station. While this section is a bit more modern, the dramatic rock gardens and artists' homes along the way are charming, and the Momosuke wooden suspension bridge just a short walk from the station is really neat. From here, you can catch a train to Shiojiri, which can take you back to Tokyo or onwards to Matsumoto. If you want to see a bit more of the trail, then overnight in Kiso Fukushima (on the same train line) and, if you arrive before 4.30 pm, visit magical Kozenji Temple, which boasts Japan's largest rock garden.

The next morning, take the train to Yabuhara and do the slightly more challenging 6 km (3.7 mile) trail that goes over the Torii Pass and takes you to Narai, the most stately of the postal towns. The whitewashed, weathered wooden buildings and old street signs, combined with the fact that they are still obviously private homes and restaurants instead of staged sets, make it a particular favourite. You can extend your walk to neighbouring Kiso Hirasawa, famous for its lacquerware, with a road of elegant shops that shows the lacquer business here is obviously prospering. There are several trains each day back to Shiojiri from both towns.

From Tokyo to Magome, the easiest option is catching the Chuo Liner bus from the Shinjuku Bus Terminal, which takes just under 5 hours to get to the Chuodo Magome stop, from where it is a 1.5 km (0.9 mile) walk into town. From Shiojiri Station, the Azusa Limited Express train departs every hour or so, providing a direct connection back to Tokyo (stopping at Shinjuku Station) or Matsumoto.

◆ *Tsumago postal town*

HIROSAKI & MICHINOKU TRAIL

It's pretty common for cherry blossom spots to not look *quite* as incredible as they do in glossy promotional shots. But, every once in a while, there's a spot that defies expectations, and Hirosaki in northern Aomori Prefecture is one of these.

From late April to early May, people come from all over the country to see the blooms in Hirosaki Park, the grounds of Hirosaki Castle. The trees around the moat cluster thickly, making it look like the iconic arched red bridge is floating on a cloud of cherry blossoms. There are around 2600 sakura trees of 50 varieties, several of which are well over 100 years old. The reason the trees look so much fuller than those in other places comes from pruning techniques that Aomori farmers use on their apple trees, allowing the cherry trees to flower with nearly double the number of buds!

Hirosaki was an important Edo period outpost in the wild north, and the area's remoteness has allowed locals to preserve the traditional buildings and Tsugaru culture, and these days it is also known for its apple orchards, which flower in May. The Fujita Memorial Garden and Choshoji Temple are also well worth visiting. Hirosaki is not a large city but is (I believe) one of the best cherry blossom spots in the country, with the fantastic backdrop of massive Mount Iwaki.

If you are going to make the trip all the way to Aomori, then I recommend extending your stay and walking the first section of the 1025 km (637 mile) Michinoku Coastal Trail, for a real taste of the rugged beauty of Tohoku. Overnight in Hachinohe (about 1 hour and 15 minutes by train from Hirosaki), where you can grab dinner and drinks in the colourful Miroku Yokocho and Hanakoji alleys, lined with little eateries and bars. In the morning, take the Hachinohe Line a few stations over to Same, where you will be welcomed by a Jaws-like statue (the word *same* can mean 'shark'), and then head to the start of the trail at Kabushima Shrine, with its thousands of black-tailed gulls.

The Hachinohe section is well marked and almost entirely flat, and there are excellent free English maps available online, making the 14 km (8.7 mile) walk between Same and Okuki Station good for anyone with basic hiking experience. Following the coastline trail, you will pass by a lighthouse, wander across majestic Osuka Beach and traverse the Yodo no Matsubara pine grove, before reaching the highlight: the Tanesashi Natural Lawn, with rolling hillocks of soft, green grass and far-reaching views of the rocky coast. Stop at the information centre for a bite to eat before continuing on the pretty coastal trail peppered with fishermen's huts to Okuki Station. Be sure to check train times between Okuki and Hachinohe in advance and adjust your start time, as there are only a handful of trains each day. From Hachinohe Station you can get a bullet train back to Tokyo, which takes about 2 hours and 45 minutes.

Getting to Hirosaki isn't hard but it does take about 4 hours. Take the Tohoku-Hokkaido Shinkansen from Tokyo Station to Shin-Aomori Station, then switch to the Ou Line (preferably on a limited express train) to Hirosaki. However, if you are coming from Sendai, the travel time is cut to just over 2 hours.

SENDAI, MATSUSHIMA & YAMADERA

If you are in Japan in early August, head to Sendai on 6–8 August to experience the largest Tanabata festival in Japan, when the Chuo and Ichibancho shopping streets are festooned with thousands of colourful bamboo and washi paper streamers made by local shops, schools and community groups.

Even if you're not visiting in festival season, Sendai is an excellent base for exploring sights in Japan's northernmost Tohoku region. There's the Zuihoden, a mausoleum to the great lord of Sendai Masamune Date, Rinnoji Temple with its beautiful gardens (and donkeys!) and tree-lined Jozenji Dori avenue. I mainly use the city as the gateway to Tohoku, as it offers train connections and interesting places within day-tripping distance.

My recommendation is to arrive in the late afternoon, check into your hotel and then head to the Bunka and Iroha *yokocho* (alleyways) to try some local food and sake, choosing a place based on your favourite sign or lantern. (You can also hire guides to go yokocho hopping with you through Tohoku Local Secret Tours, which is great fun.)

The next morning, head to Matsushima, famous for its bay speckled with tiny, pine-covered islands, and for Zuiganji, the temple that put the town on the map in the early 17th century when domain lord Masamune Date restored it and made it his family temple. The temple is surprisingly grandiose, with elaborate screen paintings, a massive traditional kitchen and a treasure hall stuffed with precious artifacts from the Date family.

Matsushima's temple-town-meets-riviera feel is quite quirky, and all the sights are walkable, including the Godaido Hall and Kanrantei tea house with bay views, and Entsuin Temple with fascinating Christian and Western-inspired imagery in the mausoleum and a rose garden. You can walk across bright-red bridges to explore the two closest islands, Fukuurajima and Oshima. Definitely take a cruise around the islands. There are a couple of companies offering different routes, including some that take you to nearby Shiogama, home to a great, old-school seafood market, sake brewery and Shiogama Shrine.

If you're visiting in early November, another great day trip is to Yamadera, a mountain temple which is actually in nearby Yamagata Prefecture. From the Konponchudo Hall at the foot of the mountain (said to house the 'eternal light of Buddhism', a flame that has burned since the temple's founding in 860 AD), you climb up 1015 steps through forest to get to the temple complex. The route itself takes 20–30 minutes, but you'll be so distracted by the statues and caves (and, in the autumn, the beautiful foliage that glows gold and red) that it'll probably take you a bit longer.

At the top, you'll be rewarded with the view of the red Nokyodo Hall perching on a craggy outcrop. Make sure to take the side path to the Godaido Hall, which offers a perfect view overlooking the Tachiya River Valley, and looks like it is lost in time. After retracing your steps, try some Yamagata cuisine at the restaurants around the base of the mountain, such as pear or cherry ice cream (as the prefecture is known for both) or soba noodles topped with chopped vegetables, herbs and soy sauce.

Whisky fans will want to make a stop at Nikka Whisky's attractive red-brick Miyagikyo Distillery, about halfway between Sendai and Yamadera, a 20-minute walk or short bus ride from Sakanami Station. Tours are free (non-Japanese speakers are given pamphlets) and include a couple of tastings, and there is a counter for paid tastings of their premium whiskies, including some that can only be bought here.

From Tokyo Station it takes 1 hour and 40 minutes to get to Sendai on the Tohoku Shinkansen. Matsushimakaigan Station is a 40-minute ride from Sendai, and Yamadera Station is 1 hour and 15 minutes.

DEPARTING FROM OSAKA OR KYOTO

With so many sights concentrated in the Osaka-Kyoto-Nara triangle, places further south tend to get overlooked.

The Kansai region is an ideal base for getting to Shikoku, the smallest of Japan's main four islands, and also has good connections to the better-known sights of Hiroshima and the Kumano Kodo pilgrimage trail in Wakayama Prefecture.

The weather in these more southern areas tends to be warmer and milder all year round but can be quite extreme and humid in the summer and more prone to typhoons. There is a distinctly more coastal, relaxed vibe, and the population density drops dramatically as soon as you get out of the larger cities, so keep this in mind on the following explorations because, if you see a shop or convenience store, it may be the last one for quite a while. If you plan to take on either of the outdoor adventures, be sure to stock up before you hit the road.

OKAYAMA & KURASHIKI

Sunny Okayama has been an important crossroads since ancient times. It's now the main connector between the mainland and the island of Shikoku, along with the smaller islands of Naoshima, Teshima and Shodoshima, which host the Setouchi Triennale, an international arts festival that takes over the islets of the Seto Inland Sea.

During the 4th century AD, this area was known as the Kibi Kingdom, which controlled trade for a large part of the country and even with Korea. The many tumulus mounds that dot the area are reminders of its power, which was then solidified in the much later Edo period when the capital of Okayama became a strategically essential castle town. Like many ports, this coastal beauty suffered from bombing during WWII, but has since come back to life with several offbeat sightseeing spots and a reputation for growing some of the best fruit in the country. It is also a good option for cherry blossom viewing without the crowds of Kyoto.

The sights in this area are a little more dispersed, but all are within 10–20-minute train rides of Okayama City. Upon arrival, the first thing to do is take a 25-minute walk (or quick tram ride) down Momotaro Dori street. Look for the statues related to the folklore hero of the same name, who was born from a peach and went on to rid Japan of oni demons. You will quickly arrive at Okayama Castle and nearby Korakuen Garden, widely considered one of the top three traditional gardens in the country.

Most of the dark, brooding castle was bombed in WWII, so the current version is a reconstruction. Access to the inner courtyard is free, but I think the view of it from Korakuen really encapsulates its period majesty. The garden was completed in 1700 and, through great dedication, has been returned to its original state, complete with beautiful bridges crossing the lotus ponds, rice and tea plantations, a crane sanctuary and seasonal flowers, particularly in the early summer.

For more Edo period charm, take one of the regular trains to nearby Kurashiki, known for its well-preserved and artsy canal area. Follow the covered *shotengai* (shopping street) in Ebisu to the main Bikan District of this former rice trading town. Take a short boat ride down the canal, lined with cherry trees and weeping willows, to see the lovely Edo and Meiji period buildings from the water. Climb up to see the town from above at Achi Shrine and consider buying some of the snazzy canvas creations in the shops (a longstanding local product). If you want to stay overnight in Okayama, this is a great area to do so as, in the evening, the quiet streets look quite magical.

If you prefer a more rural adventure, the flat 17 km (10.6 mile) cycling route between Bizen-Ichinomiya and Soja stations is a lovely way to spend an afternoon, passing rice and flower fields regularly punctuated with shrines, temples, traditional farmhouses and massive burial mounds. You can rent a bike by the station and conveniently return it at Soja. Kibitsu Shrine is a must, with its long semi-covered corridors, cherry blossoms and azaleas in spring and purple hydrangeas in June. Bitchu-Kokubunji Temple's pagoda surrounded by fields of flowers looks stunning as well. Give yourself at least 3 hours, and more if you plan to have a picnic.

It takes just under an hour to get to Okayama from Shin-Osaka Station on the Nozomi shinkansen. Kurashiki is a 17-minute ride away from Okayama Station on the Hakubi or San-yo Line, while Bizen-Ichinomiya is just 10 minutes on the Kibi Line.

OUTDOOR JAPAN

SHIKOKU 88 TEMPLE PILGRIMAGE

This pilgrimage route, which spans over 1200 km (746 miles) and circles the entire island of Shikoku, is well known in thru-hiking communities, but I think a lot of people get intimidated by the idea of taking on the entire thing. In actual fact, it is best done in smaller chunks, so that you only walk the most attractive parts of the trail and skip the long stretches that follow major roads.

For a little taste of the experience, the first 12 temples of the pilgrimage in Tokushima Prefecture combine peaceful trails, a wide variety of interesting temples, nature and good lodgings. You can expect to receive *osettai* (small gifts of food and drink) from people you pass, as there is a longstanding tradition of providing assistance to pilgrims.

While experienced walkers and hikers can take on the full 53–60 km (33–37 mile) course over three days, beginners will get plenty of lovely sights in one day going from temples 1 to 6.

The first day of the route starts at Ryozenji (Temple 1), a short walk from Bando Station, which is a 15-minute ride on the JR Line from Tokushima Station. The 17 km (10.6 mile) section between temples 1 and 6 has lots of official trail markers (along with others made by friendly locals), and the temples are not too far apart, so you feel quite accomplished. The flat walk takes you through cute towns and along shortcuts through rice fields and semi-hidden trails. There are a few options for fuelling up, with the Fujimura Bakery (about 1 km/0.6 miles before Temple 5, Jizoji) and Cafe Brisa being two tasty stops.

One of the highlights of this part of the trail (besides all the beautiful traditional houses) is staying overnight at the shukubo at Anrakuji (Temple 6). The hot spring baths are perfect after a day of walking, and the special evening ceremony is completely unique. You may be tempted to keep on going, but this is a definite must!

If you want to return to Tokushima Station the next day, ask the staff for directions to the Higashihara bus stop (a 10-minute walk away), from which there are hourly buses that will take you there in just over an hour.

The second day ups the ante, covering 22–30 km (13.7–18.6 miles) (depending on which trails you take) as you hike from temples 6 to 11. I personally opt for the more scenic Shikoku no Michi options, which are longer but avoid major roads (clearly shown in the Shikoku Japan 88 Route Guide). Make sure to check your map between temples 7 and 9, as a combination of slightly misleading signs makes it a bit tougher to figure out. Kirihataji (Temple 10) has long flights of stairs to climb, so look forward to that! The walk between the 10th and 11th temples is quite long, and crosses a large, agricultural island in the middle of a river. Just keep going and collapse at Ryokan Yoshino, where deep baths and a very hearty dinner await.

The final day on this mini-pilgrimage is also definitely the most physically challenging, as the 12 km (7.5 mile) distance between Fujidera and Shosanji is all on hiking trails with some very steep sections. This part is definitely one for experienced hikers. The trail is quite pleasant, with a combination of steep inclines and flatter ridgelines that give your legs a bit of rest. Although signs are limited and mostly in Japanese, the trail is pretty easy to follow, with a number of spots where you can stop for a breather. One of the most memorable is Ipponsugi, the highest section of the trail, where a massive statue of Kobo Daishi (the founder of the pilgrimage) greets you at the top of a stone staircase.

Give yourself at least 5–6 hours to reach the temple, and another hour to hike down through sweet farm villages to the bus stop in Nabeiwa, which has three daily buses to Yorii, where you can catch another bus to Tokushima Station. If you'd rather not wait, follow the flat main roads another 4 km (2.5 miles) into Yorii, where there are much more regular buses to the prefectural capital.

The Shikoku Japan 88 Route Guide is an invaluable resource for those interested in taking on more of the trail, as is their website, which offers trails of shorter lengths, with free maps and detailed explanations.

The easiest way to get from Osaka to Tokushima is on one of the regular highway buses, which takes about 2½ hours, and there are direct buses from Kobe. You can also use overnight buses from Tokyo to get there (although it is a very long trip) or check out the overnight train to neighbouring Takamatsu for a more unique sleeper car experience.

ONOMICHI & SHIMANAMI KAIDO

Does biking across long bridges, stopping at islands on the Seto Inland Sea and getting awesome panoramic views sound like fun? The Shimanami Kaido is a 70 km (43.5 mile) cycling route that takes you from the vertiginous and retro city of Onomichi across suspension bridges to the islands of Mukaishima, Innoshima, Ikuchijima, Omishima, Hakatajima and Oshima, ending in well-connected Imabari City on Shikoku. The route is pretty flat, there are bike rentals and drop offs available, and plenty of places to rest, refuel and even stay overnight on the islands so, depending on your fitness level, it's possible to do this only-in-Japan ride in one day.

The starting point of Onomichi is a trip back in time, a former temple town with narrow streets and staircases that wind between wooden houses, temples and lazy cats. The hills here are steep, but the views of the Onomichi Channel, massive suspension bridge and islands you will be biking through are worth the climb. Many of the houses here used to be *akiya* (abandoned or empty homes) but, through community efforts, Onomichi has attracted lots of new, often creative, inhabitants who have renovated them and brought new life to the city, with interesting cafes and small businesses. There is also a ropeway that can take you up if you want to rest your legs for the bike ride ahead.

Head back down to the port to pick up your bike. Shimanami Japan and Giant both offer rentals (which you can reserve in advance) but pay attention to which option you choose. Be sure to select one that can be returned in Imabari instead of the original terminal and opt for a cross bike or e-bike, rather than a city bike. They cost a bit more, but your legs will thank you for the convenience, lightness and (in the case of e-bikes) extra support on any hills.

Once you have your wheels, hop on one of the cheap, quick and frequent ferries to Mukaishima, where your ride begins in earnest. The route is well marked and closed to cars, so it is pretty intuitive to follow. Just look for the blue arrows painted on the ground. The main route crosses over bridges, through pretty fishing villages, past shrines and along quiet beaches where you can stop for a swim. You do not cross the entirety of each island, unless you want to make a detour, and there are a good number of eateries and shops along the way, but make sure you have water and some munchies just in case.

Give yourself extra time on Ikuchijima, a good halfway stop that also houses the charmingly eccentric Kosanji Temple, built by a successful (and grateful) businessman in the 1930s. You will find replicas of famous buildings like the gate of Toshogu Shrine in Nikko and the Phoenix Hall in Uji ... along with a delightfully creepy cave where you can see detailed reliefs of the tortures of Buddhist hell. Walk on the blindingly white marble of the large-scale art piece *Heights of Eternal Hope for the Future*, then try the gelato at Setoda Dolce near the entrance. The refreshing options made with local citrus are just the thing after a long ride. For a more substantial meal, SOIL Setoda is beautiful and friendly.

Crossing the Kurushima Kaikyo Ohashi Bridge at the end of the route, stop at the deck to take a selfie with all the islands you conquered.

The best months for this two-wheeled adventure are between March and May or September and November, as the weather is generally mild and relatively dry.

From Shin-Osaka Station, it takes about 1 hour and 45 minutes to get to Onomichi, riding on the shinkansen until Fukuyama Station and then switching to the local San-yo Line. The city is about halfway between Okayama and Hiroshima. From Imabari, there are good train connections to Hiroshima, Okayama or other areas of Shikoku, like the city of Takamatsu in Kagawa Prefecture.

OVERNIGHT TRAIN TRAVEL SECRET: SUNRISE SETO & SUNRISE IZUMO

Most sleeper trains in Japan are expensive, luxury affairs, but these two lines that regularly depart from Tokyo Station offer the experience for around ¥25,000 or less. The Sunrise Seto goes to the city of Takamatsu on the island of Shikoku, and the Sunrise Izumo goes to the city of Izumo in Shimane Prefecture, but the trains are coupled until Okayama. Both also pass through Osaka, so it can be an interesting way of travelling between Kansai and Tokyo.

Besides being a great way to save travel time, as you travel while you sleep, it's also an experience in itself. The cheapest option is *nobinobi seki* (dorm-style rooms), in which you are assigned a small area to stretch out in, with minimal partitions to provide a bit of privacy. Miraculously, these seats are covered by the JR Rail Pass for the Tokyo to Osaka section of the train service, making it an even better deal. However, I would recommend splurging on one of the private cabins for comfort and safety. The basic single and double berths are certainly not large and it is best to bring an extra pillow if you're not a fan of the bean-filled variety. But there is something so cool about watching the city lights go by as you are all tucked up and cosy, then waking up to see the sunrise over the misty hills of Okayama.

Trying to book a berth online is difficult for non-Japanese speakers so, as soon as you arrive in Japan, head to one of the JR ticket centres and get the staff to book it for you. If you avoid weekends, getting a berth is usually possible, but doing so a month in advance gives you the best chance.

DEPARTING FROM NAGOYA

Nagoya itself is not one of my top destinations, unless you're a huge fan of automotive technology or desperately want to visit the Ghibli Park. However, it is about halfway between Tokyo and Kyoto on the bullet train line, making it a useful stop, particularly when using the JR Rail Pass.

If stopping by, see if you can try some of their famous red miso–based dishes, such as miso katsu or miso nikomi udon, an earthenware bowl full of noodles stewed in the rich broth. Another cool local tradition is the 'morning service' offered by many coffee shops: if you order a cup of coffee or tea, you will get a small breakfast (maybe toast, salad, a boiled egg or yoghurt) for free!

OLD JAPAN

HIDA TAKAYAMA & SHIRAKAWAGO

Hidden deep in the mountains of Gifu Prefecture, both Hida Takayama and Shirakawago owe their untouched, traditional beauty to their remoteness and the locals' collaborative efforts to maintain their hometowns' unique charms.

The former is a particularly interesting case. During the Edo period, it was known for its skilled carpenters and quality timber. This led to patronage from the shogunate and plenty of money coming in, which explains why the houses in the gorgeous Old Town area are so well made and prosperous looking. Sannomachi Street's dark wooden buildings house shops, restaurants, cafes and a number of sake breweries (check out the Hirata brewery), most of which have been in business for centuries. Foodies will enjoy a trip to Hida, as many of the local treats feature the prized local beef, and there are two daily morning markets where you can sample other products of the region.

Traditional Shirakawago house ▸

A short bus ride away is the Hida Folk Village, an open-air museum with over two dozen traditional Hida-style Edo period houses that recreate a village. The highlights are the farmhouses with steep, thatched roofs that were moved here from nearby Shirakawago, making this a must-see if you don't have time to get to the famous hamlet.

Another surprisingly fascinating spot a quick bus ride from the station is Matsuri no Mori, a one-of-a-kind museum dedicated to the grand Takayama Festival. Enter the cave-like space to see the lavishly decorated full-sized floats, complete with the karakuri marionettes that are the trademark of the festival. Every hour, there are performances on the largest taiko drums in the world.

Those with lots of time should also consider taking the 3.5 km (2.2 mile) Higashiyama walk, which passes through the temple area of town, lined with over a dozen shrines and temples, then by the ruins of Takayama Castle and through a few quieter trails on the outskirts of town.

If you have ever seen photos of insanely picturesque thatched farmhouses surrounded by mountains and rice fields or draped in snow, good chances are they were snapped at Shirakawago, a UNESCO World Heritage site, where dozens of traditional houses from the 1800s built in the *gassho zukuri* (praying hands) style congregate in a fairytale-worthy hamlet. Many of the houses are still privately owned, but a number are open to the public, so you can see how cleverly designed these massive, strong structures are. While the area is not large, you will want at least a couple of hours to wander around the smaller lanes to get the feel of this hamlet forgotten by time.

Give yourself enough time to climb up to the Shirayama observatory point, where you can take in the whole village from above. The main area of Ogimachi is prettiest between early summer and winter. During the winter they have special evening illuminations, in which the snow-covered houses are lit up after dark, creating a truly otherworldly feel.

There are regular JR Hida limited express trains that take you from Nagoya to Takayama Station in 2½ hours and are covered by the JR Rail Pass. There are also frequent highway buses that take about the same amount of time. From Takayama, there are about a dozen buses a day to Shirakawago, which take under an hour and are best booked in advance if you are visiting during peak season. Also keep an eye out for seasonal bus tours, which often include an extra stop at other nearby scenic locations like the thatched-roof villages of Ainokura or Gokayama.

MEIJIMURA

This utter gem of an open-air architecture museum is one of the largest theme parks in the country. Within it are 67 Meiji period buildings that were taken apart, moved and then reconstructed on-site. No recreations here: everything is original and kept in splendid condition.

For those unfamiliar, the Meiji period (1868–1912) was a fascinating time of rapid change and modernisation in Japan. As they opened up to the world, new ideas, technology and architecture rushed in, with Japanese and Western concepts being mixed and matched in ways that are still an intrinsic part of the culture.

The park is divided into five zones, loosely grouped by genre. From grand private homes to an old prison, churches, a telephone exchange, schools and government buildings, you can get a good idea of what life was like during this exciting period of Japanese history. Just a few of the highlights are the facade and the lobby of the former Imperial Hotel, designed by Frank Lloyd Wright, the St Francis Xavier's Cathedral that used to stand in Kyoto, and a red-brick road lined with elegant homes, including the topsy-turvy Tomatsu House.

You can rent Meiji period outfits called hakama, a comfy split-pant that is worn with kimono, to really get into character. Be sure to also try some of the local foods, most of which are original recipes from the period. The curry pan bread available in Area 2 is particularly good, and if you are a sucker for interior design, stop for a tea break at the Imperial Hotel's tearoom. To get around you can ride a vintage bus, streetcar or even the oldest steam locomotive in Japan. Give yourself at least 4 hours to amble the old streets. You're also likely to spy cosplayers and other nattily dressed folks posing by the magnificent structures.

To get to Meijimura, take one of the two or three morning buses from the Kintetsu Bus Centre at Nagoya Station (the trip takes 1 hour and 20 minutes). There's a lot to see, so getting an early start is a good idea.

Inuyama (literally 'dog mountain') is also worth a visit. It has the oldest original castle in Japan, which was privately owned until 2005, cute Showa Alley with its wooden buildings and street food, and Urakuen Garden with the elegant Joan tea house. If you have time and enjoy weird sights, take the bus to Momotaro Shrine, dedicated to the eponymous hero of Japanese folklore, said to have been born from a peach.

EXTREME OFFBEAT JAPAN: REBUN ISLAND

This is basically the furthest northern point you can get to in Japan before entering Russian waters. This extremely remote island is known for its clifftop trekking trails, 300 varieties of alpine plants (despite not being anywhere near the elevation where these flowers usually bloom) and seafood. During weekends in the high season (from the end of May to the end of September), Japanese hikers can be seen seeking out the flowers, but if you visit towards the end of the season (or even in very early October) you will have the views basically to yourself.

The remote, austere beauty of the island, quiet tiny fishing villages, and the experience of solitude on the trails makes it feel like a true (but safe) adventure. It is possible to see the sights by car or the infrequent buses that circle Rebun, but the best way is by foot, and there are a number of different trails to choose from. English signage is limited, so preparing carefully and checking bus times are a must. Fortunately, their English maps and website are quite good.

My time in Rebun was absolutely unforgettable and, to this day, it's still the place I most wish to return to. Definitely stay overnight or longer, so you can walk at least two trails. The 5 km (3.1 mile) Momoiwa Observation Point course ends at the Kita no Kanariya school (which has been used as a film location), a perfect spot for a picnic. The much longer 13 km (8 mile) Capes of Rebun trail will eventually lead you to Cape Sukoton, the very northernmost tip of the island. On a clear day, you can see the Russian-controlled Sakhalin Islands and Todo Island, inhabited by walruses. If you hit the beaches, you might also see wild seals playing in the surf.

An interesting fact is that the average annual income on Rebun is well above the national average, as the fisherfolk harvest expensive sea urchin and the highly sought after Rishiri kombu kelp used by elite chefs. The flamboyant homes and general sense of prosperity make an interesting contrast to Wakkanai on the Hokkaido mainland, which has definitely seen better days ... although all the signs in Russian give you the feeling of being on the northern frontier.

Getting to Rebun is not cheap but isn't too complicated. The easiest way is to book a flight from Tokyo to Wakkanai (anywhere from ¥50,000 to ¥80,000 for a round trip), overnight at a hotel near the port, then take the very early morning Heartland ferry to the island. I would recommend splurging on first or second class tickets on the ferry, as you will be assigned to a surprisingly attractive shared tatami room with individual futon and pillows, so you can get another couple of hours of sleep.

WHAT ABOUT KYUSHU?!

At this point, those familiar with Japan may have noticed something missing from the guide so far. An entire land mass, in fact.

Kyushu is the southernmost of Japan's main islands and, in a way, the most dispersed, as a good section of it is made up of the Ryukyu Islands (such as Okinawa) and the Nansei Islands, the largest of which is Amami Oshima. Distances are great here, with more limited transport options so, with the exception of Fukuoka, which can be reached by bullet train via Tokyo Station in 5 hours or Shin-Osaka in just over 2½ hours, it takes careful planning and a good chunk of travel time to get around this subtropical island.

Do not fear, though, as there are bullet trains between the major cities and a number of very scenic railways (the ride to the onsen town of Yufuin is particularly lovely), so it is certainly not impossible to get around but, rather, the island merits at least a week of dedicated exploring, as the landscapes, culture and outdoor activities in Kyushu are quite distinct from the rest of the country.

To get a quick taste of Kyushu in a couple of days, it is easiest to focus on the northern part of the island, which has the best train connections to the rest of the country. For those arriving at Hakata Station, the city of Fukuoka offers a good base, with the flower-covered Nokonoshima Island and the museums and gardens of Ohori Park nearby. However, Fukuoka really shines when the sun goes down, as the lanes along the river glitter with the iconic *yatai* (street food carts) serving drinks, the famed local tonkotsu ramen and other favourites. Yatai hopping is something you can only experience here, so an overnight stay is highly recommended.

For side trips, I suggest visiting Dazaifu, about 30 minutes by train from the central Tenjin Station. This peaceful spot was the administrative heart of the entire island for over 500 years. It is centred around Dazaifu Tenmangu Shrine, dedicated to the god of scholarship and festooned with 6000 plum trees (said to be the god's favourite), which bloom in February and early March. Try freshly made umegae mochi sweets on the Tenjinsama street approaching the shrine. Komyozenji Temple and the wild escalator ride at the Kyushu National Museum are also worth a visit.

Alternatively, take the 30-minute bullet train ride from Hakata Station to nearby Kumamoto Station. From here, the main sights of the city are just a 15-minute streetcar ride away. The must-see is Kumamoto Castle, probably one of the most impressive in the country; it has resisted attacks for over 400 years. Note that it was badly damaged during an earthquake, and repairs will be ongoing until 2038. Don't miss the Suizenji Jojuen garden nearby, with its unique recreation of Mount Fuji and reproduction of all 53 stops along the ancient Tokaido road. Try the *ikinari dango* (sweet potato–filled dumplings) sold near the entrance.

Outdoorsy folks can get regular trains from Kumamoto to Aso Station and, from there, a bus to the active volcanoes and huge crater of Mount Aso. The Kusasenri grasslands look almost unreal in their perfection, with cows and horses happily grazing away. There are several trails of varying difficulty, but always check the conditions online before going, as many of the trails are closed off for safety during periods of high volcanic activity.

If this all sounds a bit too tame, then perhaps the wild subtropical island of Yakushima is for you. The entire island is a national park, covered with thick cedar forest that is home to the yakusugi, truly ancient trees that are between 1000 and 7000 years old. The untamed, lush greens and moss here are said to have inspired the Ghibli masterpiece *Princess Mononoke*, particularly the magical Shiratani Unsuikyo Ravine. If you get tired of hiking, the snorkelling and diving here are also top-notch. Most accommodation is pretty basic but, if you can, splurge on a stay at the amazing Sankara Hotel & Spa. The easiest way to get Yakushima is by plane from Fukuoka or Osaka.

Finally, porcelain and ceramics fans will adore Saga Prefecture as, thanks to longstanding cultural exchanges with neighbouring Korea, it is home to some of the country's most renowned pottery villages around Arita, Imari and Karatsu. All three are within a couple of hours by train of Fukuoka, and there are a number of companies that specialise in taking pottery fans around to see the kilns.

However, the coolest experience is at the Kouraku kiln in Arita, which holds treasure hunts in its massive storehouses. For ¥5500 for simpler ceramics, and ¥11,000 for full access to the rarer and older stock, you have 90 minutes to fill a large shopping basket with all the pieces that tickle your fancy from the warehouses of this 400-year-old kiln. Booking in advance is recommended, and they can ship worldwide.

役立つ情報

Helpful Hints

HERE ARE SOME OF MY TOP TIPS, garnered over the course of more than a decade of living in Japan, plus some secrets that experts in the travel industry use to ensure their Japanese vacations go without a hitch.

TRAVEL

Ensuring you have the best time possible in Japan starts with a bit of extra attention to planning, from timing your trip right to packing light.

TRIP TIMING

If you want to avoid dealing with crowds and booked-out attractions, plan to visit Japan outside the most popular times of the year. While the spring cherry blossoms and autumn colours are indeed magical, they also attract record numbers of visitors each year and cause hotel prices to skyrocket due to demand.

Summer is also a popular choice, especially for those travelling with children who want to make the most of school holidays. However, most of Japan is meltingly hot in July and August, with high humidity levels that totally sap your energy and leave you completely soaked in sweat within a couple of hours.

My recommendations for the best off-peak (but still pleasurable) times to visit are January, May, September and November. With the exception of January (which is ideal if you love snow and want to go skiing in Hokkaido, Nagano, Niigata or Yamagata), the weather is mild, flights are cheaper, and hotels have higher availability.

FLIGHTS

The majority of English-speaking visitors to Japan decide, quite logically, to arrive at one of Tokyo's airports – either Narita or Haneda. If at all possible, I urge you to try to get a flight to Haneda Airport.

Despite being known as Tokyo's main international airport, Narita is actually located quite far away, in neighbouring Chiba Prefecture (which is also home to Tokyo Disneyland). Be prepared for a significant train ride on the pricey Narita Express to get into the city, or a very long bus ride. If you have an early morning return flight, you may have to spend the previous night nearby, in order not to miss it.

If you can wing it, transiting via Haneda Airport is the way to go. It is far closer to central Tokyo, more walkable, has much more to see and do, and has dozens of interesting restaurants that stay open late. Despite having regular late evening flights, most food-related services are shut by 7.30 pm in Narita and the options aren't particularly exciting.

TRANSPORT

If you plan on going to the Kansai region and want to hit up at least two or three different locations in Japan, get the JR Rail Pass. You have no idea how jealous locals and expats are about visitors' ability to get the pass, as it truly saves a huge amount of money and gives you the flexibility to jump on and off trains without having to think about the cost. You can do a lot of sightseeing just using JR lines, and it also saves time searching for change or recharging transit cards.

For getting around non–JR Line trains and subways, you will also want to get a Suica card, available from the JR Travel Service centres found at most large stations and airports. Just charge it at the machines near the ticket gates, touch it to the panels on the gates and go. You can also use Suica cards to buy things at the stations, convenience stores and some vending machines. Super handy.

AVOIDING RUSH HOUR

This is especially important if you're among the more than 60 per cent of visitors who start their trip to Japan in Tokyo: if you can, try to time your arrival or departure so that it doesn't overlap with rush hour. This is good to keep in mind while sightseeing as well.

The morning rush starts around 7.30 am and lasts until about 10 am, while the evening rush begins in earnest at 6 pm and continues on until 8.30 pm or even a bit later.

There is nothing worse than getting squashed among tired people heading to or from work when you're already worn out. Not only is it stressful for you (the first time on a packed Tokyo train is something no one forgets!), but it's also likely to make you the target of annoyed looks from other passengers, particularly if you happen to be carrying big pieces of luggage with you!

LUGGAGE TIPS

Fortunately, there are some great options for avoiding being 'that' person. As a Tokyo commuter myself, seeing visitors struggling to carry their heavy suitcases up the stairs of train stations (or worse, bashing into people on the crowded trains with their backpacks) makes me feel simultaneously empathetic and enraged.

Japan – and Tokyo in particular – is tightly packed, so personal and luggage space you are 'allocated' is limited. Fortunately, as this is not a new issue, there are several options that can make getting yourself and your luggage around much easier and less stressful.

Among the best options for people staying in relatively central areas are limousine buses. Just store your luggage in the compartment beneath the bus, then sit back and watch the city pass by until you are dropped off at your hotel or the closest stop near your accommodation, then you can walk or take a cab to your final destination. If you plan to come in via Narita Airport and stay around Tokyo Station, you can even use the super-cheap Tokyo Shuttle.

If you are arriving early in the morning, another good option is sending your luggage to your hotel from the airport. That way, you can start sightseeing immediately and will receive your bags after checking into your hotel (or early the following day, if you arrive later in the afternoon). This service is safe and affordable, as many locals send their luggage home after a trip rather than deal with lugging it on the train. Yamato Transport is well known for its quick delivery services, and usually has offices in major Japanese airports. Conversely, many hotels also offer the option to send your luggage to the airport as well, which is great if you're near the end of your trip and want to travel a bit lighter.

OF HOTELS & TINY ROOMS

Unless you have the budget for luxury hotels and suite rooms, the average room size in Japanese hotels is likely to be smaller than you might expect, usually 16–18 sq metres (172–194 sq feet), although single rooms can be smaller. With limited closet space and beds that tend to be a little lower to the ground, stashing away big suitcases can be a challenge. There is not much you can do about this except consider packing light.

On a side note, if you are staying in really cheap accommodation, you may be faced with the traditional bean pillow, so check reviews before booking or bring a small pillow with you.

COMMON ASSUMPTIONS THAT CAN LEAD TO PROBLEMS

While the country prides itself on its attentive hospitality (known as 'omotenashi') and works hard to ensure visitors have a great time, there are a few cultural differences that can come as a surprise to first-time visitors.

LANGUAGE ISSUES

While signage and menus in other languages have become much more common, it is still likely that there will be times when communication is difficult. This sometimes comes as a surprise to tourists more familiar with Southeast Asia, where people seem to put a lot of emphasis on being able to communicate with visitors.

Obviously, Japan is geographically part of Asia but, traditionally, it hasn't relied on tourism to keep its economy going (although this is definitely changing) and so English-language ability was not considered a necessity. While the amount and quality of assistance in other languages have increased dramatically in the last decade, downloading a basic translation app before you go can make communicating much easier.

'I'LL JUST WING IT'

Japan became a major destination for visitors rather rapidly, and some services either have still not caught up to meet demand or are always fully booked. This goes for everything from accommodation during prime seasons to tables at renowned restaurants, and even shows or tickets for popular museums. For concerts and other events, you may well have to compete with local fans too, so it pays to be well prepared.

Basically, if there is something you really want to do, book well in advance. The magical Ghibli Museum is a perfect example of this, as they do not sell tickets at the museum itself. If you want to stay at a particular ryokan, eat at a specific Michelin-starred restaurant or book a tour, it's a good idea to lock that in as soon as your plane tickets are confirmed. Japan is a *very* organised country, so winging it is not generally a good strategy here.

'I'LL JUST USE MAPS'

Most Japanese streets do not have names and many buildings, shops and restaurants only have information written in Japanese. Being able to fire up a mapping or translation app will ensure you spend less time trying to find your destination, and more time actually enjoying your time in Japan.

While free WiFi is becoming more common around Japan, if you plan on wandering around using a map app, getting a SIM card or renting a pocket WiFi will save you a lot of stress because, if your battery dies, chances are your best-laid plans to find that secret bar or gallery will too.

'NO ONE WILL NOTICE MY TATTOO'

Despite Japan having a long history of tattoo art, visitors may find that most onsen refuse service to visitors sporting ink. This is mainly due to the fact that members of the yakuza are known for their dedication to the art, and so bath owners use this rule to keep them out ... and for fairness reasons, this extends to international visitors with no links to organised crime.

One of the easiest ways of getting around this is to stay in a ryokan with private baths, which can either be in your room or reserved in advance. With no witnesses, there's no problem! Some onsen have loosened their rules and will allow you to soak as long as your tattoo can be covered by a waterproof bandage, which they will often provide. To avoid disappointment, check out ink-friendly hot springs in advance at the aptly named Tattoo-Friendly, a useful website with lists of accommodating public baths and hot springs.

'JUST PUT IT ON MY CARD'

Even in major cities (and especially out in rural areas), there are restaurants and shops that don't accept credit or debit cards. Running around looking for an ATM that will accept your card is certainly no fun, so take out enough cash to cover your expenses, and perhaps a little more, just in case. If you do find yourself desperately seeking an ATM, there are a couple of reliable options.

While it is certainly not intuitive, during business hours Japan Post Office ATMs accept all major credit cards. Another easy option is using Seven Bank ATMs at (most) 7-Eleven convenience stores. Some Family Mart and Lawson convenience stores have ATMs that accept international cards as well, but not all of them.

HOW TO BLEND IN (BETTER) IN JAPAN

Here are some tips to help make you more attuned to life in Japan, and not to be labelled 'that tourist'.

DRESS UP

Walking around Tokyo in particular, you will see that locals are almost always dressed immaculately. Athleisure is for home or the gym, and wandering around in a sports bra and leggings is uncommon unless the person is a trainer or yoga instructor by trade.

Wearing a nice outfit and closed-toe shoes, and masking when other people do so, may make you seem like an expat who knows what they are doing, rather than a clueless (and sometimes rude) tourist.

It is unusual to show lots of skin on the upper body in Japan, so having sleeves, tops that aren't too low cut and more modest shorts or skirts will help you blend in a bit more.

Also, like many countries in Asia, the differences in temperatures indoors and outdoors can be pretty extreme, especially in summer and winter. In the summer, temperatures in places like Tokyo and Kyoto routinely go above 30°C (86°F), but buildings and restaurants will be blasting their air conditioners at full power, which means it'll be much cooler indoors. In the winter, it's the opposite, as it may be close to 0°C (32°F) outside but feel like a tropical beach in shops or on trains. By dressing in layers, you can add or remove clothes as needed to make sure you stay comfortable all day long. This also has the additional benefit of providing a bit of extra coverage when needed.

Make sure your socks are in good shape. There are many temples and traditional restaurants that require you to remove your shoes before entering, and you will be judged by the state of your socks. Just saying.

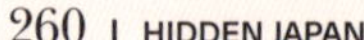

MIND YOUR MANNERS

There are many aspects to manners in Japan, but there are some in particular that you truly need to keep in mind when you visit. One is that being loud or pushy will not get you anywhere, but a calm request and lots of thanks in advance can work miracles. Avoid touching people, unless they make it abundantly clear they are okay with it (this includes tapping on shoulders and high-fives). And perhaps the most important: be considerate of other people's space.

While there are certainly local louts, on the whole, the tight spaces of the major cities (and cultural norms) mean that people try to be considerate of not obstructing others. If a train is crowded, keep your voice down and wear your backpack on the front so you don't swing around and bash it into someone. Don't block doorways or stand in the middle of the street to check your map app, but step to the side instead.

Oh, and watch out for the bathroom slippers if you need to switch at a restaurant or ryokan. Take off the ones you're wearing, slip into the bathroom ones to use the facilities, then get back into your regular slippers. It is easy to forget! Oh, and no slippers on tatami mats, ever.

Thank you

Trying to condense years of experience and visits to 43 of Japan's 47 prefectures was quite an undertaking, and it is all thanks to the direction and support of the lovely team at Smith Street Books, who have made my dreams of becoming a published author come true twice over. Other giant arigatos go to Tats, who dealt gracefully with the months of furious writing, re-writing, editing and growling at a computer screen that accompany the guide creation process, and to my parents, whose taste for offbeat travel and seeking new flavours has deeply influenced my own. A round of applause for Justine, who draws Japan just as I see it, and Michelle for making both my books look so incredible.

About the author

Chiara has spent over a decade living, working and exploring in Japan, ranging from rambles across the northernmost islands to snorkelling in the azure waters of Okinawa's many islets, always with a notebook in tow. Besides writing and helping rural areas of Japan share their stories with international audiences, she is also a professional singer, actor and announcer for a Japanese language-learning TV program on NHK, the country's national broadcaster. This is her second book with Smith Street Books, the first being *The Vegan Guide to Tokyo.* She can usually be found disappearing into an intriguing alley, hiding out at a kissaten or serving the whims of her benign feline overlords, Lupin and Michiko.

Smith Street Books

Published in 2024 by Smith Street Books
Naarm (Melbourne) | Australia
smithstreetbooks.com

Distributed outside of ANZ, North & Latin America by
Thames & Hudson Ltd.,
6–24 Britannia Street, London, WC1X 9JD
thamesandhudson.com

EU Authorised Representative:
Interart S.A.R.L.
19 rue Charles Auray, 93500 Pantin, Paris, France
productsafety@thameshudson.co.uk;
www.interart.fr

ISBN: 978-1-9227-5475-2

Smith Street Books respectfully acknowledges the Wurundjeri People of the Kulin Nation, who are the Traditional Owners of the land on which we work, and we pay our respects to their Elders past and present.

Publisher: Paul McNally
Managing editor: Lucy Heaver
Editor: Jane Ormond
Designer: Michelle Mackintosh
Typesetter: Heather Menzies, Studio31 Graphics
Illustrator: Justine Wong
Proofreader: Penny Mansley
Prepress: Megan Ellis

Printed & bound in China by C&C Offset Printing Co., Ltd.

Book 315
10 9 8 7 6 5 4 3